ADVANCE PRAISE FOR

SITE and S⊙UND

"*Site and Sound* introduces 'indie' music and its cultural context—an area of musical life that is rarely recognized by the music public, or is singled out as distinct in scholarship, but yet responsible for much of the stylistic variety and vitality of American musical life, particularly outside the major urban centers. For ethnomusicologists, Holly Kruse's book offers significant ethnographic material for comprehension of a musical culture at the interface of professional and amateur, and of private and institutional sectors of American musical culture. Presented largely through interviews with and statements by musicians, recording technicians, and members of the audience, Kruse provides insight into the musical, economic, and, most interestingly, social relationships that undergird the 'indie' musical productions and the fascinating cast of characters who live them."

Bruno Nettl, Professor Emeritus of Musicology, University of Illinois,

"Holly Kruse is one of the few scholars to have conducted in-depth research on independent record companies, and here provides a compelling and comprehensive account of the dynamics and dilemmas that characterize alternative rock culture. This is an insightful book, revealing the complexities concealed by apparently simple terms 'indie' and 'alternative.' This book should be essential reading for students of music and the media, as well as musicians wishing to understand why the contemporary recording industry treats them as it does."

Keith Negus, Senior Lecturer in Communications, Department of Media and Communications, Goldsmiths College, University of London

"In all too much popular music analysis, the concepts of place and independence become simplified into the coordinates of geography or confused with a fuzzy-headed rejection of corporate culture. Holly Kruse eloquently and effectively complicates both our sense of how particular places lead to potentially groundbreaking music as well as how independent structures of production and distribution are embroiled within and, in some cases, differ very little from the mainstream music industry. Her incorporation of numerous thought-provoking comments from participants in the independent music scene keeps the theoretical insights grounded in the day-to-day trappings of commerce. Also, her thoughtful consideration of gender reminds us that boorish behavior is not limited to the mainstream, but flourishes throughout the entertainment domain—even in precincts thought to be more sensitive to the needs of the individual."

David Sanjek, Director of BMI Archives

SITE and SOUND

M U S I C
(M E A N I N G S)

Steve Jones, Will Straw, and Joli Jensen
General Editors

Vol. 1

PETER LANG
New York • Washington, D.C./Baltimore • Bern
Frankfurt am Main • Berlin • Brussels • Vienna • Oxford

Holly Kruse

SITE and S●UND

Understanding Independent
Music Scenes

PETER LANG
New York • Washington, D.C./Baltimore • Bern
Frankfurt am Main • Berlin • Brussels • Vienna • Oxford

Library of Congress Cataloging-in-Publication Data

Kruse, Holly.
Site and sound: understanding independent music scenes / Holly Kruse.
p. cm. (Music/meanings; vol. 1)
Includes bibliographical references (p.) and index.
1. Alternative rock music—History and criticism. I. Title.
ML3534 .K82   781.66—dc21   2002073039
ISBN 0-8204-5552-0
ISSN 1531-6726

Die Deutsche Bibliothek-CIP-Einheitsaufnahme

Kruse, Holly:
Site and sound: understanding independent music scenes / Holly Kruse.
—New York; Washington, D.C./Baltimore; Bern;
Frankfurt am Main; Berlin; Brussels; Vienna; Oxford: Lang.
(Music/meanings; Vol. 1)
ISBN 0-8204-5552-0

Cover design by Joni Holst

© 2003 Peter Lang Publishing, Inc., New York
275 Seventh Avenue, 28th Floor, New York, NY 10001
www.peterlangusa.com

Contents

CHAPTER 1

Introduction

Although much has been written about the consumption and production of cultural artifacts, relatively few studies have focused on the ways in which these cultural practices are situated within specific spaces and places. In this book I examine the practices of independent music scenes—objects of varying amounts of media attention (particularly from the music press) since the 1980s—which are best understood as being constituted through the practices and relationships that are enacted within the social and geographical spaces they occupy. Those active in the production and consumption of this form of music and its ancillary texts in the 1980s and 1990s conceived of their practices as largely independent of institutions of the pop/rock music mainstream music, even though some acts thought of as "independent" in fact recorded for major labels. Recurrent in narratives of indie pop/rock is the conscious geographical and ideological positioning of the "peripheral" local sites and practices of indie music production and consumption in opposition to the "centers" of mainstream music production. As, in the late 1980s and early 1990s, forms of indie music became part of the commercial mainstream, narrative histories of indie music marked the moment as a time of the genre's decline.

By primarily using personal narratives to illuminate social, economic, and spatial practices, this book represents an approach to both popular music studies and media studies that has been somewhat neglected by media scholars, many of whom have focused on readings of media texts, overly celebratory notions of audience consumption of media products, purely institutional or economic analyses of the mass media, or highly theoretical views of media texts and processes that are difficult to connect to the lived experiences of ordinary people. Looking at the real practices of people who existed at nexi of intersecting economic, social, cultural, and geographic forces not only helps illuminate a cultural phenomenon—the emergence of independent pop and rock music as a national and international presence in the 1980s and 1990s—but synthesizes different methods and modes of analysis in a holistic manner of value in any investigation of cultural artifacts.

The idea for this project came out of my own experience as a participant in independent music scenes in the 1980s and early 1990s, and it was through the social network I developed that most of my interview contacts were found. I was particularly interested in examining in detail a phenomenon that seemed to arise not from some group defined as an exotic "Other" to my own experience, but from a group comprised of people with whom I shared many characteristics. Perhaps my association with the topic of my research caused me to lack crucial perspective in my analysis, but I hope that it gave me useful knowledge about independent music scenes that allowed me to ask productive questions of my interview subjects and show discernment when sorting through archival materials.

The chapters that follow examine indie pop/rock music's received history, its relations of production and distribution, its social and spatial relations, issues of participant identity, and this case study's place within established research traditions. In Chapter 2, archival research and the lived experiences of interviewees located at a range of independent pop/rock music sites are used to construct a narrative of indie music history, and these interviewees also point to the difficulties of defining "independent music," "college music," or "alternative music" as a genre. In the popular memory of indie music, past events were continually rearticulated: for example, the significance of R.E.M.'s breakthrough to mainstream success in the late-1980s is re-evaluated (and generally downplayed) in light of the multi-platinum success of Nirvana's major label debut album in the early 1990s. In order to understand what indie meant in the 1990s, it is crucial to look at how its history was perceived, because memories are not merely the key to understanding the history of indie music as a genre, but are also central in understanding the evolution of its economic institutions and social relations.

Chapter 3 looks specifically at the institutions of independent music production. Independent record labels specializing in alternative rock and pop proliferated during the 1980s and 1990s, and their growth created an interesting dynamic in the music industry. While many small labels professed true independence from the mainstream music industry, for the most part they were, and still are, inextricably linked to existing structures of popular music production and distribution. Sometimes independent labels were tied to larger companies because they discovered talent for major labels to recruit, sometimes because they had distribution deals with majors, sometimes because majors bought part- or full-ownerships in independent labels, and always because independent labels operated in a terrain structured by major labels. This dynamic created tension in institutions— and tension for the independent music scene participants in these institutions—that would have liked to define themselves as truly "alternative" and which sought to remain identified as local.

After an independent, or any, label has produced a record, that record must be circulated to a wider audience. Chapter 4 examines four sites of indie music distribution: radio, video, retail, and live venues. Fanzines and music journalism, while central in the circulation of discourse about indie music, were not primary sites through which the music itself was circulated, and therefore were beyond the purview of this analysis. College radio, often stereotypically characterized by free-formatting and a non-commercial structure, was a main medium through which independent rock and pop music was disseminated in the 1980s and 1990s, although video, with its national reach, was also important in the economic success of some acts. College radio stations, like independent labels, were sites of struggle between the ideal of "alternative" music institutions and the reality of major label power. As awareness of college radio's ability to "break" alternative artists grew in the 1980s, so did major label influence over college stations' programming decisions. As radio stations disseminated independent music over the airwaves, retail stores and live performance venues were the primary physical spaces in which college music was distributed. All three kinds of sites were interconnected within localities through networks of economic relationships.

Chapter 5 is a study of the social relationships that both defined and were created by late twentieth century independent music scenes, focusing in particular on how identity was constituted within the social and physical spaces of indie music. Subjects within music scenes were multiply positioned by their generic identifications, by their personal histories within localities, by overlapping social and economic relationships, by a constellation of subcultural practices, and by their gender identities. Notions of locality and interlocality are of central importance in understanding indie pop/rock music's social and economic relations and its practices, and with the mainstream success of multiple indie bands from specific localities as diverse as Austin, Seattle, and Athens, Georgia, "local sound" is an extremely salient concept. The intersection of gender and practice is also of particular interest, because while on the surface indie music claimed to operate as much as possible outside the musical mainstream, in fact the experiences of women involved in alternative music at all levels testify to the degree to which the social and economic relations of mainstream media institutions were mirrored in the structures of alternative music.

Chapter 6, the concluding chapter, situates the preceding study within the frameworks traditionally used to examine cultural products and social formations. These approaches are critiqued, and the importance of political economy, Pierre Bourdieu's notions of "habitus" and "fields of practice," and theories of space and place in looking at independent music scenes as social, cultural, economic, and local phenomena is emphasized. This chapter again demonstrates that the recurrence of themes of social/economics networks, locality, and memory in social subjects and in institutions underscores the need for conjunctural analysis of *all* social and cultural formations, of which independent music scenes are just one example.

I would be remiss in ending this introduction before thanking several people without whose help this book would not exist. Steve Jones' help, and his continuing faith in my project, ensured that this book would someday make it into print. Joli Jensen's critiques of the book manuscript and ongoing encouragement were invaluable. At varying stages of the process Chris Myers and Sophy Craze at Peter Lang were both instrumental in providing guidance. Nor can I ignore the people who were instrumental in the completion of the first version of this manuscript: Larry Grossberg and Ellen Wartella, who gave me wonderful input, as well as the confidence to believe that the research they helped guide could someday be published as a book; Nancy Baym, whose friendship and contacts allowed this project to get off the ground; and of course all the music scene participants who graciously shared their time and thoughts with me. I must also thank Mark Fenster, without whose advice, support, and manual labor at the computer keyboard the first version of this manuscript truly may not have been written. Finally, thanks to my father Elwood Kruse, who did not get to see the completion of this journey, and my mother, Noreen Kruse, who barely saw it begin, but both of whom inspired me throughout.

CHAPTER 2

Telling the Story of Independent Music

D uring the 1980s, rock and pop music put out by independent record labels, disseminated over the air waves of college radio stations, and produced in geographically peripheral locales emerged onto the national (and international) scene. This music earned its own trade paper, the *College Music Journal* *(CMJ)*, and its own chart in *Rolling Stone*, and it became the subject of music industry seminars. With the advent of college radio and college charts, it became possible for a band to break through to national popularity without airplay on commercial radio stations. In the 1980s in particular though, college radio superstars like R.E.M. and Soul Asylum found themselves courted by major labels, and disparate localities became key sources of talent for the mainstream music industry. Although by definition indie pop/rock existed, and continues to exist, on the margins of mainstream music in the 1980s, it had a major impact on the mainstream industry. Early in the 1980s, trade papers like *Billboard* and *The Gavin Report* recognized college radio as central in the circulation of emerging and alternative musics.

Even in the early twenty-first century, local and regional indie scenes still abound with low-budget fanzines that help create identities for unknowns, independent record stores that stock indie label releases, relatively freely-formatted college and/or community radio stations, live performance venues, and artists who put out music with the help of independent record labels or on their own. In the personal narratives of indie music scene participants, we will see that institutions and practices such as these are viewed as more "authentic" than those associated with the mainstream music industry. The "us" versus "them" mentality that posits "our" music, presumably created and consumed in a pure environment free of the bottom line concerns of major labels, commercial radio, and chain record stores, as authentic is one that is found among adherents of many forms of music that have at some point in their histories been perceived as marginal. In *The Nashville Sound*, Joli Jensen observes the same phenomenon in country music; like indie music, "country music uses authenticity as a generic marker, a way to define itself as both separate and worthy" (7).

The aura of authenticity attached to peripheral, non-mainstream forms of music by participants in marginal musical cultures not only defines the music as oppositional, it identifies the participants as outsiders. When marginal musics begin to cross over to the mainstream, these oppositional identities—and thus participants' senses of themselves—are threatened. A backlash of true believers against the artists or institutions that have "sold out," and a perception that the music is now in decline, usually follows (see Jensen, 5–6). These elements are present in the narrative history of indie music that follows, a narrative exemplified by Michael Azerrad in his recent chronicle of indie rock music from 1981 to 1991, *Our Band Could Be Your Life*. Azerrad argues:

> Taking music away from corporate labels and putting it in the hands of local practitioners demystified the process of making and selling records. One of the dividends of that was helping people feel OK about not fitting into mainstream culture . . . But gradually the idea radiated into the more conventionally minded precincts of society . . . [People who] had no knowledge of the history and basis of the whole movement, nor did they care to find out. (487)

Azerrad's narrative of rise and fall concludes with the pronouncement that "we won: indie rock was well established, and musicians could now earn a decent living making music even for fairly specialized audience. And yet the vitality of the music and the community was severely diminished" (499).

In the face of the perceived "selling out" and downward trajectory of the music, participants may employ a series of tactics in an effort to continually define the music and its culture in opposition to dominant musical practices. In the case of indie music, these may have included at various moments retrenchment in new "authentic" localities, the embrace of the seven-inch vinyl single, new ways of expressing a "do-it-yourself" (DIY) ethic, and the celebration of "pure pop" in the wake of mainstream success by noisier former indie bands like Nirvana.

"Indie," "College," or "Alternative"?

Because the institutions and practices of indie music were substantially about defining the music and the people associated with it as separate from dominant institutions and practices, the choice of a term to define the music and its culture is critical. My use of "indie pop/rock music" or "indie music" to describe the object of study is somewhat arbitrary; other labels, including "college rock," "college music," and "alternative music" could also apply. For those who share a popular perception of what was played on college radio in the 1980s and early 1990s, the term "college music" (or "college rock") brings to mind various guitar-based bands that began and in some cases remained on independent record labels: these bands might include mainstream successes like Nirvana, R.E.M., and the Cure as well as lesser-known bands like Superchunk. However, college radio stations were and are anything but uniform in their programming. In the United States in the 1980s and 1990s one could find college stations with Top 40 or Contemporary Hit Radio (CHR) formats, college stations with album-oriented rock (AOR) formats, and college stations with adult contemporary (AC) formats.

Since defining a musical genre based on its relationship to college radio is problematic, it is worthwhile to explore other genre labels. In 1991 *Spin* writer Jim Greer wondered whether "maybe 'college music' means alternative music—alternative, I guess, to mainstream pop. Alternative because, as Madonna put it recently, it's not popular."[1] Indeed, for many artists and businesspeople involved in the production and distribution of non-mainstream pop and rock music in the 1980s and early 1990s, "alternative" proved an attractive choice. An independent record store owner in San Francisco in the early 1990s noted that "the college music market includes independent and major labels—it's mostly alternative music. And I think 'alternative music' is kind of college music."[2] In her 1993 book *Manic Pop Thrill*, *Hits Magazine* columnist Rachel Felder used "alternative" to describe the sorts of bands one expected to hear on college radio: "British guitar" bands like the Smiths and the Fall; "American guitar" bands like Sonic Youth and Nirvana; "Miasma" and "Feedback" bands like My Bloody Valentine and Jesus and Mary Chain; and so on. Yet Felder acknowledged that the label "alternative" was not entirely satisfactory, beginning the book with this statement:

> Let's face it: The term "alternative"—which is used more often than not to describe mega-selling bands like R.E.M. and Jesus Jones as well as less than mega-sellers like, say, Tad and Jesus Lizard—is just plain inadequate. I mean, what is called "alternative" is anything but one coherent musical sound; a cross section of alternative bands is as variegated as a UN conference. (1)

Or, as a Champaign-Urbana Illinois record store manager and musician said of alternative music in the late 1980s and early 1990s:

> There are so many bands that fall into that category that can be totally different. You have bands like Public Enemy which definitely are, at least for college, the biggest rap band. And then you've got bands like Jane's Addiction, they were huge, at least in that age group.[3]

Once the boundaries of what constitutes "alternative music" are expanded, deciding what fits and what does not fit becomes even more difficult. One longtime Champaign record store employee articulated the dilemma, pointing out that many forms of music can be alternative to the mainsteam, some of which may not usually be perceived as part of an "alternative music" genre:

You can say, "What is alternative music?" It could be anything from the [Chicago independent] Touch and Go label . . . and some of the just real small labels . . . [but] there's a lot of international students, there's a lot of students from Africa that come in and buy African music. That's an alternative music.[4]

The very broadness of the term, however, made it attractive. Despite its vagueness, a booking agent at major San Francisco club of the 1980s and 1990s, preferred the term "alternative," stating "I always call [college music] 'alternative music' myself . . . [alternative music] in my mind is a lot broader than [what gets played] at college radio stations."[5]

Ultimately though, the word "alternative" continues to beg the question implied by Jim Greer: "Alternative to what?" If indeed "alternative" primarily connotes "alternative to mainstream pop," then we must wonder, as Greer did, "A lot of music that's potentially mainstream-bound fails because it's bad. Does that make it alternative?"[6] Maybe "alternative music" is specifically music designed to sound non-mainstream. If so, how do we define this sound? And what about music that sounds "non-mainstream" at a point in time, like Nirvana's "Smells Like Teen Spirit" or the Cure's "Just Like Heaven," that becomes part of the mainstream? Is this music still "alternative"?

A third term to consider is "independent," or, more precisely, "indie," music. Although there are a host of independent labels in a variety of genres—blues, rap, bluegrass, folk—the word "indie" is perhaps most commonly used to describe independent rock and pop labels. Thus referring to my object of study as "indie pop/rock" is useful. What do we say, however, about bands like R.E.M., Nirvana, and the Replacements that started out on independent labels and then moved to major labels? Did they cease to be "indie" bands even though their sound(s) did not radically change? For many fans and music scene participants though, "indie" described a sound and a point of origin more than it describes a specific economic relationship.[7] It should also be noted that a staggering number of "indie" artists who moved from independent labels to the majors eventually lost their major label deals and then continued their recording careers on indie labels.

What Is Indie Pop and Rock Music?

Indie pop/rock music of the 1980s and early 1990s is not an easy genre to define. If we were to try, for instance, to define a "sound" of the period by consulting the CMJ charts to find out what the top college radio songs were, and if we then wanted to ascertain what musical elements these songs shared, we would be faced with a list that included sounds as diverse the melodic folk-rock of R.E.M.'s "Losing My Religion," The Cult's metal-influenced "Love Removal Machine," the bouncy pop of the Go-

Gos' "Our Lips Are Sealed," and the hardcore-inspired music of bands like Hüsker Dü. Despite this diversity, an entertainment attorney who worked with college radio stars like Camper Van Beethoven and Soundgarden thought that R.E.M. was central in establishing a college radio sound during the 1980s:

> After the advent of independent, alternative bands, with maybe R.E.M. being the top of the heap, I think a lot of college bands . . . have a lot of sixties guitar influences, and may be a little more eclectic; not particularly real pop, but sort of alternative pop. And usually they [are] bands; usually they [have] guitar, bass, and drums.[8]

This account marginalizes synthesizer-based bands like New Order, Depeche Mode, and Pet Shop Boys, all of which were popular on college radio during the 1980s. Their absence indicates the degree to which by the late 1980s and early 1990s college music had come to be thought of specifically as college *rock* music.

Guitars came to be seen as the crucial element in the "college radio sound." In 1990, an executive at independent record label Alias noted that "people tend to associate [college music] with jangly, straight-ahead kind of rock bands that don't get played on AOR or CHR."[9] A former member San Francisco band Camper Van Beethoven offered a more detailed description at the time of the way guitars were used in college music:

> [One] element of it is the people who got more interested in folk music after R.E.M. and started using Rickenbacker guitars and arpeggiating chords and jangling, and they're happy using open strings in their chords; and along with that end of it, the addition of folk instruments like violin and mandolin.
>
> [But] a lot of [college music] came out of the punk stuff, and so there's a lot of harder and sort of faster guitar playing, more distorted guitar . . . you get bands that were like SST [a hardcore label] bands . . . So now we have these bands like Dinosaur Jr. or post-Hüsker Dü bands like Soul Asylum that are doing that sort of thing.[10]

The division to which this musician pointed was the widely perceived division between indie pop and indie rock. Both genres were guitar-based, but indie pop tended to be more melodic and less loud than other forms of music found in the broad genre of early 1990s alternative rock: namely hardcore and grunge, which tended to be loud and heavy; punk, which tended to be loud and fast; and more straight-ahead rock music, which tended to be more raucous than indie pop but did not quite fit into the other categories (1980s and 1990s bands like The Pixies, Smashing Pumpkins, and even Camper Van Beethoven, would fit here.)

Most of the musicians that I interviewed identified themselves as indie pop musicians, and one of the independent record labels I examined, Parasol, was and is primarily associated with this sub-genre. Individuals who identified with the indie pop tradition tend to cite as influences The Beatles, The Beach Boys' *Pet Sounds* album, various folk-rock or psychedelic pop acts of the 1960s and early 1970s (The Byrds, Alex Chilton), and punk, mainly for its stripped-down production values and do-it-yourself attitude.

Of course, just as defining a genre of "college" or "indie pop/rock" music is a problematic task, so is sub-dividing the genre. While some bands seem clearly to fit into one sub-genre or another, others are difficult to categorize. Sub-genre labels serve a useful role as, to use sociologist Pierre Bourdieu's term, a form of "practical taxonomy" through which one can divide up and make sense of the musical landscape (*Outline*, 112). Although I will use terms like "indie pop" to describe the music I discuss, the boundaries between categories are quite fluid and gray areas between sub-genres abound.

When we move back out to the more general problem of defining an overarching genre called "indie pop/rock" music we find, unsurprisingly, that outlining the musical qualities that define indie pop/rock – it features guitars, it is associated with bands rather than individuals – remains a difficult task, because a number of "indie pop/rock" or college acts simply did not fit the commonly-accepted criteria: New Order used synthesizers almost exclusively; at different moments in indie pop/rock history Morrissey (of the Smiths), Kristin Hersh (of Throwing Muses), and Juliana Hatfield (of the Blake Babies) left their bands and became a solo artists; others, like Liz Phair, were never defined by association with a band; and so on. These exceptions, however, were still generally accepted as fitting into the music genre, a fact perhaps best explained by alternative music editor at the *Gavin Report*, who said of indie pop/rock music, "it's not always sound and image, or if it's on a major or an indie. It's something like the experience of it all [that makes college music] a genre unto itself."[11]

Maybe it would be more useful to describe an aesthetic that is broader than the music itself. In his analysis of the independent label Rough Trade, David Hesmondhalgh identified "democratisation," allowing greater participation and access in media systems, as a key concept in post-punk, indie musical production (256). More simplistically, some observers saw indie pop/rock music as a "Do-It-Yourself" (DIY) cultural form rooted in the musical non-professionalism of punk in the 1970s. Indeed, Rachel Felder contended in the early 1990s that alternative (her word of choice) music was culturally significant, not because of its sound, but because "it encompasses a whole ethic." Felder explained that for a band this ethic included touring the alternative club circuit and hauling one's own equipment from show to show; for fans it entailed particular ways of dressing, acting and dancing.[12] One can assume Felder viewed these practices as constituting a more "authentic" form of musical performance than mainstream pop or rock, one in which the distance between performer and audience is minimal. She saw these practices as "an expression of 'fed-up-ness' with the status quo" (5). According to Felder, even a financially successful major label band like Nirvana shared this ethic because band members still dressed like their fans, expressed public beliefs similar to those held by their fans, and took lesser known alternative bands on tour with them (8). However, as will be seen later, the aura of "authenticity" attached to the performer-audience ethic can be rather illusory.

A "Do-It-Yourself" (DIY) attitude was an important part of the ethic binding musicians, entrepreneurs, and fans described by Felder. The indie pop/rock music landscape was and is filled with DIY enterprises: tiny record labels, xeroxed fanzines, college radio shows, and bands whose members have little musical experience. A member of a 1990s San Francisco indie pop band explained the importance of the DIY ethic:

> When college radio first started out, it was really an alternative . . . the whole idea was that you didn't need a major label to do this. It was really kind of a "Fuck You," in a way. The fact that you were on an independent label was kind of a statement. . . . It showed that anybody could make a record, anybody could play in a band, anybody could get played on college radio.[13]

It is important to note, however, that the DIY universe was a mythic construct. Felder's network of alternative fans, businesses and bands did not exist independent of mainstream influence; and while college radio expanded the possibilities for aspiring musicians, problems of access to instruments, potential bandmates, and/or recording technology, and the failure to impress gatekeepers at independent record labels and/or college radio stations, meant that it has never been true that anybody could be heard on college radio or that anyone could make a record. Still, factual problems with the DIY claim do not negate the existence of the DIY aesthetic. Indeed, the very belief that indie pop/rock music was and is DIY music is crucial in defining the genre.

Some observers, however, argued that there was nothing inherent in the music or culture of indie music that defined the genre. Instead, they saw it as an entity defined by the music industry. Seeing music specifically labeled as "college music" as an industry marketing niche necessitated a more cynical view of the music and its audience, as Jim Greer demonstrated when he wrote in the *Spin College Music Report* that

> "College music" is a marketing concept . . . You, the college student, have (no doubt unwittingly) become part of a target group, by virtue of your demonstrated willingness to spend money on anything that some marketing expert at MegaBig Records can convince you is hipper/smarter/better than the latest Elton John effort. Which is usually not hard to do.[14]

In fact, it was never a given that any music played on college radio was "hipper" than the latest release by Elton John or even Barbra Streisand. Meanings of musics and performers are ever-shifting cultural constructs and therefore sites of contestation; for instance, an album by the once "square" crooner Tony Bennett can be popular with alternative music fans.[15] Major labels in the 1980s and 1990s tried to stay aware of these shifts in meaning, largely by recruiting former college radio staffers into major label jobs in order to most effectively target the college market with particular acts and releases.

"College music" in particular became a relevant term because it could define a genre through the primary medium by which it was disseminated: college radio. Defining college music as, "The kind of music played on college radio," or, more specifically, "The kind of music on the college radio charts" avoided the complexities of describing a sound, an "attitude" of fans and bands, or industry marketing strategies—though clearly each one of these factors contributed to whether a record was distributed to, played by, or successful on college radio. A San Francisco record store owner in the early 1990s, for instance, noted at the time that "there is [a college music genre], because it would be what college radio stations play; what's on their playlists could be called that."[16] A San Francisco musician who recorded for a few different independent labels observed that college music "is probably my bands. I say that because we tend to do really well on college radio, and those related areas, like the clubs that have those kind of bands. We don't really do well anywhere else."[17]

Yet inseparable from the medium, and implied in the above statements, is the college radio (and, in general, alternative music) audience itself; in many respects, audience defines the genre. When asked whether such a thing as "college music" exists, a Champaign, Illinois, independent label founder offered this rather circular and contradictory definition, "Yeah. I'd say [it's] whatever non-mainstream-music young people are listening to . . . And you can listen to it and figure out which people like it. Like Nirvana, R.E.M., I would still consider college music, maybe because they started initially in that genre."[18] A Champaign musician agreed with this audience-centered, age-delimited definition, explaining that to him "college music signifies younger music for people who are of college age or a little bit older."[19]

Although one may question the validity of a definition of college or indie music in the 1980s and early 1990s that limits its audience to those who were of college age or a little older, it is unquestionable that understanding the audience for the music—whether one chooses to call it college music or indie pop/rock—and its context is crucial to understanding its economic, social and cultural importance. It is a mistake to conceptualize this audience as uniform and unified.

Writing in the early 1990s, author Rachel Felder, for example, over-simplistically asserted that "Alternative fans share coherent tastes and beliefs" (41). Like any other social group, music fans are cross-cut by differences of gender, socioeconomic status, sexual orientation, generational identity, ethnicity, politics and so on. Though one might be tempted to proclaim R.E.M. fans as primarily middle-class, environmentally-concerned, politically-liberal, heterosexual white males and females in their thirties and forties who also like the music of, say Natalie Merchant—and indeed, a large number of R.E.M. fans probably fit this profile—one would undoubtedly soon learn that there are R.E.M. fans who like Natalie Merchant and R.E.M. fans who despise her; R.E.M. fans who are pro-choice and R.E.M. fans who are pro-life; R.E.M. fans who are gay and R.E.M. fans who are homophobes, and so on. There are white R.E.M. fans and R.E.M. fans of color, middle-class R.E.M. fans and working-class R.E.M. fans. However, it may well be true that alternative/college/indie rock music fans share particular tastes and demographic characteristics with each other more so than with the general population.

The relationship between indie pop/rock music audiences and the music itself is always changing, so defining the genre in terms of its audience—as well as in terms of an aesthetic, and of what product the music industry labels "alternative" or what artists college radio plays—means that the definition is always in flux. The difficulty of pinning down how all these elements came together to constitute a genre was articulated by an indie label owner in Champaign in late 1991:

> The old definition [of college music], I don't think it applies anymore—that it was this pseudo-underground thing, that college radio stations would play music that other radio stations weren't playing, that you could listen to a college radio station and hear this cool new hip music . . . But the bands that were college music, which are R.E.M., the Cure and Depeche Mode, that stuff's so mainstream now. And Nirvana right now is the grossest example of the whole thing. I like their album, but the fact that you can go into Garcia's [a then-popular pizzeria in the major commercial area around the University of Illinois campus] and hear it is a little ridiculous, and sort of, I think, takes away from the college music scene . . . I don't see how people can say it's a college music scene anymore."[20]

In this attempt to define college or indie music, the label owner constructed an historical trajectory, one that was echoed by others involved in indie pop/rock music—and one common in historical accounts of other rock/pop music forms, like rhythm and blues, rap, disco and country—in which the music moved from being an "authentic" marginal music to one that was co-opted by the mainstream. His account also points to the critical roles of locality and place in stories of indie music. The theme of rise and decline and the importance of place are both central tropes in narrative histories of indie music's perceived origins and pattern of development in the U.S. Personal narratives from music scene participants and institutional/economic and social accounts of college music demonstrate how these narrative constructs articulate and/or contribute to a shared understanding of indie music's received history.[21]

Histories of U.S. Indie Pop/Rock Music Scenes

Almost all historical narratives of popular music are narratives of rise and fall. In the typical narrative, a music exists on the margins and is perceived by its producers/ consumers/observers to be a "true" and "spontaneous expression of lived experience" (Frith, "Music" 55). For example, Simon Frith describes early punk's construction by some theorists as an articulation of "the values of the punk subculture and [which], in turn, were read as a form of working class consciousness" (55). Once a musical form like punk or indie pop/rock begins to receive some recognition from mainstream institutions and audiences, it is "co-opted" by the mainstream, thereby losing much of the aura of authenticity that it held for its original audience.

The move from margins to mainstream is generally accompanied by much consternation among members of the music's core audience over artists "selling out" and marks a central moment of decline in most narratives. "Selling out" can take a number of forms, but in general it depends on the perception that an artist has changed his/her musical style or relationship to his/her core audience on the road to becoming more popular. Narratives of selling out and musical cooptation are recurrent in rock and pop music history. As music writer Steve Perry states, "The rhetoric of the sellout isn't new; the crossover critic who decries synthesized pop-funk often echoes the 1960s folkies who bemoaned the rise of the electric guitar" (54). Moreover, those who mourn the loss of a musical form's "authenticity" tend to ignore the reality that all forms of popular music are to some degree consciously constructed commodities (Frith, "Music" 55–56).

In indie music culture, the debate over authenticity was part of a larger struggle over the meaning of indie music. For many indie music scene participants, certain entities seeking to define the music (major labels, retail chains, large-scale promoters) were understood to be less "authentic" than others (independent labels, non-chain retailers, small clubs) contesting the same terrain. Mainstream popularity was sometimes expressly avoided by many scene participants who wished to define themselves by their difference from the mainstream. Whenever a band with alternative credibility signed with a major label, whenever an independent label entered into a financial relationship with a major label, whenever a college radio station adhered to playlists and rotations, the inherent tensions within a social, economic, and cultural formation that professed to eschew the mainstream success it was experiencing were exacerbated and a new version of the battle over what counted as alternative/indie/college music was joined.

Such tensions underlie the narrative of the received history of indie music. Chronology is an important framework for the narrative, especially as it charts the significance of the music's movement from the margins (when it was "authentic") to mainstream recognition (its moment of perceived decline as artists and institutions "sell out.") In addition, and not unrelated, many interview subjects made it clear that a sense of *place* was significant to them: especially since these places tended to be culturally or economically marginal localities and local spaces. Indeed, many oral and written accounts of the emergence of indie or college music privileged locality. A 1986 *Newsweek* article titled "Rock Around the U.S.A." geographically mapped college music, centering the phenomenon in three key localities: Austin, Minneapolis–St. Paul, and Boston.[22] For Rachel Felder in *Manic Pop Thrill*, locality played a more important role than history in determining what bands sounded like; she argued that within any local alternative music scene there are

> local bands both influenced by their surroundings and playing within them; such was the case in Seattle (with bands like Nirvana, Pearl Jam, Mother Love Bone), Providence (home of Velvet Crush and small factory), Washington D.C. (the base for Unrest, Tsunami, and Velocity Girl), and Portland, Oregon (where Pond came from). (14)

While she did not explain how each locality influenced bands, Felder's list of cities and bands serves as an indication of the centrality of place—and especially of "important" places—in indie or college music discourse. A particularly important site of alternative music in the United Kingdom discussed by Felder was northern England, primarily Manchester, a region of whose bands she noted:

> There is in most of these bands a common, amorphic, notable mark of cold, rainy, depressed northern England. That imprint may not be distinctly pinpointable, but it's unquestionably there. It runs through bands like New Order, which was started from the remnants of the very depressed Joy Division, whose morose elegance was an influence on many bands. And the mark runs through the Smiths and through even poppier bands like the Inspiral Carpets. It also runs through the key bands mentioned in this chapter: the Chameleons and the Wedding Present (both from nearby Leeds), Kitchens of Distinction (featuring Mancunian lead singer Patrick Fitzgerald), and the Fall. (44)

Felder privileged place over memory, but ultimately place and memory are inseparable in accounts of indie music. Particular moments and particular localities were both important parts of individual narratives of the origins and history of college music. Although the places in which they were located differed, many music scene participants identified the "moment" of punk as crucial to the development of college music. For instance, asked when indie or college music emerged as a distinct genre, one San Francisco musician replied:

> I see it starting in 1977. I was living in Davis, and I was going to high school, and my brother worked at the radio station—KDVS—so I used to do shows there. And he used to listen to a lot of stuff that was coming over from England in about '77, '78. It was stuff that was unlike anything that I was hearing on the FM stations at that point.[23]

Similarly, a club booking agent in San Francisco linked her memory of the emergence indie pop/rock music with the convergence of a particular place and a time in the 1970s:

> It was '78, '79—that's when I got involved with college radio. They still had pictures of the Doors [in the station], but there was this whole trend to hate Led Zeppelin at the same time. And there were cover bands that played the Ramones; that sort of stuff we had in Chico, California.[24]

Another Northern California musician located his awareness of college radio and the indie music played on it at the moment at which he started college in the late 70s: "I guess it was around '77, '78, when I first went to college, oddly enough. Fall of '78 is when I went to college, although it was starting to happen about a year before that."[25]

Others placed the origins of indie or college music as a genre a little later, in the early 1980s, but still tended to identify the moment not just with a time but also with a place. For instance, a prominent indie musician recalled the year 1980 as being particularly important. He stated, "I remember [1980] vividly, because that when I was really beginning to listen to music all the time, and that was when I was first starting to hear about clubs in Los Angeles."[26] Similarly, the founder of a Midwestern indie pop label recalled:

> The first I ever knew about [college music] was the Athens [Georgia] scene . . . when I first got into music I heard about the Athens scene and that clique: R.E.M., Let's Active, dBs, Turning Curious. It was '81 when the first R.E.M. single came out. It was right when that single came out when everything seemed to start coming out of Athens and North Carolina . . . and that was a huge scene.[27]

Many people associated with the San Francisco indie pop scene located the genre's appearance as a national phenomenon in the early 1980s as well, but rather than pointing to Athens, Georgia as the key site, they emphasized the important role played by local college radio stations in establishing college music. When asked when indie pop/rock music appeared, one San Francisco–based musician said:

> I'd say the early eighties. When I moved up here, our manager was a DJ on KSFS, which was the San Francisco State station; and actually it was through him that I became aware of college radio. Then he worked at KUSF. It was at that point that I realized that college radio is the only type of radio where some of this music could be played.[28]

A local entertainment attorney went so far as to say that "in San Francisco the prototype of college radio, and maybe throughout America, is KUSF. And KUSF started in 1980," thereby linking the emergence of college music with the establishment of KUSF as an alternative music station.[29]

The importance of place in histories of indie pop & rock music cannot be over-emphasized; despite the differences between individual narratives in the particular times and sites pinpointed, the necessity of locating music within both a temporal and geographical context cross-cuts almost all such narratives. The practices of making and listening to music were always located in specific places and times. These places and times carried individual significance, but some became part of a larger discourse in which certain moments and certain places were understood as particularly meaningful.

A Chronological Narrative of Indie Music

By pooling oral and written narratives of indie rock/pop music's emergence and de-velopment one can arrive at a chronological narrative of indie music. Specific themes, events, bands, and localities appeared repeatedly across individual ac-counts; and all accounts agree on the general trajectory the music took in the 1980s and early 1990s.

In attempting to locate indie pop/rock music's point of origin, most sources agreed that British and American punk rock music of the mid-seventies played a central role in shaping the ethos of North American indie pop/rock music. But many also pointed to earlier influences, like American "garage" bands and the "proto-punk" of the late 1960s and early 1970s, which shared with punk rock and indie music a certain disdain for professional musicianship, while being less con-frontational than punk. An early 1980s issue of *Spin* magazine listed "The Top Ten College Cult Classic Albums," and, as testament to the widely held belief that a retrospectively named "proto-punk" had a significant impact on college music, three of the albums named were recorded before 1970: The Velvet Underground's *White Light/White Heat* (1968), The Stooges' eponymous 1969 album, and *Kick Out the Jams* by MC5 (1969).[30]

The degree to which "proto-punk" bands inspired future indie music artists is questionable, however, since most indie musicians were too young to have heard these albums when they were first released and only discovered them a decade or more later. British (and American) punk rock music of the mid-seventies seems by far to have been a more direct influence on indie music and was frequently cited by interview subjects. For instance, one owner of an independent record store argued that indie music "really came out of the punk and post-punk scenes,"[31] a perception echoed by Rachel Felder, who wrote, "the roots of this music can be found in the punk movement of the late seventies, which shunned the musical conventions of the time" (3).

An executive at an independent record label placed indie pop/rock music's origins in the mid-to-late seventies too, and she claimed that what was significant about that time was not merely the emergence of punk, but also the formation of audiences for all kinds of alternative music:

> After the disco period, I think there was something in the underground that was definitely growing, that was just so disheartened and disillusion with what was getting played on the radio. More people started finding different types of music.

> Punk was just such a huge turning point in the development of college music. It gave people something to rally behind; it was really an alternative at that point. Bands like the Sex Pistols and the Vibrators led the way . . . [they] gave bands after them an audience, [they] gave them a base to build on . . . I don't really see anything that challenged the major label system before that.[32]

Yet writer Scott Decker, ignoring the influence of New York punk bands like the Ramones, argued in *CMJ's* tenth anniversary book that British punk's effect on American music was not immediate:

> [In 1979] in Britain, the punk revolution was already over two years old and its impact had become far-reaching. Its overall mark on America, however . . . was negligible; in fact, the most attention it received was in February '79, when ex-Sex Pistol Sid Vicious died of a self-inflicted drug overdose in a Manhattan jail cell awaiting trial for the murder of his girlfriend, Nancy Spungen. (10)

A *Gavin Report* alternative music editor agreed that punk's impact in the United States was delayed, but she claimed that once punk music and its aesthetic arrived in the U.S., its influence on the development of college music was significant:

> . . . by the time punk really got to America, it was about 1979; and in New York and especially in Los Angeles there was a whole do-it-yourself thing. So there were all these bands making records and pressing them and distributing them.[33]

Los Angeles and New York were the cities most often mentioned as sites of seminal American alternative music scenes. The May 5, 1980 issue of *CMJ* included a cover story on Los Angeles bands which featured punk/hardcore bands like Black Flag, X, and the Germs, and pop bands like the Go-Gos and the Plimsouls (Decker 15). Along with prominent New York City alternative acts of the time like the Bush Tetras, Lydia Lunch, and Talking Heads, these Los Angeles bands were seen by many to represent the earliest stage of indie pop/rock music's development, during which the "do-it-yourself" ethos was firmly established (Fletcher 7; Decker 19).

In addition to American bands, British, Australian, and Irish bands were prominent in the narrative of college music's early history. For instance, in the early eighties, British "neo-psychedelic" bands like Echo & the Bunnymen and Teardrop Explodes reached audiences through college radio airplay. British acts like The Smiths, The Cure, XTC, Robyn Hitchcock, the Psychedelic Furs, and Jesus and Mary Chain, and Australian acts like Midnight Oil, the Church, and Hoodoo Gurus were college radio favorites in the 1980s. But these acts occupied rather different positions in college music history than most American acts, because foreign bands were not implicated in local scenes for American listeners in the same way as American acts. Occasionally, as with the Manchester "scene" of the late eighties, the locality from which foreign acts emanated was made salient to American audiences, though a British locality's significance is clearly not the same to an American listener as it is to a British listener.

The appearance of the B-52's in the national spotlight in the late 1970s, followed by the early 1980s critical praise for R.E.M., contributed to a media "buzz" about the Athens, Georgia music scene that helped to shift the narrative of college music away from the entertainment centers of New York and Los Angeles (and also away from punk and hardcore) and to the periphery, where DIY rock/pop was being produced. Athens, Georgia became, in college music discourse, the prototypical college music "scene." A 1993 issue of *Spin* featured an article called "A to Z of Alternative Music" which included the following entry:

> Athens, Georgia. The town that made "college rock" a three-letter word in the early '80s: R.E.M., who along with the B-52's, Pylon, and dozens of other quirky, jingly-jangly combos came out of the cracks seemingly all at once, setting the stage for leagues of imitators for years to come.[34]

The B-52's emerged from Athens in the late 1970s to gain notice at New York alternative clubs like CBGB's, and the band signed to Warner Brothers in 1979 (see Brown, 47–69). When R.E.M. also gained national attention a few years later, Athens became central in the indie music narrative. This excerpt from Andy Schwartz's 1982 *New York Rocker* interview with R.E.M.'s Peter Buck, Mike Mills, and Michael Stipe illustrates how, in the early 1980s, Athens came to be articulated as the first geographically-peripheral alternative music center:

> To hear them tell it, R.E.M. could have happened anywhere, *is* happening in cities and towns across the nation, miles from the media centers. Athens is accidental, if not incidental. That the Georgia university town also gave us the B-52's, Pylon, the Method Actors, Love Tractor, and the Side Effects, is, according to Peter Buck, "just a coincidence." Or maybe not . . .
> Mills: "It's just that when a band comes to play in Athens, everybody goes to see 'em and has that kind of interaction . . . That's how we got together."
> Stipe: "Also, as far as new bands coming up [to NYC]–the B-52's brought Pylon, Pylon brought the Method Actors, the Method Actors brought Love Tractor . . ."

Mills: "Plus there are some [Athens] club owners who are willing to let the new bands play. The 40-Watt Club, the guys at Tyrone's–they provided a place for somebody to get up and do something different. There are people everywhere who would listen to the new stuff if they could only get exposed to it."[35]

In the narrative of indie music, Athens was important not only because it produced notable alternative bands, but also because it signified the possibility that any locality with the right elements—in the case of Athens, an an alternative college radio station (WUOG), alternative clubs in which to play (Tyrone's, the 40-Watt Club), an independent record store (Wuxtry)—could become an indie music mecca. Rachel Felder downplayed the importance of R.E.M. in her examination of alternative music by remarking that the band was "like a yuppie alternative . . . cool, but not frightening, jangly in a very American way . . . to me, the band is not all that interesting on a musical or cultural level" (155). To dismiss R.E.M. as not interesting on a cultural level is to ignore the important ways in which a locality becomes meaningful to those who do not live in it. Had no Athens band followed the B-52's into the national spotlight, perhaps the "Athens scene" would never had existed as a popular construct, and there would have been no real precedent for the "Seattle scene" of the late-eighties and early-nineties. Because of Athens' distance from the media centers of New York and Los Angeles, the town and the bands associated with it enabled a discourse that linked indie music identity and authenticity with locality. In the early and mid-1980s, as Tony Fletcher notes in his biography of R.E.M., "would-be bohemians" flocked to Athens and formed bands (78). Ultimately, R.E.M. and the B-52's were the only Athens bands to enjoy mainstream success (and the B-52's moved to New York City in 1979), and after the mid-1980s the indie music narrative shifted to other local scenes.

By the mid-1980s, the print media were focusing more attention on Athens and other localities. *CMJ* spotlighted a number of American "movements" in 1984, including the "paisley underground" on the west coast, led by the 3 O'Clock, the Bangles, and Rain Parade; the Boston indie scene, including Mission of Burma, Volcano Suns, and Dumptruck; and various "roots rockers" like Jason and the Scorchers, the Del Fuegos, Rank and File, and True West (Decker 35). Even the British music press announced the existence of an American independent music movement: in 1985 *Melody Maker* ran a four-part series called "State of the Union" on American alternative acts. During the same year, a number of indie bands, including Hüsker Dü, the Replacements, and Green On Red, were signed to major labels (Fletcher 78). By 1986, American local and regional alternative music scenes were getting widespread coverage in the mainstream media. *Newsweek*, for instance, averred that "Some of the best music isn't in the big cities: it's in Hometown, America" and looked at alternative music activity in cities like Austin, Boston, and Minneapolis, far removed from East and West Coast entertainment capitals of New York and Los

Angeles.[36] The *Village Voice*'s Pazz & Jop polls of the early and mid-eighties tended to celebrate geographically-peripheral bands like R.E.M., the dBs, and Hüsker Dü. Indeed, in the mid-1980s much alternative media attention was focused on Hüsker Dü and fellow Minneapolis bands the Replacements, and Soul Asylum.[37]

Many sources claim that it was during the mid-eighties that college radio established itself as a medium of importance to the mainstream music industry and that indie rock music solidified into a recognizable genre. More and more independent labels like Enigma and Big Time signed distribution deals with major labels, and major labels began to divert more of their resources to college radio marketing. One musician interviewed stated that college music "defined itself around the mid-eighties—'84 or '85—because there were so many bands. Labels and radio had to call it something."[38] Another musician expanded on this:

> . . . college radio had a really obvious period of growth, and then by the time that [we] put out [our] first record, it was just finishing defining itself . . . in 1985 the concrete was definitely beginning to harden into a form.[39]

Within the discourse of college music history, the moment of definition marks the point at which the genre went into decline. Bob Mould, formerly of Hüsker Dü, remembered the mid-1980s as a time during which independent music production and distribution was starting to fall apart:

> [A] milestone was in late '85 when Hüsker Dü went from [independent label] SST to Warner Brothers, the beginning of my now-aborted tenure with major labels, watching a scene that for five years had a lot of strength and energy and cooperation start to come apart at the seams, at least that's what I thought.[40]

Mainstream attention to a formerly marginal music meant that at a time when indie pop/rock music's earliest adherents largely believed that the music was being co-opted and made less authentic, broader audiences became aware of bands which had up to that point enjoyed only cult popularity. In 1987, for instance, R.E.M., Squeeze, and the Cure all crossed over from the college and alternative charts to success on the *Billboard* pop chart (Decker 51). By January of 1988, R.E.M.'s album *Document*, released on the independent I.R.S. label, had sold one million copies (Fletcher 103).

The latter years of the 1980s and the early years of 1990s have been articulated in the discourse of indie pop/rock music as essentially a continuation of the infiltration of alternative bands into the mainstream. 1991, however, is a particularly significant year in the narrative of indie rock history, marked by two events: (1) the commercial success of Nirvana's *Nevermind* album, and (2) the first Lollapalooza concert tour, a popular and profitable touring "festival" of alternative bands. Both events generated a substantial amount of debate over whether indie or alternative acts were "selling out" when they reached a wide audience. What counts as "selling out" constitutes a rather wide range of practices and events. As Dave Laing explains in *One Chord Wonders*, his examination of British punk rock, the model of selling out consists "of something to 'sell out' (a cause, a vision, a pact with the fans) and somewhere to sell-out to (the record industry, occupying a separate space from that of the original pure creation)" and has been part of rock discourse since the 1960s (106-107).

Who has sold out and who has not is a site of much contention and of very fine, and sometimes inexplicable, distinctions in music communities. For instance, music journalist Ted Friedman, in a comparison of several college radio stars who moved on to mainstream success, asserted in the early 1990s that "[as] one of the very few women in popular music who really rocks, Sinead [O'Connor] served her public well in graduating from cult hero to mass icon," but that

> by the time [R.E.M.'s major label debut album] *Green* was released, the ironic distance between R.E.M. and their audience had turned sour with contempt. The crass, tired "Stand" is one of those songs that could never be a hit single for an unknown band, but is inoffensive enough to coast into the Top 40 on name recognition. When Michael Stipe introduced the song in concerts by saying, "this is the stupidest song ever written," he wasn't joking, and it wasn't funny.[41]

The pronouncement that R.E.M. had sold out and Sinead O'Connor had not was an expression of personal opinion; an equally valid argument could be made to support the opposite contention. This sort of disagreement has been prominent in anti-mainstream music circles for decades. As the excerpts from Friedman indicate, in indie music discourse "selling out" pertained both to the aesthetics, the perceived "authenticity" of the music, and to the relationship between an act and its audience: e.g. Sinead O'Connor remained in some way "true" to her audience, while R.E.M. did not live up to its end of the bargain and instead turned to producing material unworthy of its core audience.

Similarly, the quintuple-platinum success of Nirvana's second album and major label debut, *Nevermind*, inspired heated debate over whether the Seattle band had sold out. Unlike R.E.M.—whose fifth album was their first million-seller, whose sixth album was their major label debut, and whose crossover from the college to the pop charts was gradual—Nirvana's chart success seemed to come out of nowhere and created divisions among its fans. Some believed that Nirvana remained an "authentic" voice of the underground despite its mass popularity, a view articulated by Rachel Felder:

> By going outside the "alternative" demographic, Nirvana eased its way into the mainstream. But by sticking to its original alternative guns—by still doing interviews with fanzines, by sustaining its smash-it-up sound, by approaching icons of the

rock 'n' roll establishment like (as weird as it may sound to anyone from the sixties) *Rolling Stone*—with an adamantly "fuck you" attitude (by wearing a t-shirt reading "CORPORATE MAGAZINES STILL SUCK"), the band affirmed its alternative identity. Which is not to say that other bands haven't . . . expanded from their initial base through [the] mainstream media without "selling out". . . Nirvana has just done it recently, quickly, and with a lot of chutzpah . . . All three members [of Nirvana] have let fans know that a band could be on a major label, maintain the gruff bite of its original charm, and still hit the charts. (8 & 89)

Others strongly disagreed and maintained that Nirvana "sold out" by leaving Seattle independent label Sub Pop and signing with David Geffen's DGC label, a subsidiary of Warner Brothers. A harshly-worded article by Samuel Nathan Schiffman in the underground music fanzine *MAXIMUMROCKNROLL* titled "Nirvanification" laid out some of the arguments against Nirvana:

Even though Nirvana are probably wonderful human beings who have no idea that they're destroying our way of life, we are all within our rights to wish their destruction . . . Nirvana's success says that it's O.K. to fuck over not only your friends, but also the value system from which your career was built. If the complex support system which enabled SubPop to thrive did not exist their [sic] would be no Nirvana . . . Because of Nirvana's success we are witnessing a breakdown in the system . . .

Whether *Nevermind* is a piece of shit or a masterpiece is beside the point. The point is that like Elvis, Nirvana's success has metamorphosized them from being a representation of the counterculture to being nothing more than a mainstream caricature of us all. Wearing a "Corporate Magazines still Suck" t-shirt on the cover of *Rolling Stone* means nothing.[42]

By signing with a major label and selling over five million records, Nirvana lost its alternative credibility with many music scene participants, including Schiffman.

Like Nirvana's success, the success of the Lollapalooza tour, which showcased alternative bands, inspired debate over the question of whether alternative music has "sold out." Conceived by Jane's Addiction and Porno for Pyros lead singer Perry Farrell, the first Lollapalooza tour in the summer of 1991 was one of the few profitable tours during a summer in which the concert industry was struck particularly hard by the recession.[43] Although Farrell was praised by many in indie music circles for resisting corporate offers to sponsor Lollapalooza, others, like critic Evelyn MacDonnell, believed that the tour still fell victim to commercial impulses. She wrote of the 1992 edition of the tour:

Unfortunately, Lollapalooza doesn't have an ideology capable of resisting the pull of the marketplace. Conceptualized as a reactive forum rather than a model for revolution, much of the show comes across as packaged rebellion.[44]

Strong opinions such as these made Lollapalooza a key part of the terrain on which the meaning of college music in the nineties was contested.

As indie pop/rock music increasingly became part of mainstream American culture—indeed, the music and its stars came to be used to sell products like Gap clothing and Nike shoes[45]—the debate over its "authenticity" became more vital for those who seek to assert identities oppositional to the dominant culture. Many members of the original audiences for alternative acts believed that bands can no longer express the "truths" of and for those original audiences once the bands' fan bases have grown beyond their original audiences. For early fans of a band or music, its crossover to mainstream popularity represents, as Simon Frith describes it, an "ideological struggle between artistic truth and commercial compromise" (Frith, 1988, 130). Few took the happy view of writer Jim Greer, who observed that the mainstream's embrace of indie music meant that

> if you're tired of the sort of tried-and-true corporate rock that's been shoved down your throat for the larger part of your adolescence, you're going to have a lot more good music to listen to. It means that there'll be . . . more Top Ten records like Nirvana's—good bands in the pop charts, what a concept![46]

Greer's interpretation of the ramifications of alternative music's movement into the mainstream ran counter to the prevailing narrative of indie music history. Rather than seeing the music's assimilation into the mainstream as its downfall, he saw it as the mainstream's salvation. Such diverse readings indicate that the meanings and history(-ies) of college music will remain contested sites for the foreseeable future.

Conclusions: R.E.M. in the Definition and History of Indie Music

No band better exemplifies indie pop/rock music's historical trajectory than R.E.M. The band, founded on punk's "do-it-yourself" ethic, was made up of members who met when they all lived in the same college town. It continued to be based in a college town, received heavy college radio airplay well into the 1990s, spent several years on an independent label before signing with a major, and thus was in many respects the prototypical indie or college band. When R.E.M. was formed in 1980, three of its four members were attending college, a situation analogous to that of many other indie bands—from Santa Cruz's Camper Van Beethoven to Boston's Blake Babies to Champaign's Poster Children—that formed during the 1980s on college campuses, far from the entertainment capitals of New York and Los Angeles. And rather than booking dates in large cities, R.E.M.'s tours in the early 1980s took the band to cities like Greensboro, North Carolina and Memphis, Tennessee.[47] Not only was R.E.M. central in developing a pattern of regional and national touring that would be followed by many other indie bands, the group was also crucial in establishing college radio as a viable medium. CMJ founder Bobby Haber argued that R.E.M. was one of the first bands that could "be called the medium's own . . . that could sustain [itself] solely on college radio and its spinoff media: underground press, mom and pop retailers, and a loosely structured club circuit."[48] Within this network, the band found itself crossing paths and making friends with a variety of other bands that were also helping to define the genre, like the Neats and the Lyres from Boston, Hüsker Dü and the Replacements from Minneapolis, and Black Flag and the Minutemen from California (46). Critic Robert Christgau maintained that even in the 1990s, R.E.M. remained "definitive college-radio idols."[49]

R.E.M.'s career in the 1980s and 1990s paralleled the received narrative of college music's rise and fall. Formed by members who were influenced by New York-based proto-punk and punk musicians—especially Television and Patti Smith[50]—R.E.M. embraced the do-it-yourself ethic espoused by American and British punk bands. Patti Smith's idiosyncratic vocal style was a particularly important influence on lead singer Michael Stipe. He read an interview with her in which, according to Stipe, Smith said that "anybody could do it. And I took that very literally . . . I thought, 'If she can sing, I can sing.'"[51] In a similarly DIY vein, R.E.M.'s self-taught guitarist Peter Buck stated that all of R.E.M.'s earliest songs begin with the A chord because, "it was the only chord I really liked"; and he claimed that in 1981 when the band was at the top of many critics' lists, R.E.M. was essentially "three chords and a six-pack of beer."[52]

An initial DIY attitude toward music production followed by growing professionalism was not only characteristic of indie/college music in general, but of R.E.M. in particular, during the 1980s. Like many indie bands, R.E.M.'s first release was a seven-inch single on a micro-indie: 1981's "Radio Free Europe"/"Sitting Still" on Hib-Tone (Decker 27). In 1982 R.E.M. signed a five-record contract with an independent label, I.R.S., despite major label interest, because, according to Peter Buck:

> If we had gone with Columbia or Warner Bros., they would have put us on the bottom line of a big showcase. We didn't see the point of going with someone who didn't understand what we were doing. We wanted someone small who would let us learn. And the way we did it, we went from being pretty bad, to being okay, to being pretty good with some problems, to being a good band. (Quoted in Brown 192)

R.E.M.'s first EP, *Chronic Town*, and the two I.R.S. albums that followed, *Murmur* and *Reckoning*, were produced by North Carolina indie pop musician Mitch Easter, whose underground acclaim from his work with R.E.M. led a number of indie bands, from Champaign-Urbana's Turning Curious to Northern California's Game Theory, to seek out his services as a producer. 1983's *Murmur*, in the college music narrative, is a seminal album of the genre; as one reviewer noted, "this LP lured the majority of its listeners into the Athens sound that would inspire countless imitators, primarily manifested in Peter Buck's remarkable guitar riffs."[53] The album reached number two on the CMJ chart, number 26 on the *Billboard* album chart (the re-recorded version of "Radio Free Europe" from the album peaked at number 78 on the *Billboard* singles chart); and a *Billboard* writer observed that just prior to R.E.M.'s appearance on the charts in 1983 that "this Athens, Georgia quartet would have been considered too abrasive for pop radio; but the airwaves are gradually opening up to what used to be underground music" (quoted in Fletcher 52). Members of R.E.M. did indeed see themselves leading the college music underground into the mainstream, as Buck indicated in a 1983 interview: "We like to think of ourselves as the tip of the iceberg. We're not the most commercial band in the world, but we're one of the most accessible of the new American bands" (quoted in Fletcher 57).

Soon after R.E.M. released its third I.R.S. album, a headline above a 1985 *Billboard* article announced, "R.E.M. Surprised By Its Success, 'Fables of the Reconstruction' Is Group's Breakthrough."[54] The declaration was indicative not just of a band's success, but of a whole genre that was being in large part defined within the social and institutional practices of college radio, musicians, record companies, retailers, trade papers and the music press, and fans. R.E.M. released two more albums of new material on I.R.S.: *Life's Rich Pageant* (1986) and *Document* (1987). With *Document* the band achieved its first *Billboard* Top Ten album, and a single from *Document*, "The One I Love," was R.E.M.'s first Top Ten single. This breakthrough occurred at a moment in the indie music narrative at which the genre, having peaked in the mid-1980s, was seen as in decline. "The One I Love" was the song that made R.E.M. safe for Top 40 radio. According to Don Dixon, co-producer of R.E.M.'s first two albums, its crossover success would not have been possible at an earlier moment. Dixon stated that "Regardless of what 'The One I Love' sounded like when it came out in 1987, had it come out in 1983 on *Murmur* it wouldn't have got[ten] radio play" (quoted in Fletcher 102). So by the time R.E.M. signed with Warner in 1988—and four years before Nirvana reached the Top Ten with "Smells Like Teen Spirit"—R.E.M. had prepared the mainstream for future crossovers by alternative bands; and therefore, in the view of some, assured the co-optation and decline of indie music.

R.E.M. (or Nirvana, or the Cure, or any alternative act that achieved success on the *Billboard* album or singles chart), as part of a discourse surrounding the question of "selling out," became a metaphor for the conflict over commercialism in indie music as a whole. R.E.M.'s long-term relationship with I.R.S., its decision to remain in Athens, its support of little-known independent bands and so on allowed some, like *CMJ* columnist Jeff Tamarkin, to construct R.E.M. as a popular band that retained its alternative credibility:

Managing to expand within the stylistic framework it set for itself . . . R.E.M.['s *Document*] did what it did commercially largely on the basis of being a great band rather than playing any kowtowing music industry games. Its success was a testimonial to keeping one's head in place in the face of the pressures of success.[55]

Likewise, *Spin* writers Mark Blackwell and Jim Greer argued for R.E.M.'s retention of non-mainstream credibility long after the band had attained mainstream success, even though in the late 1980s

> longtime fans cried sellout and critics yawned, having long ago written off the band as having betrayed its early promise . . . [R.E.M.'s 1991 album] *Out of Time* serves as a reminder that R.E.M. has never played by the established rules, that they're as far from a mainstream band now as they were from a "college radio" band (whatever that's supposed to be) then.[56]

Yet within this discursive terrain, reaching a wide audience necessarily means "selling out" a little. Although individuals may quibble over whether songs like "Stand" or "Shiny Happy People" (or Soul Asylum's "Runaway Train" or The Cure's "Just Like Heaven," for that matter) aimed for a lower common denominator than the band's earlier, less commercially successful material,[57] popularity often alienated fans simply because the band, as part of the mainstream, could no longer be alternative or oppositional to it. Peter Buck acknowledged that R.E.M. had lost many of its original fans with mainstream recognition, but according to him, "That's fine. A lot of people like bands when they're smaller—and I'm one of them" (quoted in Fletcher 119). A narrative that raises questions about whether a band or a genre has "sold out" is in fact a narrative about personal and collective identity: it is about how music scene participants position themselves in relation to particular bands, to the mainstream, and to sets of situated practices defined in opposition to the mainstream.

More than any other band in the 1980s, R.E.M. embodied the contradictions and tensions between mainstream/margins, authenticity/artifice, and local/national. In regard to the third dichotomy, R.E.M. was particularly important because of the way in which the band was constructed in subcultural histories and media discourses as a product of and participant in *localized* musical practices. Recurrent among narratives that variously defined the band in terms of its musical style, its influence on other artists, its relationship to a specific generation and social class at a specific point in time, its interactions with the economic structures of underground and mainstream music production and distribution, and its members' location within a far-flung social network, was the importance of R.E.M's identification with the culturally peripheral locality of Athens, Georgia.

In a 1981 *Atlanta Journal-Constitution* article about the Athens music scene a reporter wrote, "It's rare that where a band comes from takes on nearly as much importance as what it's playing" (quoted in Brown 187). In indie music, it was not only the music itself but also where its practices were located (or where they were *not* located) that was essential in the production of meaning. In the description of the structures of indie music's industrial production and distribution that follows, I will demonstrate that despite the trends of centralization and globalization within the music industry, businesses like independent record companies, college radio stations, and independent retailers struggled to assert alternative and even oppositional identities by situating themselves both physically and discursively outside of the spaces of the dominant media institutions.

CHAPTER 3

Producing Independent Music

Independent record labels specializing in rock and pop proliferated during the 1980s and early 1990s, and their growth created an interesting dynamic in the music industry. Many small labels established their "authenticity" by professing true independence from the mainstream music industry. Yet even though most were located in towns and cities relatively far removed from the capitals of the mainstream industry, New York and Los Angeles, for the most part these indies and their situated local and interlocal practices were inextricably linked to existing structures of popular music production and distribution. Sometimes independent labels were tied to larger companies because they found talent for major labels to recruit, sometimes because they had distribution deals with majors, sometimes because majors bought part- or full-ownerships in independent labels, and always because independent labels operated in a terrain structured by major labels. This dynamic created tension in institutions—and tension for music scene participants—that wanted to define themselves as marginal or "alternative" (and thus non-commercial, true, real, authentic), and which sought to remain identified with peripheral localities (again, non-commercial, true, real, authentic.)

The Mainstream Industry

By the end of the twentieth century, five multinational companies—Warner and its affiliated labels, US-owned by AOL Time-Warner; Sony, including Columbia Records, with ownership in Japan; European company Vivendi Universal, which owned both MCA and Polygram; British-owned EMI Group, including subsidiary labels Capitol and Virgin; German company Bertelsmann, which owned BMG, RCA, Arista, and other labels—had become responsible for defining the environment in which most music production and distribution took place. Although some of the players have changed in the past few decades, with companies like Warner Music and Universal being absorbed into even larger conglomerates, the situation in which a few major companies dominate the music marketplace has not changed in recent decades. By the 1980s, as Robinson et al. state, the majors were vertically integrated companies with their own facilities for production, manufacturing, and distribution of music product (41). In addition to these functions, major labels enter into a variety of relationships with independent labels and therefore have a profound impact on the ways that all types of alternative musics are produced and distributed, since in recent history the majors have controlled over ninety percent of recorded music distributed in the United States (Robinson et al. 52). Before we can understand the specific conditions of independent pop/rock music production, we need to look at the contemporary industry environment in which all recorded music had been and continues to be produced.

Any explanation of the relationship between the mainstream music industry and marginal cultural formations must take into account the economic structures that condition this relationship. Even the most marginal forms of cultural production are always available for incorporation into the mainstream, because they are positioned in relation to apparatuses of mainstream production and consumption. All rock music, as Simon Frith points out, "is capitalist music" (*Sound Effects* 272). When faced with potentially disruptive marginal musics, mainstream institutions attempt to maintain their dominance by either 1) ignoring these forms of music, or 2) bringing them in, but employing procedures for incorporating their threatening elements to minimize the disruption of orderly consumption (Laing, 75). In the cases of punk in the 1970s and rap in the 1980s, major labels opted to bring these musical forms in because they did not want to miss out on the potential profits that might be generated by marginal musics that could prove to be the "next big thing."

The music that came to be thought of as "college music" in the 1980s was not viewed by the mainstream music industry as a particularly "disruptive" music. Major record companies, however, perceived alternative music's systems of independent production and distribution to be potentially damaging and began moving in the mid-1980s to integrate independent music sounds and structures into their own organizations. In their attempts to bring independent rock and pop music into the mainstream, major labels often used and manipulated existing indie music social networks (in, for instance, their use of former college radio personnel to pitch major label releases to college radio stations); and they also influenced social relationships and meanings. By signing independent label acts and thereby fueling debate about whether these acts were still "authentic" or whether they were "sellouts," the majors forced music scene participants who defined themselves, their practices, and their institutions in opposition to the dominant industry to disown some artists, locations and practices and take up others in order to remain outsiders.

Staying a step ahead of mainstream co-optation was not easy in the late twentieth-century media environment. During the last two decades of the twentieth century, media industries were undergoing simultaneous processes of fragmentation and consolidation. Fragmentation resulted from the numerous advances in communication technology that enabled small firms to enter the market: in desktop publishing, video production and audio recording. But consolidation accompanied fragmentation, as larger companies took over those upstarts and other smaller counterparts (Smith 2–3). Some consolidation in media industries involved mainly major players and was largely hardware-driven, as companies like Sony, primarily a producer of consumer electronics, purchased software-producing companies like CBS Music and Columbia Pictures, thus ensuring that there was product available to play on Sony technology. There was also non-hardware-driven consolidation, as in the case of the Time-Warner merger, in which two media software giants joined forces to form a fully integrated audio-visual conglomerate (Tunstall and Palmer 38–39). When America Online merged with Time-Warner, the preeminent Internet content and service provider took over the behemoth corporation.

Developments in media ownership indicated a trend, not merely toward concentration of resources but toward globalization. The multinational nature of contemporary media ownership is beneficial to those in control, for it provides them with a variety of international markets in which cultural products can be sold without going through complicated negotiations over rights, distribution, and related issues. Furthermore, a multinational media company can shift valued personnel from one subsidiary to another, draw upon knowledgeable and often cheaper work forces within the various countries in which it is based, and shift the relative balance of resources invested in various markets in concert with shifts in regulatory and legal climates (see Smith). The goal is to create a smoothly-operating unit in which all parts act in "synergy"; in other words, the subsidiary companies contribute different resources to the multinational, creating a vast organization which is capable of achieving, through vertical and/or horizontal integration, the sort of control of a market that cannot be achieved by one subsidiary company (or even a subset of the subsidiaries) on its own.

The major record labels, like other multinational media organizations, seek synergy through their strategies of diversification and vertical integration. Currently media companies are growing faster than the economies of the United States, Europe and Japan. Whether recent strategies will be successful remains to be seen. Warner Brothers took on an enormous debt load in its merger with Time, as did Sony when it took over Columbia (McChesney 27, Tunstall and Palmer 213–36). But the late 70s and early 80s were disastrous years for the music industry, and many economic trends in the industry during the past two decades can be seen as attempts to regain economic solvency. In 1979 the music industry's earnings fell 11 percent, the first decline since World War II, with CBS Records' earnings alone declining 46 percent from the previous year (Dannen 5). And while music business figures like CBS Records President Tommy Mottola credited the industry's recovery in the 1980s to music videos and to technologies like the expensively priced CD,[1] which allowed company profits to increase even as unit sales declined and cheaper vinyl formats were phased out, it was clear that structural overhauls were also necessary: some of which led the major labels to turn their attention to geographically peripheral indie labels as sources of both talent and new institutional practices.

Record industry reorganization has taken and is taking place on a number of different levels. Before discussing the establishment of various relationships between major labels and independents, I would like to briefly examine the other ways the music industry has attempted to cope with an environment that has changed significantly since the 1970s.

Over a decade ago, an issue of the music trade paper *Billboard* devoted a special section to label heads' opinions about where the music business was headed. Several pointed to areas of increasing concern which highlight the ways in which the mainstream music industry had been reorganizing itself in an attempt to insure its survival. Marketing was a primary area of concern; Hale Milgrim, president of Capitol Records, stated:

> I feel that marketing is the entire process of exposing and selling music to the public: promotion, press, in-store placement, club airplay, etc. . . . In the future, we are going to have to rely as much on all these and other areas as on radio airplay—especially in light of the currently heavily formatted status of radio, where there are fewer and fewer outlets which will take chances with new music.[2]

Al Teller, chairman of MCA Music Entertainment Group, cited the changing nature of retail outlets as a primary reason for the need to develop more innovative marketing strategies:

> On the retail side, there are a handful of accounts, large chains of stores with centralized buying, that are responsible for over half the retail business. Stores are becoming home entertainment centers, not just audio retail outlets, which means that we're constantly facing shrinking shelf space.[3]

Compounding the problem of lack of shelf space at the retail level was the desire of retailers to sell major CD releases at under ten dollars, a desire to which record companies have never acceded, which likely strained relations with retail outlets even more, and which, in the years since this *Billboard* issue, has made the Internet marketplace particularly attractive to major labels.

Indeed, while Ed Rosenblatt, president of Geffen Records and DGC Records, argued in 1999 that, "We're a healthy business at the moment," he also warned, "we must never stop finding new ways to motivate the customer to walk into a record store"[4] (and now, presumably, to buy music online)—especially since this "health" is founded on a mountain of debt, inflated CD prices, and control of most recorded music distribution, as will be seen later in this chapter. Record companies have increasingly turned to licensing music for use in films, television, and advertising and to repackaging back catalog material as ways to motivate consumption.[5] We must also keep in mind that the record industry is relatively small; as Frederic Dannen pointed out in the early 1990s "Americans today spend about the same amount on breakfast cereal . . . as they do on compact discs, tapes and records" (15). The music business does not have the resources to withstand major economic downturns, and parent corporations can only be expected to absorb losses accumulated by their music division for a short period of time.

An additional complicating factor is the nature of the consumer that recorded music has traditionally attracted. Tunstall and Palmer characterize recorded music as a "one-off" medium; as with books, magazines, and visits to a movie theater, records and even Internet downloads are bought or sought out by consumers on an irregular basis. "Cash flow" media, on the other hand, are used by consumers on a continuing, and usually daily, basis, as is typical with newspapers and television (5). Record companies are therefore faced with the challenge of either routinizing consumer purchasing behavior (through record clubs, etc.) or expanding the customer base by bringing in new groups of purchasers.

The increasing globalization of the music industry through the 1980s and 1990s, and into the twenty-first century, is seen largely as an opportunity to bring in new consumers, either consumers in markets in countries or regions previously untouched by industry products or consumers in corporations' home country(-ies) newly exposed to forms of "world" music. The conviction in the 1990s that the global expansion of the music industry created a bonanza of markets was exemplified in this observation by the president of Geffen Records: "with the changing global situation, the opening of new and exciting markets, we must begin to develop and comprehend a more worldwide perspective."[6] Major label heads increasingly voiced the notion that "musical achievement and popularity is not restricted by . . . geography."[7]

Yet clearly the argument that the concept of one mainstream is outmoded, that instead "there are many musical streams"[8] for the music industry to tap, does not merely apply to the transnational context in which multinational corporations penetrate new markets and co-opt indigenous music for mass production and worldwide distribution. Another important way in which major labels attempt to diversify their product lines and appeal to a wider range of audiences is by entering into a variety of relationships with independent labels.

Independent Labels

Independent record companies as a rule are relatively small-scale operations that usually originate and try to operate outside—through their geographic locations and/ or their locally situated practices of production and distribution—of the established mainstream organizations that dominate the music industry. Robinson et al. claim that indies "were started to record ethnic or regional music ignored or maligned by the majors" (41), though this definition clearly needs to be expanded to include other forms of subcultural, non-regionally defined music, like punk. Moreover, their statement that "Some independents are only production companies. They produce a limited repertoire, usually only a few artists whom they hope will make it big" (41), indicates that independent labels seek to reach a wider audience and, presumably, to make a profit, with acts that "make it big." In fact, most independent label owners traditionally have not expected to make money from their acts; for instance, the owner of one small indie explained that in founding and operating his label he has lost "lots of money. But that's all right. The label's fun."[9] Most indie label owners enter the field primarily to make music they like more widely available to select audiences. As a 1987 *Rolling Stone* article explained, most American indies are not profitable and walk a perilous financial tightrope, because they "release commercially marginal records and usually have only minimal promotion budgets to spread the word over an enormous expanse."[10]

However, over the decades a few independent labels have been quite financially successful. "Independents" come in a range of sizes and forms: from multi-million-dollar corporate operations like I.R.S. in the 1980s, to medium-sized labels like Alias, to small labels that concentrate on producing singles rather than full-length albums, like Sunday, many of which are operated out of houses and apartments. A few indies—among them A&M, Motown, Virgin, and Island—become very large in their own right and are then bought by majors. The variations between independent labels are underscored by Mark Fenster, who points out that, "Some independent labels produce music that seems quite similar to that produced by major labels, while others might have no relation to mainstream popular music whatsoever" (89). Because of this Ian MacKaye, co-founder of Washington, D.C.–based indie Dischord, noted in the early 1990s that "the word independent is quickly losing any meaning."[11] This statement may also be true because "indie" described, and still describes, both a type of music (most commonly thought of as music characterized by a particular "do-it-yourself" guitar sound, regardless of whether it appears on a major label or an independent) and a system of production (music put out on independent labels).

Although there are long-standing independent labels that concentrate on blues (Alligator Records in Chicago), gospel (Malaco in Mississippi), and bluegrass (Sugar Hill in North Carolina), the do-it-yourself- production ethos of independent pop/rock music was most obviously linked to the production practices of punk rock. In fact, the now-defunct indie label Rough Trade was the home of American college radio favorites Camper Van Beethoven and the Butthole Surfers in the 1980s, and it originated as a British pub and punk rock label in the 1970s. Indies like Chiswick and Stiff were formed in Great Britain in the early-to-mid 1970s to create an outlet for pub rock artists like Nick Lowe who were ignored by the mainstream industry. These independent labels were important in the emergence of punk in Britain, since punk in part favored the same "do-it-yourself" (DIY) attitude as pub rock, eschewing traditional music industry institutions.

The punk ethos celebrated the lack of formal musical training among its musicians, the release of punk records on non-major labels, and the promotion and distribution of punk music through non-mainstream channels (such as The Cartel, a system of independent record distribution that was founded as an alternative to the major labels' distribution pipeline). For the most part, the indies that arose with punk were located outside of London, the center of the British music industry, just as many American indie and pop rock labels formed away from Los Angeles and New York. The dissociation from the geographical and economic spaces of mainstream music practiced by punk was part of, as Dave Laing argues in *One Chord Wonders*, the "'small label economics' pioneered by Stiff and Chiswick . . . [which] proved that to start a record company only a few hundred pounds and not a vast bank loan was needed" (6–17). As Laing also argues:

> One irrevocable result of the punk era was a major change in what might be called the economic psychology of making records. Whereas the making of an album had previously been envisaged by most aspiring musicians as comparable in scale to the making of a cinema film (and therefore as far out of reach), punk showed that the recording could be the equivalent of a magazine or paperback book. (118)

The influence of punk on independent pop/rock music was more on the philosophy of production, which said that anyone anywhere could make a record, than on stylistic elements of the music.

The DIY ethic, of course, extends beyond independent labels to other sites of independent music dissemination, such as booking and promotion. Yet the whole DIY mythology that shrouds indie music begins to fall apart under close scrutiny. In an article in the American punk fanzine MAXIMUMROCKNROLL, Ben Weasel quoted an alternative music promoter, who stated,

> I think a lot of bands act like they believe in [DIY] but that's only because they're not drawing these huge crowds yet. Once they get bigger, they totally forget about all those ideals.[12]

Weasel added that, "Although most of the people I talked to support the Do-It-Yourself ethic, a lot of bands and labels get to the point where they can't do everything themselves."[13] The mythology of DIY, however, and the existence of independent music institutions, has always encouraged indie bands—and therefore, indie labels— to form and put out music in hope that by relying on the mechanisms of independent music production they can reach a segment of the alternative music audience.

While major labels have large Artists and Repertoire (A&R) departments to seek out and sign new talent, small independent labels have proportionally smaller A&R staffs, if they have staffs, or at least individual staff people, who specialize in this task at all. Indeed, label owners, managers, or employee collectives tend to make decisions about what records to put out, and young bands often find the accessibility of decision-makers at independent labels—and the very proliferation of indie labels—an incentive to record their music with some hope that it will be released by a record company. The rise of independent labels in the United States in the 1980s and early 1990s was accompanied by an increase in the number of bands recording their music (as opposed to simply performing it live). A member of the Seattle band the Walkabouts attributed Seattle's prominence as an alternative music mecca in the early 1990s in part to the increased interest of local bands in recording their music; he noted:

> A lot of people weren't even poking their heads out the door [five years ago]. They were just sitting there woodshedding. Then a lot of people collectively started thinking about getting into recording studios instead of making live music the central focus. It was . . . the whole independent record thing; you'd be reading about the stuff happening in Minneapolis, in Athens [Georgia], and God, those people were making records.[14]

Similarly, a member of a very popular Champaign band observed that while "there were more bands" active in Champaign in the early- to mid-1980s, there were "a lot more bands with tapes" by the late 1980s.[15] Though small local labels are unable to pay these bands or solo artists advances before recording, the larger indies of the 1980s and 1990s like Sub Pop, Homestead, and Frontier were able to fund the production of records and videos, and therefore provide an incentive for bands to commit to two or three record deals with them. Such deals did and can be detrimental to a band, however, if the band wishes to seek a major label deal and is bound by an indie contract.[16]

Bands and artists sometimes find themselves on indie labels with whom they are generally happy, but they feel trapped by the label's image. The San Francisco–based band The Sneetches released records in the United States on Alias, a San Francisco label that has generally associated itself with alternative pop, and in England on Creation. One member of the band complained about the "neo-psychedelia stigma" attached to bands on Creation, remarking that, "All those Creation bands, like Primal Scream and the Weather Prophets, have had to face this same problem."[17] Still, indie label reputations are useful for letting both bands and consumers know what kind of music the company is generally interested in signing and releasing, even if bands occasionally feel unfairly categorized by virtue of releasing something on a particular label.

The diversity of sub-genres within independent rock and pop production (hardcore, pure pop, alt-country, industrial) points to the existence of what one member of an East Coast indie pop band once referred to as "subundergrounds."[18] Each subunderground has its own distinct economic network of, in the words of *MAXIMUMROCKNROLL* writer Samuel Nathan Schiffman, "bands, promoters, radio station, fanzines, charlatans, and hucksters who [get] their jollies propagandizing and promoting whatever wave of pasty-faced mooks . . . just crawled out of the garage."[19] Subundergrounds allow relatively obscure bands and labels to reach audiences most receptive to their musics.

Independent labels thus provided a means in the 1980s and 1990s, before the Internet boom, by which bands and individual artists otherwise unable to put out and distribute a record, CD or tape could do so. Even today, because of the difficulty in getting unknown bands noticed amongst the thousands and thousands of bands with music available on the World Wide Web, indie labels perform an important function. Yet independent labels are not problem-free. Some indies, like some majors, develop reputations for poor business practices. Ben Weasel once argued that SST was, "the granddaddy of indie corporate rock" and "is notorious for shafting its bands in favor of bigger profits for its high level executives."[20] In general though, the problems facing artists in dealing with indie labels result from the relatively limited scale on which most indies operate. For instance, the recession of the early 1990s had a particularly deleterious effect on independent labels, many of which did not have the financial resources to ride out the economic downturn. Although the recession was by no means the sole cause of Rough Trade's financial troubles, it certainly was a contributing factor; and it caused layoffs at labels like Important/Relativity (now owned by CBS) and Sub Pop.[21]

Independents have always had a tough time competing with majors, because while major labels are vertically integrated and control their own pressing, promotion and distribution of product, independents seldom have this sort of control. Unlike major labels, indies rarely have much money or many employees to advertise and promote releases. In addition, independent distribution, as will be discussed more fully below, remains a rather unsatisfactory system compared to major label distribution, both because of delays in payments by distributors to labels and because distributors are reluctant to take many records from small labels until they know there is a demand for the product. Small indies generally lack the reassuring sales track records of major labels, as well as the promotional budgets that major labels have at their disposal to push product.[22]

Independent labels seem especially to suffer when they try to compete directly with the majors. In the mid-1980s, major labels began adding alternative promotion departments to promote alternative artists on major labels to independent pop/rock and commercial alternative radio stations. Independent labels usually lack the resources to staff large promotion departments, but increasingly in the

1980s they found themselves competing with majors for airplay on alternative radio outlets. Greg Workman of San Francisco indie Alternative Tentacles argued at the time that it was suicidal for indies to try to promote their releases at the same level as majors:

> [Indies] have people whose jobs it is to work records up college radio charts or to send promo copies to some important magazine in Dubuque, Iowa or something and they're playing this game of alternative marketing, which major labels have now. They have full time employees whose job is, "I've got to get 20 ad[d]s on this record this week to college radio stations." And I happen to believe that some of the best independent labels and some of the biggest are falling right into this terrible, terrible game and they're in really bad shape.[23]

Island Records, one the largest indies of recent years, found itself unable to compete with the majors in international marketing and distribution, and its resulting financial troubles eventually led to its sale to Polygram (Robinson et al. 51). There are a variety of arrangements independent labels enter into with majors, for often these deals are the only way that indies can be competitive in the marketplace.

Independent Distribution

Distribution has been a problem area for most independent labels. Independent labels have not historically had their own distribution arms as the major labels do, and therefore have lacked control over their ability to get product into stores. Most independent labels would like to be able to depend on distributors that are not associated with major labels to fulfill their distribution needs. When punk emerged in England, independent labels making punk records often wanted their records to be available nationwide, and many sought to achieve this goal without the help of the mainstream music industry, instead relying on non-major distributors like Pinnacle and Spartan, or the newer network centered around London's Rough Trade record store and label. Rough Trade linked up with other stores and distributors across Britain, providing an independent system of distribution for punk and new wave records (Laing 18).

Independent distributors in the United States modeled themselves on Rough Trade and were able to provide independent labels access to national and even international markets. In the early 1990s, Urbana, Illinois-based label Parasol may only have pressed about one thousand copies of any of the seven-inch vinyl records it produced, but it was able to disseminate its releases across the U.S. through five distributors—Cargo (Chicago), Twin City Imports (Minneapolis), Dutch East India (New York), Boner (San Francisco), and T.C.I.—as well as internationally through

Semaphore in the Netherlands, Roller Coaster in Britain, and Summer Shine in Australia.[24]

Parasol used some of the larger independent distributors in the United States. By the early 1990s, there were three powerful independent distributors in the U.S.: Dutch East, Caroline Records, and Important. These three companies, like the late Rough Trade, rose to prominence as distributors with their own in-house labels, and the competition between them to arrange exclusive distribution deals with labels became fierce. A then-buyer in distribution at Rough Trade explained in 1990:

> Everyone is trying to snatch up little labels to kind of [establish] a monopoly on the market. So retail stores, chain stores, are forced to buy from that distributor. Let's say we got the whole Alias catalog, and the agreement was that . . . we have an exclusive distribution deal with them, so that Caroline, Important, Dutch East wouldn't have Alias. Then Alias puts out this great new record; then everybody's going to have to buy from us.[25]

With indie distributors vying to amass exclusive deals with indie labels, clearly the impulse towards consolidation was and is not the sole preserve of the major labels. The trend appears even more ominous when one discovers that by the heyday of independent production and distribution in the 1990s, Sony owned half of Important, the largest independent distributor; and Caroline was partly owned by Virgin, which was turn owned by multi-national Thorn-EMI.[26] The "independence" from the mainstream music industry of many independent distributors was certainly questionable.

Moreover, indie distributors have tended to act in some ways like major label distributors. Largely because of the competition for exclusive deals, independent distributors in the 1990s grew more conservative in their decisions about what records to distribute. Samuel Nathan Schiffman wrote in his *MAXIMUMROCKNROLL* article "Nirvanification" that Caroline Records would no longer associate itself with releases put out by bands themselves or by small independent labels, and Cargo, T.C.I., and Dutch East were "very reluctant to take a chance on anything which will not sell."[27] The largest independent distributors, like the major labels, sought to minimize their risk by becoming more selective about the product on which they chose to expend their resources.

Somewhat paradoxically, the major complaint that independent labels and their artists had about independent distributors in the late-1980s and early-1990s was precisely that indie distributors did not operate more like major labels: and, interestingly, that locally situated and identified indies were not getting national coverage from these distributors. At Alias Records, which was distributed by Important, Dutch East, and Midnight, among others, one concern was that independent distributors didn't provide the same kind of blanket national coverage that major label distribution did. In the words of one Alias staff members, "sometimes there are a lot of open spots, and you just never know what territory is going to get covered by whom."[28] Not only can independent distribution often result in some areas of the country not receiving a label's releases, the volume of product any independent distributor can handle is limited. A former member of the band Camper Van Beethoven explained:

> Even if you take California, if you were to put out a record independently distributed, it would get say three copies in three record stores, maybe four record stores, in San Francisco, which extrapolated would mean three or four thousand copies around California. But if it were a major label release, there would be, say, three copies in twenty record stores in San Francisco, which extrapolated is a potential of 10,000 records to be sold in the state of California—or, more, 20,000 maybe.[29]

Independent distributors were also frequently criticized for their unreliable reimbursement of labels for records they ordered. Some labels complained that they were never reimbursed for records they shipped to independent distributors. A more common complaint, though, was that there was often a significant delay between the time records were shipped and the time the distributor paid the label. As a producer/engineer of indie bands noted:

> [The distributors] of independent labels sell to record stores and mark up the price a bit from what the bands wants . . . but they don't pay the bands until the record is actually sold.[30]

Some labels, like Chapel Hill, North Carolina's Merge (founded and owned by members of the band Superchunk) chose to deal with smaller independent distributors like Scooby-Doo, Get Hip, and Ajax, rather than Caroline, Important and Dutch East, because they found that the delays in payment for orders and reimbursement for sales were longest with the larger independent distributors.[31]

Although problems with independent distribution led some labels and artists to seek business arrangements with major labels, others, in the interest of maintaining an alternative system to the mainstream music industry, sought and continue to seek to make the best of an unsatisfactory situation. Independent music production is permeated by the collective memory of a utopian past during which "anybody could have released a little punk rock record, get it into any underground, and even some chain-run stores. If the music was good they could have sold a few thousand copies.[32] The desire then was to reinvent this blissful state. For instance, writing in MAXIMUMROCKNROLL, Samuel Nathan Schiffman called for the establishment of

> some kind of underground distribution and information service. . . . A business which could sell to stores and mail order alike. A business which wouldn't have to

cower to the for-profit only concerns of the major labels. Maybe we play by the same rules as the big guys, yet stay within our own moral aesthetic. We can beat them at their own game, only we would use our profits to further our own interests.[33]

The histories of organizations with goals similar to these, such as that which follows of the original Rough Trade collective, illustrate that lofty goals tend to fall by the wayside in an environment where labels' very survival often depends on their ability to provide a range of artists and audiences with choices preferred by those constituencies to the choices being offered by other labels, both major and independent.

Independent-Major Label Relationships

Problems in systems of independent production and distribution often led artists and indie labels to enter into relationships with major labels in order to better reach a particular audience, or to reach a wider audience. The discussion of independent distribution points to the problems that small companies often experienced in making sure that the product they put out was available to potential customers. Because of the difficulties encountered with independent distribution, one of the first sorts of relationships an independent label might have sought with a major was one in which the major took over distribution of the indie's records. The opinion of the co-founder and co-owner of Washington, D.C.'s Dischord Records, Ian MacKaye, was probably shared by many people at independents: "The only thing major labels can really offer is distribution."[34]

Major Label Distribution

Major labels allow independent labels to compete in the marketplace because the process lets major labels, in the words of Mark Fenster, "cooperate with, colonize, or take over those companies and musics that become financially attractive" (93); distribution is at least superficially the relationship that an independent label can enter into with a major label that is the least threatening to an independent label's image of integrity. The major label in this relationship is not necessarily trying to lure artists away from the indie it distributes, nor does the major necessarily own a financial interest in the independent label. In many respects, an exclusive distribution agreement appears to be mutually beneficial: it allows the major label to use its already operating distributions system to reap financial benefits from a product which the label did not pay to produce, and it allows the independent label to get significant quantities of its releases into chain and other retail stores not normally serviced by independent distributors.[35]

Still, making exclusive distribution agreements with independent labels is an-other way in which major labels solidify their control over the production and dis-tribution of music. In his book *Hit Men*, an account of the American music industry in the 1970s and 1980s, Frederic Dannen describes the oligopolistic structure of the industry and noted that major labels maintain control over the music marketplace not merely by signing artists and putting out their records, but also by controlling the channels of distribution through which most recorded music passes. Starting in the late seventies and continuing to the present day, the major labels began making deals to distribute many of the notable independents, including Motown. Through vertical integration, major labels established, according to Dannen, "a huge 'pipeline' [that] must be filled all the time or else it does not pay for itself." This pipeline consisted of "sales branches, warehouses, and shipping depots . . . [which] need tremendous volume to keep them running at capacity" (112). In other words, once this massive distribution apparatus had been constructed, it required a con-stant flow of products to remain cost-effective. Thus, in order to supplement their own releases, majors make distribution deals with independents, guaranteeing a steady flow of product to push through the pipeline. The process of intense consoli-dation that began taking place in the music industry over a decade ago required even higher product flow to maintain vertical integration, so there was an increas-ing incentive for majors to handle distribution of independent label releases.[36]

Some have argued that the only way an indie can expand is by entering into a distribution deal with a major. Wendy Harte of the independent label Frontier ex-plained why her company entered into a deal with BMG during the indie label boom of the late 1980s by noting, "We wanted our bands to have better distribu-tion, but do the promotion ourselves." Part of that deal meant that BMG's publicists "handle[d] the *Rolling Stone*-type features. [BMG] would make sure [articles on Frontier's artists] run. The indies just can't do it; the majors can."[37] And while one might argue that independent labels give up a lot when they sign a distribution agreement with a major label—they tend to receive less money for each unit sold than they would from independent distribution, for instance, and they often face accusations of "selling out" from within the indie market—the advantages for a label of receiving advances before the release has sold, receiving payment more quickly when product sells, and better retail placement make signing a deal with a major label necessary to the economic survival of many independents.

This isn't to say that all large or growing independent record companies found it necessary to enter into exclusive arrangements with major labels during the 1980s and 1990s. Jim Nash, owner of Chicago's Wax Trax Records, claimed that Wax Trax could "sell six figure quantities [of bands] like Front 242 without major label distri-bution."[38] Moreover, an independent label like Wax Trax might well have found that major distribution would be more of a hindrance than a help; Nash observed: "If we had In the Nursery albums in a K-Mart, I don't know if it would mean much for sales. The names of our bands, like the Revolting Cocks, run into censorship things with a lot of big distributors."[39] However, even those labels that did not themselves enter into relationships with major labels often found that their talent rosters provided a farm club for major labels looking to sign new artists.

Major Label-Owned Independents

Before looking at how the majors recruited talent from indie labels, it is useful to examine the phenomenon of major labels that were dissatisfied with being limited to distributing music from independent labels and wanted to be more deeply involved in the process of developing indie acts. Major labels in this position had two choices: they could either buy an existing indie or start their own in-house "independent" label. Many of the most prominent independent labels of the 1980s and 1990s were at least partly owned by major labels. These included I.R.S., in which EMI bought a fifty percent interest; Enigma, half-owned by EMI; Tommy Boy, which is still fully owned by Warner Brothers; and Caroline, fully owned by Virgin (and thus by EMI).[40] We might understand this trend, which *New York Times* popular music critic Jon Pareles referred to in the early 1990s as a "shopping spree" on the part of major labels,[41] as representative of a periodic cycle in which an upsurge in independent musical production is quickly followed by successful attempts by the mainstream industry to compete in the independent marketplace. During this "period of recuperation," major labels often buy many of the most successful independent labels.[42] This is a logical move for major labels to make, because, as Keith Negus explains,

> Incapable of comprehending where new trends are occurring, cumbersome and unable to maneouvre quickly enough to attract fresh talent, the major labels wait and then rush after the repertoires of small independent companies who have already "tested" the commercial potential of their new talent. This is the well-recounted tale of the major companies continually co-opting or swallowing the small "indie" companies. (*Music* 34)

Yet just because a major label owns a substantial or full interest in an independent, the independent has not necessarily given up its autonomy. Pareles noted that in order not to tamper with the perceived "instincts" of an independent label that it buys, a major label will often promise the independent the continued ability to sign whomever it wants and develop the new talent it chooses. For example, First Warning, partly owned by BMG, signed artists who often had very little commercial potential, and BMG did not have the right of first refusal on an artist; in other words, First Warning was essentially free to sign whomever it wished with no interference from BMG. If a band on First Warning moved to a full-fledged major label, that label was not necessarily BMG. BMG, as part-owner of First Warning, of course benefited financially from whatever deal First Warning struck with another major.[43]

An "independent" label started by a major would naturally tend to have less autonomy than an existing independent bought by a major. While a major record company might accept that by starting its own "independent" label rather than buying an existing one it would lose some of the credibility associated with a known independent, by starting its own "independent" label it still hopes to reap some of the benefits of the more compact organizational structure of a small, independent company. These benefits might include a more compact bureaucratic structure which allows a small management team more freedom to be closer to and act quickly in response to emergent musics; an opportunity for more personal relationships between the company and its artists; and the public perception that the label, as a semi-independent entity specializing in a narrow range of genres, has more credibility than the major label that spawned it (Fenster 94–95). For instance, EastWest America Records, founded within the Atlantic company, signed little-known bands in the early 1990s which had been marginally successful on college radio, like Clutch and For Love Not Lisa.[44] Charisma was started within Virgin/Capitol-EMI, and its roster included the well-known British alternative pop band Curve; it also put out an album by Champaign-Urbana alternative rock band Titanic Love Affair. Interscope was created within the Warner empire, and while still part of the Time-Warner corporate structure (it is now part of the Vivendi Universal empire), it successfully signed alternative rock bands like Helmet and former Wax Trax act Thrill Kill Kult. Small, in-house "indies" at major labels often make signing with a major more attractive for an indie band.

Signing Independent Label Bands to Major Labels

Belgian political economist Bernard Miege notes that in the culture industries, no matter how corporate the production process becomes, companies are compelled to maintain an aura of artistic activity; products of the culture industries "must continue to bear the stamp of genius and uniqueness, and not appear to be emanating from research laboratories" (46). In other words, even large media companies want to be associated with products considered by audiences to be expressions of "real" experience. It therefore makes sense that in the 1980s and 1990s, major labels looked to locally situated independent pop/rock labels as sources of new talent. The "Do-It-Yourself" mentality associated with many independent labels gave the artists on those labels a sort of instant cachet and "authenticity" with major labels—working one's way up through the independent pop/rock music ranks appeared to indicate an artist's integrity. As Simon Frith observes, major labels tended to use independent labels as sources of "credible stars" (110).

In Frith's discussion of the changed nature of talent recruitment at major labels during the 1980s, he quotes Island Records' founder Chris Blackwell's observation that, "[N]owadays people get a record contract, buy the instruments, make the record, then have the videos force-fed to the media" ("Video Pop" 109). Certainly this is the case with some acts, like those that begin as a producer's or manager's concept, such as En Vogue in the early 1990s or The Backstreet Boys a few years later. This, however, is not a new phenomenon, as 1960s hits by the Byrds and the Monkees, on which the listed band members did not play instruments, demonstrate. Moreover, Frith's contention that by the 1980s there was "no live circuit left for unknown groups to build up fans and credibility" (109) ignores the independent pop/rock circuit that was central in building followings for bands like R.E.M., and the thrash metal circuit that helped make stars of Metallica when the band was getting little-to-no radio or video airplay.

Frith proposes two models to explain how the music industry finds talent: the pyramid (or "the Rock") and the pool. The pyramid, according to Frith, is how artists used to attain star status. Under the pyramid model, artists would start out playing local shows, then regional shows, then put out a record on an independent label, then sign with a major label, and so on. During the late 1970s and the 1980s, Frith contends, the industry shifted to the pool model, in which the multinational record companies "fished" for material in a pool of "ideas, sounds, styles, and performers" ("Video Pop" 113); independent labels were important in that they were part of this pool. While the notion that the pool has replaced the pyramid can explain how acts like Celine Dion and Destiny's Child get signed to major labels and quickly rise to the top of the charts, it is less useful in understanding why acts like Nirvana in the early 1990s or The Offspring today[45] might appear next to such acts on the charts. Rather than assuming that the pool has replaced the pyramid, it might be more helpful to think of these two models as co-existing, and then trying to understand the dynamics of this relationship. Mark Fenster points out that "Alternative bands . . . represent the possibilities of retaining the 'pyramid' model of development by [giving record companies the opportunity of] creating, handling and profiting from acts and genres that can be developed into consistent record sellers over a long period of time" (123).

When major labels began to go "fishing" for talent at independent labels, they in fact recognized that they were acquiring acts that had worked their way through the lowest levels of the pyramid via the independent system of music production. For years the major labels have looked at independent record companies as "minor leagues" for developing talent. A 1986 *Rolling Stone* article noted that often indies "act as farm teams for major labels hesitant to invest in acts that don't immediately fit into an AOR [Album-Oriented Rock Radio] niche."[46] Rough Trade certainly saw itself as fulfilling this role. Although in part Rough Trade wanted to establish a production and distribution network independent of the mainstream industry, it also wanted to work, in one former Rough Trade executive's words, "almost as a farm system, where we would help establish a band and get a couple records out, get them on a tour, and then they could go on to better things."[47]

The notion that bands could work their way up through the independent system and earn a major label contract was structured into the industry. A former program director at Foothills Junior College's noncommercial pop/rock radio station KFJC, in the San Francisco Bay area, described how this system worked:

> A lot of artists assume that they'll work their way up, and [independent labels are] a logical stepping stone. The major labels use indies as minor leagues for the music industry. They watch what happens there, and if it's good, they bring 'em on up to the big time. The bands get their show there, and if they don't cut it, they're bumped back down to the indie label, Warner Brothers distribution, cult status. . . . I think there's a definite plateau there—an industry-created plateau.[48]

With the relative success that major labels had in the late 1980s and 1990s with bands recruited from indie pop/rock labels, and the reification of this process within the music industry, the use of independent labels as "farm teams" has continued. Some observers see this as a disturbing phenomenon; critic Robert Christgau remarks that "the indies' farm-system function is self-evident." For him, this function degrades independent labels. He hopes "SST, or Alias, or at least Rhino turns into the HighTone or Shanachie of aging 'alternative rockers,'" the latter two being independent labels that have not tended to act as stepping stones to the big time for their artists.[49] Others, like this longtime San Francisco area indie pop musician, saw the farm team structures in the early 1990s as reflecting more poorly on the major labels than on the indies:

> Now it's like college radio is a testing ground for the major labels. It's sick. It's like they put their little feelers out, and if you do well as an independent pop/rock band, then maybe they'll sign you. It seems like they really want to struggle. It almost seems like signing a independent pop/rock band is more of an excuse to not put money into a band.

> A lot of major labels want the band to already be at a certain point, and then all they have to do is pump money into it and distribute it, and they don't really seem to do anything with the band.[50]

Seattle scene veteran Grant Alden agreed, observing that "[t]he record industry feeds on regional scenes (Athens, Minneapolis, Austin, Seattle) like sharks on fresh flesh."[51]

Looking to regional/ local scenes and independent labels for acts made economic sense for major labels in the 1980s and 1990s. By then the majors were investing between $250,000 and $750,000 per act each year on a number of new artists, because even if only a few of these artists sold well, the record company would make a profit.[52] And where better to look for new acts than to the larger independent labels where they could find artists with already-established track records? Signing bands that had put out releases on independent labels ensured that the band had a degree of "street credibility" and made selling records to alternative music audiences less difficult. In the words of Gerald Cosloy of independent label Matador: "It's a lot easier to sign an indie band . . . than to start off from scratch with a fake alternative rock band."[53] Clearly R.E.M., the first act to move from independent label (I.R.S.) and college radio stardom to major label (Warner) and mainstream chart success, is a case in point. R.E.M. released four albums and an EP on I.R.S. before they were signed to Warner Brothers, and thus had built up a sizable audience. The albums that R.E.M. has put out on Warner have each sold over one million copies, with the second Warner album, 1991's *Out of Time*, selling over four million.

Nirvana, on the other hand, had a more dramatic impact when it released its first album for the Time-Warner-owned label DGC in 1991. Unlike R.E.M., which had already released several records—including a top ten single—when it signed with a major label, Nirvana had only released one album (*Bleach*, on Seattle's Sub Pop label) when it signed with DGC for the relatively small sum of $550,000. According to Robert Christgau, Nirvana's 1991 multi-platinum DGC debut album, *Nevermind*, was projected to ultimately bring in $50 million, a 9000 percent return on DGC's original investment.[54] Moreover, while the traditional narrative of the relationship between independent labels and major labels is one in which the independent label is forever the victim as major labels continually "steal" the best indie acts, in the case of Nirvana the band's major label signing actually benefited the independent label. Because of the deal the label made with DGC when Nirvana left, Sub Pop receives royalties on every copy of *Nevermind* sold—this deal alone brought Sub Pop back from the brink of bankruptcy.[55]

Many observers of the alternative music scene argued that Nirvana's mainstream success was only possible because of its success among fans of independent music. The director of alternative music at DGC credited word-of-mouth within the indie audience for getting the album *Nevermind*, and in particular the single, "Smells Like Teen Spirit," off to impressive early sales: "there's never been a time when the indie buzz was so qualitatively important . . . we've never had such instantaneous response to everything we did to market an album."[56]

Word-of-mouth created excitement about the album's Los Angeles release party, excitement that continued with the quickness with which independent pop/rock and commercial alternative radio stations added "Smells Like Teen Spirit" and led to large and enthusiastic audiences on the tour scheduled to coincide with *Nevermind's* release. Soon after the album came out, MTV played the "Smells Like Teen Spirit" video as a "World Premiere Video" on its alternative music show, *120 Minutes*; the clip also began airing on MTV's *Headbangers Ball*, attracting heavy metal fans, and eventually it became part of MTV's regular rotation. Audience requests to AOR and Top 40 stations ensured that the song got airplay on mainstream commercial radio.[57] With Nirvana then, the music industry was able to bring up from the "minors," so to speak, the audience and interest the band had generated while it was with the "farm team" (Sub Pop) and capitalize, through timely promotion, on the existing curiosity in the independent music community about Nirvana's second album.

However, neither the Nirvana example nor the R.E.M. example was paradigmatic. Even before Nirvana broke through to the mainstream, New York City hardcore band Helmet was the subject of a fierce bidding war between Warner Brothers and Interscope, both of which, interestingly enough, were divisions of Warner's overarching company, WEA (which stands for Warner, Elektra, and Atlantic—Interscope was developed as subsidiary of Atlantic). Helmet, which had put out one album on a Minneapolis label Amphetamine Reptile, eventually signed with Interscope for one million dollars. Interscope's goal was undoubtedly to achieve the same kind of crossover alternative/metal success as Nirvana and Faith No More; but *Spin* writer Jim Greer correctly predicted at the time of the band's major labeling signing that "Helmet's idiosyncratic and, most important, largely tune-less version [of alternative music] is going to confuse more people than it attracts."[58] So far, Helmet has not crossed over to a mainstream audience.

There was obviously a desire by the mid-to-late 1980s on the part of the mainstream music industry to expand its borders to encompass independent or alternative rock and pop, genres that had previously been considered fringe musics. An important reason behind this expansion of borders was that during the eighties and nineties major labels were recruiting graduates with significant college radio experience to work in departments like Promotions and Artists and Repertoire (A&R). A 1987 *Rolling Stone* article gave the examples of Fred Ehrlich, who was recruited by CBS Records out of college radio and had risen by the age of 25 to the position of director of independent pop/rock marketing, and of Matt Williams, the 26-year-old director of A&R at Virgin America.[59] A&R departments, as noted earlier, even today are almost exclusively staffed by men, and they are responsible for finding new talent, signing acts to contracts, and for serving as the act's liaison to the label once the band is signed (see Frith, *Sound Effects* 102–105). The significance at the institutional level of replacing A&R men who had grown up on the music of the fifties and sixties with college radio veterans cannot be underestimated. At major labels there was a perception in the 1980s that A&R needed to be in "closer touch with music at its sources,"[60] especially with the activity in regional and local independent pop/rock music scenes.

The change in the make-up of A&R departments was not lost on indie music artists. As fellow participants in independent pop/rock music culture, musicians and college radio staffers shared similar knowledge, tastes, and experiences. In the

1980s some artists, like Dan Stuart of the band Green on Red, were encouraged by the presence of former college radio personnel in major label A&R departments:

> There are so many people in A&R departments now who had come up through college radio and who are signing bands. I know guys I saw three years ago when I was playing for a hundred dollars a night, little independent pop/rock kids, who are not wearing suits and working for CBS. That will change things.[61]

Others, however, did not see this as a trend that helped independent pop/rock music on the whole. One San Francisco musician saw the change in the composition of A&R departments as potentially dangerous to innovation in the mainstream industry:

> When the major labels picked up all the independent pop/rock music, it happened because a lot of people that were working in college radio were getting jobs with the major labels. Previously what had happened was an A&R guy had been someone who was an ambassador; it had nothing to do with the music. A&R people would say, "This band seems kind of popular. Let's sign them and see what happens."
>
> Now the A&R kids are saying, "I know what's popular. This is popular. I know what's good. This is good. I can tell you guys 'cause I'm young like these kids are." Before, A&R people would say "I don't know. Let's check it out and see what happens." We got a lot of good bands that way twenty years ago.[62]

Another Bay Area musician agreed:

> In the old days record company A&R men were less cool, but more convinced that they had to go out and find the new sound. And they were going to tell people what the new sound was rather than going in with this really sure of themselves demographic kind of an idea.[63]

Whether the changing-of-the-guard in A&R decreased or increased the quality of music released on major labels is certainly a debatable question, and one on which participants in independent music scenes remain divided. And, as will be seen at the end of this chapter, signing with a major label has not always been particularly beneficial to an act.

Subsequent Relationships

As ways both of potentially increasing profits and of being seen as purveyors of authentic (and still often locally identified) musical experience, distributing independent records, signing independent label acts, and buying and/or creating independent labels were, by the 1990s, fairly well-established major label practices. By that time too the major labels had incorporated a few more novel ways of competing with independents into their repertoire. In looking for new talent, majors were not restricting their search to established independent label acts; the big record companies began pursuing little-known bands.[64] And after rejecting all vinyl formats in the 1980s, in the early 1990s the majors began to issue some releases on 7-inch vinyl in order to better target the alternative audience. Flipper (Def American/ Warner), the Melvins (Atco/ Atlantic/ WEA), Mudhoney (Reprise/ Warner), and House of Pain (Tommy Boy/ WEA) are examples of bands that released songs on 7-inch vinyl for major labels in the early 1990s.[65]

Though some observers might view the majors' re-embrace of the vinyl single as hypocritical, it was clearly part of a new strategy for reaching fans of independent music in the wake of Nirvana's breakthrough mainstream success. A particularly curious recent trend of the early 1990s was in distribution, where, despite the problems with independent distribution, major labels actually used independent distributors rather their own distribution arms to better reach alternative music audiences. For instance, BMG used Dutch East India to distribute records for Beggars Banquet and Silvertone; Geffen and DGC used Cargo to distribute vinyl singles; and Tommy Boy, owned by Warner, was wholly distributed by independents rather than WEA. In addition, Polygram set up its own "independent" distribution company, in order to sell records directly to small, independent records stores, a market which traditionally had not been well-served by major label distribution.[66] Gerald Cosloy of Matador pointed out the irony of these distribution developments:

> Major labels are supposed to take bands away from indies because indies have shitty distribution. Now the majors are saying, "We've figured out a way to sell your records through indie distribution." As a marketing tool, it's of questionable value.[67]

As industry critic Jason Cohen wrote, resorting to independent distribution to sell product was "almost an admission [by] the majors [that they] can't do the jobs they hired on for when they signed indie-based bands."[68] While the move towards independent distribution to market alternative/ independent pop/rock music might simply have been an attempt to increase the major labels' audience share, it may also have meant that major labels no longer expected their alternative acts to sell 100,000 or more copies of a release and compete successfully with more obviously commercial acts in order to stay on labels' rosters.

Specific Independent Labels

Obviously, not all independent labels chose to enter into financial relationships with major record companies. Three indies that in the late 1980s and early 1990s largely chose not to enter the major label distribution pipeline were Rough Trade (a fairly large independent production, and formerly, distribution company), Alias (a medium-sized independent label), and Parasol (a small indie that at the time specialized in seven-inch singles and mail order). Each label prized its freedom from the constraints a major label relationship might involve, yet none of the three companies was free of financial and/or management problems.

Rough Trade

Rough Trade was founded in the U.K. in the 1970s with exactly the sort of objectives outlined by Schiffman above, and informed, as David Hesmondhalgh writes, by "a leftist or anarchist critique of corporate capital" and strove to maintain a system of internal democracy in opposition to the dominant industry (259). In London, Rough Trade, with its distribution arm, in-house label, and record store, was central in disseminating punk and new wave music. It joined with other independent distributors and small stores to form "the Cartel" (Laing 18). Rough Trade sought to mirror the vertical integration achieved by the major labels by controlling the process from production to retail sale. Although it survived corporate reorganization in 1986 (Hesmondhalgh 269), ultimately Rough Trade overextended itself in the pursuit of this goal and declared bankruptcy in 1991. Before looking at the reasons for Rough Trade's collapse, I want first to look at the history of Rough Trade and then at the market niche it occupied in the United States.

Rough Trade's U.S. office was established in 1980 in Berkeley (moving later to San Francisco) by label founder Geoff Travis as a distributor of British imports.[69] Rough Trade, Inc., as it was known, was owned by Rough Trade, U.K. and remained fully dependent on the British company for operating capital until Rough Trade declared bankruptcy in 1991.[70] As in Britain, the retail store in the United States was a center of independent music activity, first at its location in North Beach, then in a space in front of the distribution office south of Market on Sixth and Folsom. A former of Rough Trade employee recalled the second location:

> [They were] teeny rooms—a horrible part of town, no one walks through there. But . . . people used to come from all over to go there, 'cause it was just known [to have] the coolest imports. People would drive in from all over the Bay Area. . . . [Rough Trade] wouldn't do any major label stuff—it was real conscious of the whole independent scene. And real big in reggae, and other types of music: African and Calypso and punk rock and European and experimental.

> There were close bonds between the people at Rough Trade back then with Re-Search Books and Magazines and Ralph Records and Subterranean; they were all friends and would help each other out. Survival Research Laboratories was part of it too. Just kind of a real underground, [a] subculture of artistic, creative, subversive-at-times [people].[71]

The relatively non-hierarchical structure at Rough Trade in the United States until the late 1980s undoubtedly contributed to the underground sensibility. According to the former employee:

> When I started . . . Rough Trade was still a collective. Everyone had equal say as to what we [wanted] to put out. Whenever there was any talk of putting out [a] band, everyone voted on it. It was real lax. People would drink beer at work, smoke pot and everything. It was a total hippie commune.[72]

Things changed in early 1988 when Rough Trade CEO Robin Hurley instituted a five-year plan, opened a label office in New York, and forced the U.S. company to operate in a more business-like manner. A former Rough Trade buyer maintained that this was "necessary to survive—we had to get organized like a company." The goal was to allow Rough Trade in the U.S. to expand so that it could truly compete with the majors while continuing to put out independent music. In the second year of the five-year plan, Rough Trade, Inc. was still important as a distributor of both established independent labels, like SST and Wax Trax, and similar independents. In terms of the artists on its in-house label, Rough Trade sought to expand beyond the indie rock genre which encompassed its best-known acts so that it could be perceived as, in the buyer's words, "more of a rounded label," signing country artists, for instance.[73] He saw Rough Trade as "a growing label that is getting more organized and putting out bigger things that are going to sell over ten or twenty thousand copies, unlike the way it used to be or the way some independents are." However, Rough Trade was unsuccessful at changing perceptions. While in the second year of the five-year plan Rough Trade was "getting identified with bigger bands that [were] getting on MTV like Galaxie 500 and Mazzy Star and Victoria Williams," in the end people still tended to identify the label with bands like the Smiths, the "poppier underground rock stuff."[74]

Besides signing a greater variety of acts, Rough Trade tried to compete with the majors by increasing the reach of its distribution, so that, as the Rough Trade buyer stated in 1990, "bands will not see an advantage in going to a major, other than possibly a larger advance at the beginning, or a fancier ad somewhere." By the late 1980s and early 1990s some in the independent scene were unhappy with Rough Trade's plans:

> the way people are talking in the industry now, they're referring to some independents as majors. . . . And so we are kind of going that route. Some people . . . have slagged Rough Trade in the last year or two, saying "Oh, they're being a major label, they want to put out these things that are going to sell X amount, they don't care about grassroots idealism, the new Cabaret Voltaire or the new punk band or whatever, they just want to get a major band.[75]

The Rough Trade buyer did not directly refute this criticism, although he did point out that, "Rough Trade is still signing independent bands," and that it could "still be seen [like other indie labels] as almost a farm system, where we can help establish a band, get a couple records out, get them on tour, and then they can go on to better things," thus indicating that Rough Trade was fulfilling a traditional function of large independent labels.

Yet Rough Trade, Inc. was more than a traditional independent. Although the buyer in the early 1990s was hesitant to view other indie labels as Rough Trade's competitors, he did believe that Rough Trade competed in the marketplace with those few companies

> that do the same thing we do. That would be Important Records, Caroline, and Dutch East India [because] they're distributors, and they also have in-house labels that they manufacture and promote and distribute and all that. So these are our definite direct competitors. Like I wouldn't say Alias is a competitor. If you look at it like, "Oh wait, they could sign a band that we could sign," then they're a competitor, but it's really not fair.[76]

Rough Trade occupied at least two niches in the market, operating both in the highly competitive world of independent distribution and the superficially noncompetitive world of independent labels. Certainly success at Rough Trade was measured in different terms than at smaller labels included in this study, like Champaign-Urbana-based Parasol. At Rough Trade, making it onto the college radio charts—either *College Music Journal* (CMJ) or the *Gavin Report*—was an important objective.[77] Likewise, the goal stated earlier of selling more than 20,000 copies of many releases is far beyond the expectations of many independent labels.

Yet Rough Trade in the United States did not exist only within the context of a national market; it is also important to understand how Rough Trade—encompassing both the record company and the retail store—was defined by and interacted with the community of San Francisco. We cannot overlook the role that the retail store played, and continued to play through much of the 1990s, in identifying Rough Trade with the San Francisco community. The store will be discussed in detail in the next chapter. In looking at the record company, we find that there was a tension between its role as a national producer and distributor of independent music and the perception that Rough Trade was a San Francisco label. Many of Rough Trade's American acts were based in Northern California, including Camper Van Beethoven, Mazzy Star, the Ophelias, Short Dogs Grow, Mr. T Experience, and Fuel. Moreover, some of the labels manufactured and distributed by Rough Trade, like Heyday, had several San Francisco–area artists on their rosters, thus contributing to Rough Trade's image as a San Francisco label. The fact that so many Rough Trade artists resided in the Bay Area did work to the company's promotional advantage, however; it allowed Rough Trade to organize showcases of the label's bands at local clubs. Yet the tension remained. As an employee stated early in the 1990s: "It's not like we are San Francisco's label; we're national and international."[78]

The conflict over Rough Trade's identity as a national and international label rather than a local independent label highlights the problems inherent in its expansionist tendencies, in its attempt to maintain a visible presence in a local site outside of the centers of mainstream music production, while at the same time working to transcend local identity. The fragmentation of Rough Trade's local identity was largely responsible for the company's demise: it wanted to be both an independent and a major label, a local and a national/international business. Rough Trade's struggle was between maintaining the perception of its integrity as an indie label and distributor with a connection to and an understanding of the local, the symbolic site of indie music, and following a plan to achieve financial success. Finally, in the third year of the five-year plan, Rough Trade failed at both.

The general consensus is that Rough Trade in the United States was too ambitious and financially overextended itself in an attempt to secure desirable bands like the Butthole Surfers and high quality staff people. According to the woman who bought the San Francisco Rough Trade retail store in the 1990s when the label filed Chapter 7 bankruptcy and liquidated the company in May of 1991, Rough Trade in Britain "was suffering and did not want to extend the money to the U.S. company like it was supposed to. The money had already been spent here."[79] In the U.K., an effort to expand Rough Trade's distribution business resulted in an expensive move to a larger space and a disastrous attempt to computerize operations. When these factors were combined with the bankruptcy of a large British one-stop and distributor that owed Rough Trade four million dollars, the U.K. company found that it did not have the resources to extend to the U.S. company to continue its expansion. Rough Trade, Inc. in the U.S. was forced to borrow money.[80] Simon Frith argues that indie success in a depressed marketplace was the cause of the British company's cash flow problems. In its capacity as a distributor, Rough Trade Ltd. found that while it was distributing more releases for more independent labels and generating more hits, the company had spread itself too thin, since it lacked the infrastructure (for instance, the distribution arm had yet to move into its new, computerized facilities), to adequately handle all the product it was introducing into the marketplace.[81]

Although most industry observers attribute Rough Trade's problems to mismanagement in the U.K. company, the U.S. company had problems of its own. Several independent labels had signed pressing and distribution (P&D) deals with Rough Trade in the U.S. In other words, smaller indies would locate and record new artists, then Rough Trade would actually manufacture the records and get them into stores.

Many of these indies complained that Rough Trade had exclusive P&D deals with too many small indies—seventeen or eighteen—and the company's resources were strained. As Randy Kaye of Genius Records, a label that had a P&D deal with Rough Trade, observed: "They weren't concentrating enough on each label. We were told that they were only going to take on three or four labels."[82] At the same time, Rough Trade in the U.S. had its own in-house label, and American artists on the Rough Trade roster complained that they were not being given adequate attention by the U.S. company.

Relations were particularly strained with Rough Trade's most profitable American band, the now-defunct Camper Van Beethoven. Camper's relationship with Rough Trade began as a P&D deal. In the spirit of the DIY ethic, Camper formed its own label, Pitch-A-Tent, and put out its first record, with the help of Rough Trade, in February 1986. The P&D deal with Rough Trade meant that once it had recorded the music, Camper didn't immediately have to use any of its own money to have the album manufactured and distributed. Rough Trade gave Camper ninety days to pay back these costs, by which time the record had sold 3000 copies and the costs were recouped. But the relationship with Rough Trade was not problem-free. A member of Camper Van Beethoven recalled:

> We did have a number of tours where it was like, "Why haven't they gotten the record here yet?" We'd ask Rough Trade, "What the hell's going on, you guys? You're supposed to send out our new record. They have our old record, they're still playing 'Take the Skinheads Bowling.'"[83]

A bandmate agreed:

> We would ask, "Why the hell isn't the record in this town?" and Rough Trade would answer, "We don't know, we just didn't think it was a very good market." We would say," "What do you mean it's not a good market? Did you look at our tour itinerary?"[84]

Relations between Camper and Rough Trade were not improved when Rough Trade fired the company's U.S. label manager and liaison to Pitch-A-Tent, Steve Connell, as part of the implementation of the five-year plan. Moreover, the new label manager hired a director of publicity who was thought by the band to be quite incompetent. Camper left Rough Trade soon after the shake-up and signed to Virgin.

Rough Trade's U.S. operation experienced problems on many levels: problems with the parent company in Britain, problems internally with its own staff, problems resulting from its exclusive deals with struggling independent labels, and problems with artists on its own in-house label. Of course, all these problems were interrelated and demonstrate the difficulties of combining poorly managed economic expansion with a desire to maintain indie authenticity.

Alias

Alias is a medium-sized label that was heavily associated with the San Francisco indie-pop scene in the early 1990s. When the label started in the late 1980s it maintained both a headquarters in Los Angeles and an office in San Francisco. Even after the two offices were consolidated in the Los Angeles headquarters—a process undertaken in 1991 in an effort to reduce redundancy, primarily in promotional activities—its small roster of recording artists was disproportionately populated by Bay area acts, including American Music Club, Harm Farm, X-Tal, the Sneetches, and the Loud Family. In early 1989, Alias had only two bands (Too Much Joy and the Sneetches), but by the end of 1990 there were eight acts putting out records on Alias. By early 1993 Alias had expanded its roster to twelve acts, including perennial critics' favorite Yo La Tengo, based in Hoboken, New Jersey, and Midwestern bands the Skeletons and the Magnolias.

Unlike Rough Trade, which was founded with more ambitious goals, Alias was started, according to an employee who had interned at Alias in its early days, "by a few people who thought it would be a good idea to put a record out, but nobody really knew what they were doing. Eventually those people kind of fell off, one by one."[85] In 1989, when Alias released its second and third records (one by the Sneetches and one by Too Much Joy) there were just two people working in the San Francisco office. Though the label had been around for about two years, it was only in 1989 that it became active in releasing records. In subsequent months the San Francisco office added a part-time publicist, a retail director, a radio promotion assistant, and a label manager, giving Alias a combined total of six employees in its two offices. By early 1993, Alias employed ten people. While the label's growth was steady, Alias did not become a major indie. Unlike at Rough Trade, where the United Kingdom branch was able to export managers with record company experience to the U.S., at Alias, according to one executive in the early 1990s, all of the employees "learned day-to-day what to do and what's required of us." She explained:

> None of us really knew what a label was, what a label's supposed to do, but we each knew our own area. I was totally familiar with college radio . . . [but] I didn't want to deal with commercial radio. I didn't want to know about commercial radio; I didn't really know a lot about community or NPR stations. It was all just a hands-on type of thing. Which is great, because it gives you a little bit more confidence in going into places that people say you shouldn't go. And maybe [you] even become more successful at it because you don't know.[86]

This sort of amateur-ness that resulted in a learn-as-you-go approach made smaller independent labels attractive to some bands. A member of the Sneetches remarked, "I'm glad we signed to Alias—they allow us to make records the way we want to."[87] For an Alias employee, the most important thing was that Alias marketed "quality" music; she was careful to stress that Alias didn't release "a throwaway, something we just regret releasing or that we felt bad about putting out there." The professed goal at Alias, as at most small and intermediate independent labels, was not to sell records: "We've never really been after money per se, and all the stuff that has to go into making it, as in really getting great chart numbers."[88] As we will see later, for many bands of the 1980s and 1990s, the advantages of staying with an independent label, such as the freedom to make non-commercial records, were outweighed by the disadvantages, and they sought deals with larger independents or major labels.

As has already been discussed, distribution is the primary limitation faced by independent labels. Although later in the 1990s Alias did enter in distribution agreements with major labels for some of its acts like Archers of Loaf, in the early 1990s Alias did not have any such agreements, but all the large independent distributors did carry Alias releases. Nationwide distribution allowed Alias to have a fairly high profile as an intermediate-sized independent in the national marketplace. An important part of gaining national recognition, according to an Alias executive of the 1990s, "was definitely signing bands out of the area and looking for talent out of the area."[89]

In spite of the nationwide search for talent in which independent labels engage, Alias, like all the other labels included here, did not perceive itself to be in competition with other labels. Although the former Alias executive interviewed acknowledged that Alias didn't "have as much clout as a Frontier or Sub Pop," she didn't characterize those labels as competitors. Rather, she opted to focus on the similarities Alias shared with other labels of the 1980s and early 1990s: Mammoth in North Carolina (which is now owned by the Walt Disney Company), for instance:

> I would think we are approaching the same stature or are at about the same point as Mammoth . . . I think they've been around about the same time [as we have]. They have great bands; they've had the Downsiders, the Blake Babies, and Black Girls And it's interesting, because we're all really getting along with them; they're great people.

> I don't think it's even really a rivalry. We work together more often than not. All of us have friends there, know people there. We actually lean on each other a little bit.[90]

Discourses of community recur in discussions of the national marketplace of independent music. Each label saw itself as putting out a unique product; discourses of difference then infiltrated the constructed community, as this Alias executive demonstrated in 1990:

I don't think we really compete with anybody at this point, because . . . we're not stuck in any one genre necessarily, so I don't think sound-wise that we're really competing with anybody. Nobody's putting records that sound like The Sneetches out. . . . I don't see much competition, but I see weird niches that we have to work ourselves into because there aren't other bands that sound like ours out there.[91]

Of course, having bands like the Sneetches and the Loud Family contributed to the perception of Alias as a "pure pop" label, creating a tension between the professed desire not to be "stuck in any one genre" and broader perceptions. In fact, because the first two reasonably well-distributed records that Alias put out were by The Sneetches and Too Much Joy, people at Alias believed that from the outset Alias was perceived as an indie pop, college radio label.

In order to have more control over its label image, Alias put quite a bit of effort into marketing its bands. When sending promotional material to record stores, for instance, Alias tried to make it unique or otherwise memorable (e.g., posters autographed by band members), since the label was relatively small and limited in the quantity of materials it could send out. Also, considering the small number of releases that Alias put out, it was important for the label to make a good first impression on retailers in order to get rack space for its limited catalogue.

Alias also put a fair amount of effort into supporting bands that were on tour. It helps a label's level of recognition to have a band on a national tour, as when Too Much Joy was out for fifteen weeks straight. Alias tried particularly to track bands through places where their records were doing well. But bands out on the road were expected by the label to work at becoming better known, according to a label employee:

When [a band is] out there we try to do everything possible. Everything has been pretty much in-house. There's usually one to two to three radio interviews in every city. We try to do live in-stores. Even if [record stores] don't want to do in-stores, we send the bands out there and make sure their records are there. . . . If their record's not there and they're playing that night they will go up to the counter [and say], "I really want to buy this record!" and not tell them it's theirs.[92]

Although Alias closed its San Francisco office in the 1990s, its tenure in the city and the large number of Bay Area acts that were signed to the label continued to contribute to the identification of Alias as a San Francisco label throughout the 1990s. Some argued that Alias was the only label of the 1980s and 1990s besides Heyday and Alternative Tentacles to be identified with San Francisco that made a name for itself on both a local and national level. In the early 1990s an Alias executive maintained that, "there are other [local] labels that are signing local bands . . . but [they] don't have the distribution for a commercial push that we have."[93] Yet while Alias relied heavily on the Bay Area in its search for talent, to a degree it tried to distance itself from the locality. Before the San Francisco office was closed, the interviewed Alias employee observed that it "takes a lot for us to sign somebody locally. . . . If there's a really good band in San Francisco, we're usually right on top of it."[94] For a medium-sized label like Alias, it was important to maintain a local identity in order to have access to artists and their fan bases, but it was also important to transcend local identity to have at least a small presence in the commercial music marketplace.

Parasol

Parasol, based in Urbana, Illinois, typified in its early years a late-1980s and early 1990s indie label trend: the move towards the 7-inch vinyl format. Just as the mainstream music industry was completing its phase-out of vinyl LPs and 45s, independent labels were finding the 7-inch vinyl format a cheap and effective way of circulating the music of new bands, many of which did not have the extensive repertoires required to fill up a normal length CD or tape, to underground audiences.

The 7-inch trend was referred to by *Village Voice* critic Robert Christgau as "vinyl revanchism . . . rhetorically rebellious commodity fetishism, and possibly something more" (9). In fact, this self-conscious effort by some indies to refuse the range of formats decreed saleable by major labels has existed since the majors began to phase out vinyl: it was noted in 1990 by independent pop/rock 'zine *The Bob*. At that time the best known 7-inch indie was the New York City–based Singles Only Label (SOL), founded by Hüsker Dü frontman Bob Mould, but *The Bob* also mentioned labels like Chicago's Touch and Go; Lawrence, Kansas' Leftover; Bellingham, Washington's Estrus; and Iowa City, Iowa's Bus Stop.[95]

Parasol emerged at the intersection of two distinct vectors: one is the emergence of the 7-inch single as an important marketing tool in indie rock in the late 1980s and early 1990s, and, most notably in this case, indie pop; and the second is the history of indie music production in Urbana-Champaign. The rise of the underground 7-inch market seemed to coincide with the mainstream industry's determination that the vinyl phonograph record was no longer a profitable, and therefore viable, format. Independent labels, and especially smaller indies, were reluctant to abandon the cheap vinyl format for CDs. Indies not already affiliated with major labels through Pressing and Distribution (P&D) deals usually had existing agreements with vinyl pressing plants and did not have the available capital to initially invest in more expensive CD production. On the other hand, most indies did not want to be relegated to the production and distribution of cassette tape, since the stigma attached to cassettes was that anyone could put one out. Undoubtedly part of vinyl's appeal to independent companies selling alternative rock and pop was that the major labels' effort to make the format obsolete in effect made whatever appeared on vinyl, especially 7-inch vinyl, more oppositional to the mainstream.

Furthermore, the format catered to a rather narrow audience: those who still owned, or were willing to purchase, the outmoded turntable technology.

The 7-inch underground of the late 1980s and the 1990s encompassed a range of independent music, though the two genres that most commonly appeared in this format were hardcore and indie pop, with some labels, like Olympia, Washington-based K, releasing music in both genres. Unlike the larger independent labels discussed up to this point, which resembled major labels in that they rented office space, many of the smaller indies—including hardcore-oriented labels like Sympathy for the Record Industry and Amphetamine Reptile, as well as North Carolina–based Merge Records, British indie-pop label Sarah, and Parasol—were at least at one time operated out of apartments or houses.

The indie pop underground in particular seemed to be dispersed across several micro-indies found on both sides of the Atlantic. The 1992 . . . One Last Kiss pop compilation, the first release on the Lancaster, Pennsylvania spinArt label, featured tracks previously available only as 7-inch singles on labels such as Parasol (Champaign-Urbana), Bus Stop (Iowa City), K (Olympia), Slumberland (San Francisco), and Playtime (Manchester, England).[96] Though there was an indie pop tradition in the Champaign scene that could be traced to the early 1980s, Parasol was the first local 7-inch label that released a significant number of records.

Throughout the 1980s, a number of bands of the indie pop or rock ilk appeared on the Champaign-Urbana scene, and several released albums, singles, and/or tapes on local labels like Office, Trashcan, and Popsicle.[97] The existence of small local labels and the availability of cheap recording equipment enabled bands to have recordings available locally without relying on signing major label or major indie deals. According to Trashcan co-founder Chris Corpora, Trashcan's entire purpose was "to break the local scene."[98] Several Trashcan releases, including the first Poster Children tape, as well as Parasol releases by Champaign-Urbana band Twiggy, were recorded by a local scene participant in his home. The accessibility of the technology meant that local bands were able to reach larger audiences.

A 1989 newspaper article examined the Champaign music scene and declared, "Champaign-Urbana is on the verge of becoming a trend-setting music scene with national influence."[99] While this optimistic prediction did not come to pass, several local bands or artists did get major label or major indie deals in the late 1980s and early 1990s. These included the Poster Children, which released a single on Seattle's Sub Pop label, as well as records on Frontier, Twin Tone, and major-owned Sire, and who have charted high on modern rock and alternative radio charts;[100] Titanic Love Affair, which signed with Charisma; Adam Schmitt, who was on Warner Brothers; former Champaign musicians Ric Menck and Paul Chastain, whose band Velvet Crush signed a five album deal with Warner Brothers in the United States and Creation in Britain, and whose first album entered the CMJ college radio chart at number twenty and went as high as eight;[101] and Last Gentlemen, who signed with Zoo.

Others, like Lonely Trailer, while recording only sporadically and for small labels, were known outside the area through independent distribution and word-of-mouth.

The sense that Champaign-Urbana was a regional scene of some national significance was undoubtedly important to Parasol's visibility. Within the Champaign-Urbana scene there were a few notable local labels in the early 1990s. In addition to Parasol there was 12 Inch Records, started by Rick and Rose of Poster Children, which put out, for instance, a 45 and CD for local band Hum. Parasol, however, was an older label and better known outside of the local area, as evidenced by the *Spin* article on . . . *One Last Kiss* compilation that mentioned Parasol bands White Town and Our American Cousins.

Parasol's first single was by Our American Cousins, a New Jersey band, and was released in the summer of 1991. Parasol's founder Geoff Merritt had in fact been active in the Champaign-Urbana scene for several years, working at the now-defunct record store the Pop Shop in the early 1980s and then opening his own video and music rental store, That's Rentertainment, in 1984. With a local musician he started Popsicle, a tape label, and later Picturebook, a singles label that put out four singles during 1985 and 1986; neither label aspired to release music by artists from outside the local area. When the musician left town in the mid-1980s, Picturebook left with him, and Merritt concentrated on his store[102] and on selling other labels' records at collectors' conventions and through fanzine ads. While spending the summer of 1990 in San Francisco, according to Merritt:

> I decided I was gonna start [putting out singles], because Brian [Kirk of Bus Stop] was doing it, and it seemed really cool. And then I must have mentioned it in one of my ads or something, or mentioned it to somebody that I was going to start, and this . . . Cousins guy called and sent me a tape, and [I decided to] put that out. And then I got back and I talked to [Champaign musician] Nick [Rudd], 'cause I always thought he was great, so we put his stuff out.[103]

By the mid-1990s the Parasol roster had grown to include local artists and bands Blown, Sidecar Racers, Three Hour Tour, Sarge, and non-local acts Our American Cousins, White Town, Cowboy and Spingirl, and, from Britain, Strawberry Story. Merritt called all this music "guitar pop stuff," and noted that Parasol bands tended to be labeled "indie guitar pop." However, he pointed out that a band like R.E.M., which, while starting out on indie labels and often described as having an "indie pop" sound, in fact records for a major label. He tended to identify his bands as true "indie" bands because they recorded for a very small label, as opposed to a band like R.E.M. He thus contended, "If you're talking with anybody that normally deals with the majors, they're thinking of 'indie' as though R.E.M. is still an indie band. For me, on our level, we're an indie pop label. But that's only if you're talking with our little [circle]." In her 1992 *Spin* article "Jangly, Fuzzy, Cute, and Twee," Gail O'Hara defined the indie pop put out by small labels like Parasol, Bus Stop, K, Harriet, and Slumberland as "an anti-rock subgenre favoring singing over yelling and jangly/fuzzy guitar."[104] Evelyn McDonnell, writing in the *Village Voice* in 1991, labeled the same genre "'love rock' or 'cutie music,'" and described it as "a sweet folk-pop . . . regressive, primitive, acoustic, small."[105]

Whatever the disputes about the name of the genre, the preferred format of most labels releasing indie pop singles was in the early 1990s the 7-inch single. When asked why most Parasol releases of the early 1990s were 7-inches, the label founder replied:

> Because they're the best—they're the best format. We do a few CDs, mainly because the bands want to. I think most bands we're dealing with don't have enough material to do an album. You could stretch them out to an album, and it would suck. 45s are great. You put on a 45, you listen to it, and you're done—put on something else. 45s are cool, and you get the little picture sleeve.[106]

Putting out 45s was clearly meaningful because it was, at least on the symbolic level, anti-hegemonic; and because 7-inch singles were relatively cheap, they were attractive to low-budget operations like Parasol which tried to reach small, select audiences. 7-inches offered potential consumers unfamiliar with particular bands an opportunity to buy records and find out whether they liked bands without spending considerably more money on a CD.

Parasol was certainly not alone in the indie pop 7-inch market. But like representatives of larger indies like Alias, Parasol's founder refused to define labels comparable to Parasol as competitors, with the exception of Slumberland: "the moment somebody puts out a cool record, all of a sudden Slumberland is all over them trying to get them to put out a record with them." Other labels on the whole, however, were not seen as competition:

> There are other labels that do the same stuff, but we're not in it to make money and people that do it on the same level as us aren't competitors. There's Four Letter Words out in California, there's K Records out in Washington, who are all very cool and very friendly, and we trade with each other to get more stuff.
>
> We're just doing it because we like it, and if somebody has good music we'll put it out.[107]

With the exception of Slumberland, the indie pop underground was characterized as one happy, transnational community.

In order to reach the "community" of indie pop fans, after Parasol's launch the label employed a variety of marketing devices. Parasol ads offering product through mail order ran in fanzines like *Puncture*, *Emma's Hip Pocket*, and *Four Letter Words*.

Parasol also had a mailing list of mail order customers and sends them frequently up-dated lists of available stock (and today sends it not just through the postal service but also via email.) This stock included not just Parasol records but releases on other indie labels. In fact, a 1993 magazine round-up of nine specialty music mail order companies discussed Parasol without even noting Parasol's function as a record label:

> Parasol stocks tons of domestic indie-pop (Sunday, Simple Machines, K), English and Aussie imports (Sarah, Summershine), kiwi [New Zealand] pop (lots of Flying Nun), used stuff, collectibles, 'zines, as well as techno, industry, and hardcore.[108]

To access an audience for its own releases larger than that which can be reached through alternative media outlets, Parasol had to get its product in record stores. The record stores in which Parasol releases could be found were the alternative stores that stock 7-inch vinyl, so this left them with a limited number of outlets. Within this market, however, Parasol got fairly good distribution, as its founder and owner explained in 1991:

> We're selling all over the U.S. We're selling records in England, Australia, the Netherlands, Germany—not in huge quantities. We only press a thousand of any-thing we do, but we've got distributors in all those places, and we've got five distrib-utors in the U.S.: Cargo in Chicago, Twin City Imports, TCI, Boner Records in San Francisco—the big ones for the most part. And then Viskit and Roller Coaster in England, Semaphore in the Netherlands, Summershine in Australia.[109]

Through this network of independent distribution and mail order, what would ap-pear to be a small local label was able to transcend local-ness and reach an almost global subcultural audience.

Ironically, at the outset Parasol did not have as much success selling records in Champaign-Urbana as it had outside the local area. Parasol releases were carried by Record Swap and Record Service in Champaign. And while Record Swap was fairly receptive to stocking the records, Record Service was been reluctant to sell them; it was "like pulling teeth to get them in there."[110] Perhaps this is because few Parasol releases had sold well locally. The label's head admitted that Parasol didn't "do any-thing locally. There isn't anything to do locally." Singles by Champaign music scene veteran Nick Rudd did not sell well in Champaign: his first single on Parasol sold eighty copies in England and one at Record Swap, the store at which he worked at the time. However, singles put out on Merritt's "noisier" Mud label by local bands like Hot Glue Gun and Honcho Overload early in the label's history sold fairly well in Champaign. This was attributed this to the familiarity audiences in the area al-ready had with those bands: "But as far as buying stuff that they don't know about, they don't do it anymore. At least not around here."[111]

The unwillingness of consumers to buy the records of bands with which they were unfamiliar was perceived by Parasol as impeding its ability to get exposure for local bands. While others saw Parasol as important in getting local music to the public, those at the label argued that despite a roster laden with local talent, Parasol was not doing them much good in the local area: "I'm just putting out singles, and nobody's buying them." This was perceived as different from a time in the early 1980s when there was more of a sense of community in the Champaign scene:

> It used to be a single came out in this town and everybody bought it. *Stabs in the Dark* [a 1982 compilation album of Champaign bands] came out and everybody bought it whether they liked the stuff or not, because it was local. And now, if it's not Honcho Overload, if it's not Hot Glue Gun. . . . I guess there's something wrong with putting out 45s because a lot of people don't even own turntables anymore, but even so, people should buy this stuff.[112]

Nostalgia for a lost community had an economic basis in this case: true membership in the community was thought to be expressed through the consumption of a specific product. Interestingly, it was at this moment, when the Champaign scene was most in the national spotlight, that one of its key participants saw the scene as at its least cohesive. Yet national identification of a "Champaign scene" came when participants in this scene were connected in some way with entities that both transcended and were defined by locality: Parasol and the other "local" indie pop 7-inch labels, like Slumberland and K; or Poster Children and other harder indie rock, even "grunge" bands of the early 1990s, notably Chicago's Smashing Pumpkins, Minneapolis' Soul Asylum, and various Seattle bands (Nirvana, Soundgarden, Mudhoney).

Major Labels and Independents:
Advantages and Disadvantages for Artists

Although the three labels featured in the case studies—Rough Trade, Alias, and Parasol—operated in the early 1990s without major label involvement, there were clearly advantages for artists to the major label arrangements I have discussed. For the most part, the primary advantage of signing a major label contract was better distribution, though major labels could also provide other services to artists that some independents can or do not. In the 1980s and early 1990s at Washington, D.C. independent label Dischord, for example, bands received no tour support and were responsible for booking their own shows and supplying promotional materials.[113]

When an act began to receive widespread national recognition, it often began to look for a deal with a major label or an independent with major label distribution because of the limitations of independent record companies. A member of a popular 1980s indie band explained:

> With an independent label, it can be very frustrating to watch a record that you've worked intensely hard on, and the radio mailing list is done competently—and then watching the record climb, but no advertising underneath it, no solicitation for reviews.[114]

Even when an artist was cynical about major label practices and wanted to maintain indie credibility, the advantage of being on a major label could outweigh the advantages of being on an independent label. A Northern California musician stated:

> It's really, really important to be on a major label. A major does a lot more for you. If you look at the Top 10 in college radio, it's almost all majors nowadays; and the more time passes, the more it's like that. A major can buy its way onto *Billboard*. I haven't been on a major, and I don't see this happen with my own eyes, but everyone says the industry is bought and sold.[115]

By citing the services a major label can provide, artists were no doubt trying to deflect criticism that they would be "selling out" if they signed with one of the majors. The defensiveness of independent label-based musicians who see advantages to a major label contract is demonstrated by this explanation of major label merits by a musician in a one-time Alias pop band:

> If we could have an independent label that could give us what a major label could give us—it's not a major label deal in itself. Unfortunately, the way things have become you need a major label in order to really be heard, or in order to really progress and move on, or to even have the vaguest semblance of making a living at what you're doing and to be able to survive. And that sucks.

> It's not that we really want to be on a major label just because it's a major label. It's because the way things are structured, it's almost as if you're forced into that.[116]

And, in fact, some indie acts were happy with their major label deals. When R.E.M. signed with Warner Brothers in 1988, it had reached a point in its career at which it was selling one million units of its releases, and band members felt that that was the maximum volume of product that I.R.S. could handle. Furthermore, R.E.M. had not successfully expanded its audience in Europe, most importantly in the United Kingdom, and R.E.M. believed a lack of enthusiasm for the band on the part of I.R.S.'s overseas distributor, CBS International, was responsible. R.E.M. was impressed by the roster of alternative artists that Warner Brothers had signed—including fellow

Athens, Georgia band the B-52's and Minneapolis band The Replacements—and by assurances from the company that Warner's overseas division would make marketing R.E.M. in Europe a top priority.[117]

Some independent music-type artists eschewed the independent label "farm system" and signed their first contracts with major labels. One Champaign, Illinois musician, for example, had been offered a contract by Frontier, an independent label, when Warner Brothers expressed an interest in him. After a year of negotiations Warner offered him a contract; that was, according to the musician, "the happiest day of my life," in great part because, in his opinion at the time, "Warner is really one of the few labels that has a really, really high standard of good quality records coming out. There's not a lot of schlock that Warner puts out."[118] With his first Warner album, the label provided some services many independents could not have:

> Warner did a really good job of getting the record out to the press . . . we were in *Billboard* and *Rolling Stone*, and there was a lot of fanzine stuff, which gave it really good reviews.[119]

Despite the lackluster sales of his debut album—only between 15,000 and 20,000 units—Warner lived up to its reputation as an artist-oriented label by giving the musician substantial freedom in recording his follow-up effort, which he produced and mixed.

For artists like this, except for the discrepancy in available resources, there appears to be little difference between signing with an independent label and signing with a major. As major labels seek to bring musics that have dwelt on the fringes into the mainstream, the aesthetic differences between major labels and independent labels diminish. Kevin Shields, guitarist for British band My Bloody Valentine (which was dropped by the British label Creation), commented on the lack of difference between independent and major labels:

> In England, the only difference between a major and an indie is that the major and an indie is that the major has a bigger cash flow. There's no other difference.

> The important thing is the people you work with. The majors vs. indies issue has become irrelevant, because nowadays so many independent labels interfere with you more than the majors would.[120]

But the view held by Shields did not necessarily represent the consensus of indie pop/rock musicians in the 1980s and 1990s. For the most part, relatively successful indie artists viewed major label deals as a necessary evil. Often alternative acts found themselves in losing situations at the start when they signed with a major. The standard major label contract stipulated that recording costs were repaid out of the royalties earned by the artist rather than out of gross receipts, which means that the record company could be making money off of an album long before the artist sees any royalties. It was, and remains, a system in which only million-selling superstars could see a reasonable return (Dannen 143). One indie musician described how the major label approach to royalties works:

> At an independent label, we get paid full royalties on every song. Major labels won't sign people unless they give up their publishing rights, so the major label controls at least the administration of the publishing. Plus, major labels have a controlled composition clause, which means they won't pay for more than ten songs per record.

> If you record any covers, whoever owns the publishing rights to those songs gets paid first. You get paid for any leftover songs that you've written. Which means if you're putting twelve to fourteen songs on a record, you may only be getting paid for eight of them. This is different from our first three records, which had sixteen, seventeen, eighteen songs on them, and we got paid—we still get paid, if the records sell—the whole royalty rate per song. That's the sort of contract you cannot make with a major label.[121]

When R.E.M. signed with independent label I.R.S. in 1982, the band agreed to accept modest advance payments in return for a greater share of the royalties. The contract was unlike one they would have been offered by most major labels. R.E.M. liked the contract because it made the band less financially beholden to the record company and therefore, they hoped, less under the company's creative control.[122]

Creative control was cited by artists as one of the primary advantages of independent labels, although some artists (like Kevin Shields of My Bloody Valentine) complained that even at independents bands may run into a great deal of label interference. In *One Chord Wonders*, Dave Laing observes that in general independent record companies are more likely than majors to allow musicians latitude, since they lack the bureaucracy needed for creative micromanagement and the all-encompassing desire to maximize audience and sales possessed by major labels (21). Though this may be somewhat less true today than it was in the mid-to-late 1970s, it remained true in the 1980s and 1990s that most independent labels tended to concentrate on their own narrow target audiences rather than a larger, less differentiated audience. Because of the absence of complex bureaucratic structures, the owners of independent labels usually displayed a greater degree of commitment to individual artists than major record companies.[123]

At major labels, artists often found themselves in conflict with decision-makers over creative choices. For instance, an indie pop artist who was allowed significant freedom in recording his second Warner Brothers' album found that during the making of the first album he had to acquiesce to the company's decisions about which of his songs should appear on the record. When Warner executives decided that a particular song should be the first single off the first album, the artist disagreed but could do nothing about it.[124] Moreover, he was not pleased that Warner chose the musicians to play on the first record and that the company failed to promote the record. While he respected the quality of artists signed to Warner and the label's ability his records out to the music press, this artist had misgivings about how he had generally been treated at the label:

> I don't think it's any secret that there wasn't any promotion for the first album. We never even did a video. It is sort of difficult at Warner Brothers, unless you make an incredible first impression on people, to get them to remember who you are. There are so many artists on that label.[125]

Like this musician, Camper Van Beethoven had problems with the major label to which they eventually signed, Virgin. Many of the conflicts were over creative decisions:

> The pressure's there in terms of major labels' expectations. There are production standards. A lot of the time you find these are not so much production standards as economic standards.[126]

Problems with major labels were so prevalent among alternative rock/pop acts that signed to majors that the issue was spotlighted at the 1991 CMJ conference. One panel, called "Signed, Sealed, and Abandoned," focused on what artists should do after being dropped by a major.[127] Many artists, like indie pop musician Matthew Sweet, who signed his first record contract with CBS and later moved to the small label Zoo,[128] actually sold more records after losing their major label contracts. In some cases though, the lack of attention paid to bands by the major labels that signed them permanently harmed bands' careers. A Champaign, Illinois record store owner noted that local bands Combo Audio and the Elvis Brothers signed major labels contracts in the early 1980s, but both bands were quickly dropped, and their careers never recovered. [129]

The problems associated with signing to a major label were well known to indie rock/pop artists of the 1980s and 1990s. Thus, few aspiring musicians were willing to admit to a desire to record for a major label. For most, openly seeking to record on a major label was a sign of "selling out." Also, artists were aware that the road to indie rock/pop stardom was littered with bands that signed major label contracts, released single albums, and were never heard from again. When asked whether a major label deal would be a goal at some point in the future, a Champaign drummer replied, "I hope not." Instead, his goal was

> to have Parasol or Bus Stop say, "I want to do your solo project." That would be one of the best things that could happen in my life. There are some good independent

labels that it would be nice to be on, but mainly the label itself doesn't matter as long as the music gets around.[130]

A dilemma arose, however, when one asked, "as long as the music gets around to what number of people?" If a musician wanted her/his music to reach more than a few hundred or a few thousand people, s/he had to consider major label distribution and major label contracts.

The encroachment of major labels onto the terrain of independent labels was not a new or surprising phenomenon in the last two decades of the twentieth century, but it did underscore the degree to which independent music production was fragmented. Independent labels and indie music artists struggled to ground themselves in their localities and at the same time liberate themselves from identities that were exclusively local, and they sought to both target select audiences and reach as many potential consumers as possible. The tensions between authenticity and artifice, periphery and center, and independence and co-optation underlying the personal narrative histories of indie music scene participants were played out in the economic arena. In this terrain of shifting practices and identifications, to say that major record companies intruded into the local spaces of independent music production, stole the best ideas, and subsequently destroyed the independent music marketplace would be a vast oversimplification. Moreover, looking at the production of independent pop/rock music in isolation from the systems of indie music dissemination and the contexts in which independent pop/rock music was, and continues to be, consumed gives us only a partial understanding of its economic and social formations.

CHAPTER 4

Disseminating Independent Music

After an independent label—or any record label—has produced a record, that record must be circulated to a wider audience, even if it is just a local or regional audience. Four important sites of indie music distribution in the 1980s and early 1990s were radio, video, retail, and live venues. College radio, stereotypically characterized by free formatting and a non-commercial structure, was the main medium through which indie rock and pop music was disseminated, although video, with its national reach, was also important in the economic success of some alternative acts.

College radio stations, like independent labels, were sites of struggle between the ideal of "alternative" music institutions and the reality of major label power. The tensions between local practices and mainstream aesthetics and economics, and between authenticity and commercial logic, manifested themselves in offices and over the airwaves of college radio stations. As awareness of college radio's ability to "break" indie artists grew in the 1980s, so did major label influence over college stations' programming decisions. These tensions were felt too at retail stores and live performance venues, which were the other primary physical spaces in which indie music was disseminated. Although all of these sites were subject to influence from the dominant industry, they were also places of situated local practices, interconnected within localities through networks of economic relationships.

College Radio

When one thinks of indie pop and rock music of the 1980s and early 1990s, or "college music," one generally thinks of music played on nonprofessional, non-commercial (and thus more "real" or "authentic") student-run college radio stations at disparate colleges and universities located across the United States. College radio, however, was not the only mode of broadcast dissemination of independent pop and rock, nor did all college radio stations play the sort of independent music commonly associated with college radio. College radio was generally perceived as being primarily comprised of student-run stations that served reasonably large campus communities and whose playlists tended to emphasize independent rock and pop; however, this stereotype did not apply to all, or even most, college stations. So how did the approximately 1200 college radio stations of the time fit into the overall radio environment?

Because radio was no longer the primary entertainment medium in the last two decades of the twentieth century, radio stations found that they could best compete for audience members by specializing in particular formats to attract demographically narrow target audiences. The resulting proliferation of formats meant that in a major radio market like San Francisco, a college radio station could carve out a niche for itself and attract a substantial fragment of the radio audience. By the early 1990s, while some radio stations chose to follow Album-Oriented Rock (AOR) formats, alternative college radio stations were one of the few radio outlets, besides stations with Urban, Modern Rock, or Contemporary Hit Radio (CHR) formats, to play new releases (Barnes 46).

College radio came to inhabit a key position in alternative music culture and the alternative music marketplace, but this position of importance was a late twentieth-century phenomenon. Although one of the earliest experimental broadcast radio stations was 9XM, established at the University of Wisconsin in 1915, for the most part early radio in the United States was controlled by corporations like Westinghouse, which created programming in order to create demand for the radio receivers they manufactured. In 1922, educational entities held 74 of the 500 station licenses; however, the percentage of universities that held licenses dwindled after 1925, due to a lack of money to fund stations at schools, the increasing commercial domination of the airwaves, and the undesirable frequencies assigned to college stations.[1] It was only in the late 1940s and early 1950s, when the FM band opened up new frequencies for broadcasting, that college stations began to flourish (Fornatale and Mills 126).

Through the 1950s and early 1960s college radio received little outside attention because college radio stations were generally low power operations with few off-campus listeners, and these stations did not report to any trade magazine charts. In the mid-1960s, however, a handful of shows on college radio stations began to be noticed, like Tom Gamache's "Tee Time" show, which began in 1966 on WTBS, the Massachusetts Institute of Technology's thirty-watt, student-run FM station. Gamache played his own records and aired fake commercials (many dealing with marijuana) in his satire of commercial radio. He later moved his show to Boston College's WBUR, which had a 20,000 watt signal (Fornatale and Mills 133).

The popularity of shows like Gamache's encouraged more colleges to develop their own FM stations. Although some media observers, like the *Village Voice*'s Richard Goldstein, consistently wrote about what was going on in the sixties at college radio stations, and while many college radio personnel moved on to careers in commercial radio, for the most part college radio remained unnoticed by the music and broadcasting industries (Fornatale and Mills 134). College radio in the late 1960s and in the 1970s was simply not seen by these entities as a place where new artists could be usefully introduced to the public.

It was not until the late 1970s that new music programming at college radio stations began to take hold. Music journalist Anthony DeCurtis explained:

> By that time, the open formats that characterized progressive [commercial] FM radio—itself created as a response to the narrow strictures of Top Forty AM stations—had been almost completely eliminated. At the same time, the punk movement had spawned a host of British and American bands with rabid followings and nervous sounds that didn't quite settle comfortably next to the high-gloss sonic finish of Fleetwood Mac and Eagles records. Inspired by the punks and given free rein, as long as they didn't burn their studios down, college programmers began tracking discs with a glee best expressed in the dictum articulated by Faith Henschel, music director at KCMU at the University of Washington in Seattle: "Everything can fit your format."[2]

A San Francisco–based indie musician who graduated from the University of California at Davis in the early 1980s recalled that college radio gained music industry recognition in the late 1970s largely because of:

> the breakdown of free-format commercial radio. Once DJs could no longer play what they liked, you had a small but significant number of people, mostly college age people, [who said] "we want radio where we play what we like." So college radio kind of was there before that, but started being an important industry forum, indicator, because there was no other place where DJs actually played what they wanted.[3]

In the early 1980s, college radio stations were crucial in bringing then-indie label bands like R.E.M. and U2 to the attention of college audiences. However, it is important to note that significant differences existed between college radio stations; for instance, as I will discuss in more detail shortly, there were, and still are, both non-commercial and commercial college radio stations. There were also many college radio formats in the 1980s and 1990s, including mainstream (AOR, Urban, Top 40, etc.) and alternative formats: formats more associated with "selling out" than with "authenticity" by fans of marginal musics. Furthermore, significant differences could even be found between stations that programmed alternative music. The San Francisco area is a large radio market—one that can support a number of college radio stations as well as commercial stations (including a commercial alternative station)—and within this market there were clear differences in the 1980s and 1990s in how the major college stations were programmed. For example, the University of San Francisco's station, KUSF, celebrated in the early

1980s for its innovative programming, became increasingly dependent on rotations and college charts, while the University of California at Berkeley's station, KALX, which switched to a free-form alternative format in 1977, continued to allow DJs to play almost anything they wished. In 1992, the music director at KALX reported:

> As music director I don't tell people what to play. I don't have heavy, medium, or light rotation. We put everything pretty much out for DJs to play . . . Things regularly make our Top 100 that are just demo tapes . . . bands . . . have given us.[4]

A member of a San Francisco indie label pop band appreciated KALX's open format, noting at the time that:

> KALX is a great station because a lot of the time they won't stick to a format, they'll just play a variety of things; they'll have shows that center on one genre of music, and you can hear stuff that you've never heard before.[5]

Stations like KALX remained close to the prototype of the "authentic" college radio station, yet in truth college radio had never been as "free-form" as college radio mythologists would have us believe: many college radio stations were formatted from the beginning. The program director in the early 1980s at KFJC, the radio station at Foothill College in Northern California, recalled:

> [One] thing about KFJC was [that] it was fairly well run by the students and the students only. When I [was] program director, the station was [on] 24-hour[s] a day [and played] what was called New Wave music . . . I block programmed. There was no actual playlist [DJs] were forced to play, but [they did have to play] thirty percent new music. Their playlists were checked. We had systems, and I think it worked.[6]

Moreover, KFJC was included in the Arbitron ratings book, which was unusual for a college station. And in fact, KFJC's numbers in the 1980s (and 1990s) were better than those of many of the commercial stations in the San Jose/South Bay market.[7] Undoubtedly the power boost from ten watts to 250 watts the station received in 1980 helped to it expand its audience considerably.[8] The early success of KFJC, and the following testimony from Gerard Cosloy, founder of indie label Matador, indicated that early college radio's "independence" was largely a product of nostalgia:

> [c]ollege radio was never a bastion of independent records. Actually it's much more open to independent records now than it was seven or eight years ago . . . Obviously major labels still dominate it . . .[but] [y]ou didn't see independent records on the cover of *CMJ* or *Rockpool*, at least not very often, not nearly as often as you do today.[9]

Certainly, however, in the days before the music industry paid much attention to college radio playlists, music and program directors felt less compelled to follow strict formats. By the mid-1980s, the proven ability of college radio to break new artists caused major label representatives to establish relationships with college radio music directors, resulting in a tendency for many music directors to emphasize programming major label releases over records received from independent labels. The perception that college radio was more loosely programmed than commercial radio may still have largely held true, but as Ted Friedman and Raymond Rogers noted in a 1990 issue of *Spin* magazine: "At some stations rotations are so strict that DJs have little freedom of choice."[10] I.R.S. Records promoter Lori Blumenthal added that "it's not so much that college stations have changed but that the industry and climate have changed. College radio stations are being treated like commercial stations [by record companies], and they shouldn't be."[11] Statements like these point to a perception that as the 1980s progressed, the glory days of college radio were ending, and a narrative of decline was taking shape.

Musicians whose work did not fit easily into categories like "alternative rock" and who did not have records that chart high in *CMJ* or *The Gavin Report* found the growing regimentation of college radio troubling. One musician complained:

> a lot of the college radio stations don't really have the alternative playlisting anymore, because they have specific rotations. It used to be specific DJs would be really interested in things across the board, and they would play them. . . .rather than having to play Sinead O'Connor's record once every four hours.[12]

One of the stations to which he was referring was KUSF, the University of San Francisco's station, which, though often cited as one of the important and prototypical college radio stations of the early 1980s,[13] was later perceived by many Bay Area listeners to be too conservatively programmed. A booking agent for a prominent San Francisco club observed that "KUSF is really formatted . . . for the past couple years [their playlists are] kind of right off the *CMJ* charts."[14] DJs at KALX worked under less stringent guidelines. According a former music director in the early 1990s, "[s]ome college stations . . . have formats or . . . programming where you must play this cut once an hour," but at KALX the only rule is that DJs must play four new songs an hour.[15]

One problem that arises when discussing college radio charts, playlists, and formats is the temptation to assume that formatting and programming according to the charts are bad; and thus that college radio stations that followed these practices in the 1980s and 1990s were somehow less "authentic." The notion that free-formatting was an outlet for true broadcast expression, and that limitations on what was played on college radio constituted a way of "selling out" and catering to mainstream sensibilities, echoes the trajectory of rise and fall outlined by music scene participants in their personal histories. There were, however, dissenting narratives of college radio. For some there was a rather distasteful politics associated with the sort of loosely formatted college radio deemed by many to be authentic. As a member of a San Francisco indie pop band explained in the early 1990s, "the thing I hate about college radio is that they're always trying to educate you, they're always trying to show you how cool the DJ is."[16] The philosophy was made explicit by the former program director of the University of South Carolina's radio station, who stated, "You have to give the people what they want, but you also have to give them what's good for them."[17] The idea, where it did exist and as *Rolling Stone*'s Anthony DeCurtis put it in 1986, that "[c]ollege radio staffers tend to believe that their programming ought to educate, not simply reflect, listeners' tastes" [18] became rather outmoded as the 1980s progressed, as major labels exercised increasing influence on the majority of alternatively formatted college radio stations.

The change in the last two decades of the twentieth century in major labels' involvement in college radio was dramatic. In the early 1980s, major labels in general paid little attention to what college stations played: in fact, college stations tended to be poorly serviced by the majors, often having to pay for the major label releases sent to them.[19] However, when college radio began to be noticed for its role in breaking eventual multi-platinum-selling acts like R.E.M. and U2, major labels started actively trying to influence playlists at college stations. Major labels perceived the college student market to be populated with music-loving individuals eager to spend money on tapes and CDs—and college radio was the most obvious way to access this market.[20] While it is questionable whether airplay on college radio alone was enough to create a mass audience for a release, college radio popularity could generate a "buzz" for a song, CD, and/or artist, which might then have translated into video airplay on MTV, more bookings and more prestigious bookings for live performances, articles and reviews in magazines and fanzines, and so on.

Major labels reached college radio stations most directly through the alternative music promotion departments that began springing up at majors during the 1980s and that were formed almost exclusively to get records played on college radio (and, to a lesser extent, commercial alternative radio stations). Promotional pressure exerted by these departments at major labels on college radio music and program directors generally consisted of phone calls asking that the station play particular releases.[21] A promoter might have called a music director every day for several weeks requesting airplay for a particular song. By doing this, major labels hoped that eventually a relationship would develop between the music director and the promoter, causing the music director to strongly identify with the people at the label and be more open to the promotion department's requests (and thus, in the minds of many college radio listeners, to "sell out"). Major labels were often successful at achieving this goal, as evidenced by one music director who quite simply said: "I just hate to say no."[22] Moreover, the large number of college radio music directors in the 1980s and the 1990s who were offered major label jobs after college was further indication that relationships in which music directors had vested interests in pleasing labels often developed.

Major label interest in and influence on college radio pointed to the perceived medium's reach and to its special niche in the radio market: it seems doubtful that large record companies would expend significant resources on college radio promotion if the medium was not infiltrating an important market. When looking at how college radio of the 1980s and early 1990s fit into both the overall radio market and specific local markets, it is tempting to conceptualize college radio as a monolithic medium—a temptation that should be avoided. In fact, not all college radio stations of the time followed alternative music formats, and college radio was not the only form of radio that programmed alternative music.

Although when one thinks of "college radio," one tends to think of student-run, noncommercial, alternative music-formatted stations, historically there have been a number of essentially student-run stations that have adhered to more traditional formats like AOR, Urban Contemporary, and Contemporary Hit Radio. In addition, many college stations were and are commercial, accepting paid advertisements and operated for profit. *Billboard* estimated at the end of the 1980s that ten percent of all college stations in the United States followed mainstream formats.[23] These stations included Syracuse University's WJPZ, which used a Top Forty and dance format; Lincoln University's KLUM (Jefferson City, MO), which followed an urban format; and Nassau Community College's WHPC (Garden City, NY), which programmed adult contemporary music.[24]

The decision by a college radio station to adopt a mainstream format could have resulted from one or many of a variety of reasons, none having to do with the authenticity of the listening experience or the promotion of locally situated musical practices. Some program directors argued that college stations with mainstream formats better prepared broadcasting students for careers in commercial radio. Others cited the nature of the audience. For example, at Siena College in Albany, New York, research in the 1980s showed that students were unhappy with the alternative music programmed by WVCR, the college station. Plus, WVCR found itself in a unique situation: because of the proliferation of college stations in Albany, alternative formatting did not provide an alternative to what was available on other stations.[25] Thus WVCR switched to heavy metal and album rock. Another example was found at commuter schools like Nassau Community College which took their older, non-resident student populations into account. Without a dormitory population, these colleges sometimes chose to program for the surrounding community, thus opting for, in Nassau Community College's case in the 1980s, an Adult Contemporary format.[26]

A college station with a mainstream format often found its identity less overtly defined by other college radio stations than it did by commercial stations within its particular market. When a college radio station was also a commercial station, the relationship to non-college commercial stations was even more noticeable. For instance, the University of Illinois' student-run commercial radio station, WPGU—until 1993 an album-rock station that switched to a Modern Rock format—has always competed with local commercial FM stations. A WPGU music director acknowledged, "we're definitely in competition for advertisers."[27] Clearly then a station like WPGU has occupied a very different market niche in a college town than have many college radio stations. The former WPGU music director observed:

> I think we fit in as the station in the market that is your chance to hear rock and find out what's happening, what's new, what's hip, what's cool . . . In essence we are trying to break a lot of new bands . . .[28]

As a commercial station, WPGU has historically not only competed with other FM stations for audience share, it has also been in competition with these stations for advertisers' dollars. Moreover, for several years WPGU reported its playlists to *Radio & Records*, an industry trade paper. In the 1990s the station lost *Radio & Records* reporting status to a competitor when that competitor became the number one rock station in the market, according to the Arbitron ratings.

From its establishment in 1967 until 1993, WPGU was an album rock station, and this made the station a site of contention. In 1992, before WPGU switched to a Modern Rock format, its music director complained:

> We get pressure from the college students to be more alternative, because they think that we are the college station. And in essence, we are not the college station. We are a commercial rock station catering to Champaign-Urbana . . . And then you go the other direction, and you get people who've been listening to WPGU for 25 years . . . who call up and say "What the hell is this XTC-Matthew Sweet shit? Why can't you play more of Mellencamp and all this stuff I'm familiar with?"

> So you get pressure from both sides . . . It's good, because the people who've been listening to us still listen to us because they like the station . . . And then you get the college students who listen to us even though they don't like us, or say they don't like us—they listen to us because that's the closest they're gonna get. If they're looking for the new music, they're gonna get it here, even though they have to struggle through Mellencamp and the Black Crowes and whatever else that they find sickening.[29]

In support of the notion that many local music fans found WPGU's AOR format "sickening"—and presumably this is in part another way of saying "inauthentic"—a local Champaign-Urbana musician remarked at the time, "I'm always so blown away when I go to another town and I hear their college radio station, because PGU is—I hate to get on anyone's case—but they're really awful."[30]

For most Champaign-Urbana listeners who wished to hear alternative music radio shows, the only option was the community radio station, WEFT. WPGU did not see WEFT as a competitor for its audience. As a community radio station, WEFT's overall philosophy has always been to provide the community with programming that is not otherwise available. In Champaign-Urbana in the 1980s and into the 1990s this included independent rock and pop. Within its programming mix in the late 1980s, alternative rock and pop occupied about twenty percent of WEFT's slots: generally, some weekday afternoon, evening, and late night slots. Of course, WEFT also devoted slots to a number of other types of music and programming that were not otherwise available in the area, including alternative news and information, world music, bluegrass, folk, and jazz.[31]

For listeners looking for alternative rock/pop on the radio in Champaign-Urbana, WEFT was a rather frustrating source of material. As a local musician noted, WEFT tended to be "so sporadic, it's hard to know when you turn it on what you're going to be hearing . . . and it doesn't really count in terms of charts or in terms of the way that major labels perceive getting radio airplay."[32] Indeed, community radio as a whole was often overlooked by record companies and charting services as an outlet for alternative music. The early-1990s head of college radio promotion at California-based independent record company Alias was not familiar with community radio, only with college radio, when she started at the company, and consequently she didn't know much about how to service community stations. This situation existed at other labels as well, and those at Alias thought that they were notable for their promotion to and record service for community and NPR stations.[33] Of course some college stations, especially those at community and junior colleges, in many ways resembled community radio stations. Foothill College's KFJC, for example, occupied a somewhat different niche than the other college stations in the area, KALX and KSFU, because KFJC was community-based. For the small fee required to enroll in a radio class, anyone, including non-college students in the community could work at the station.[34]

Even in a large market with several college radio stations, like the San Francisco Bay Area, college stations of the 1980s and early 1990s seemed not to see themselves in competition with each other.[35] As the music director at the University of California at Berkeley's student-run station, KALX, put it at the time:

> I don't think any of us think of ourselves as competitors. There's a lot of other college stations in the area, and there's a lot of really good ones. For the most part, relationships are amiable. Sometimes between individuals they aren't, but I think for the most part we're all interested in other people's programming and other people's shows.

We have good relationships with KFJC, down south from here, and we're even plan-ning on doing a thing where the DJs will trade for a day. It's more like that than competitors. There's really nothing to compete over. We're non-commercial radio, so it's not like we're selling ads.[36]

There was a sense among some that each Bay Area station occupies its own geo-graphical niche: KALX covered the East Bay, KUSF covered the North Bay, and KFJC covered the South Bay.

Beyond the boundaries of locality, however, college radio stations existed within a national marketplace in which some stations were especially central. From the early eighties, for instance, KUSF, the University of San Francisco's station, had, ac-cording to a former KUSF music director, cultivated a national reputation, "[a]nd it served us well in record service. The more we exploited it, the more people would seek us out, and then the greater the reputation would become." He continued:

in fact, it was really no different and probably a lot worse than most college radio stations. It was just circumstances, it was just another group of college students en-joying the machinations of faux stardom. But the geography made it a bigger thing.[37]

Stations like KUSF and WUOG at the University of Georgia (Athens) enjoyed na-tional prominence for many years not necessarily because of the innovativeness of their programming but because of the localities with which they were associated. As with independent record labels, college radio stations even today find themselves at the intersection of locality and a national marketplace (which, in the case of col-lege radio, is most noticeably represented in the form of national college radio charts); the sense of the local is largely constituted by recognition within a national marketplace, and recognition within a national marketplace contributes to the for-mation of a local identity.

Individuals at college radio stations, unlike most people active at independent record labels, often stressed in interviews the important roles played by locality and local music in the constitution of their stations' identities. Obviously a radio station does not have the geographical reach available to even a small independent label, which can reach national and international audiences through independent distri-bution and mail order; many college (and community) radio stations are unable to reach audiences beyond a ten to twenty mile radius of their transmitters. College radio is an inherently local medium, and college (and community) radio stations, to varying degrees, articulate their identities as constituted by locality. For instance, because KALX at the University of California at Berkeley de-emphasized major label releases, on-air space was opened up for local acts. According to a former KALX music director:

I think KALX and other college stations are really important in [disseminating local music], because we're not as interested in getting the major labels played to death . . . so there's a lot of room for local people to come in. They come in a lot for interviews, we'll put [their tapes] on the air, and 45s put out by local bands get added for play. And usually these groups are pretty visible in the area, so DJs will at least check them out, and if they like them, they'll keep playing them.[38]

Another former Bay Area college radio station music director agreed that college stations were important in getting local independent music to the public, and pointed to the nature of the locality as crucial in generating an audience for local music.

The [KUSF] audience really enjoys hearing [local music] and supporting it in clubs, which is a lot different from the San Jose market [of KFJC] where nobody goes out at all. In San Francisco you have people who are going out five, six nights a week. People go out every single night and see local bands, not national touring acts. Or [they see] both.[39]

While the commitment to local music programming may have varied from college station to college station, depending on the nature of the market and the audience, even a commercial AOR college station like the University of Illinois' WPGU set aside airtime specifically for local music programming. In the early 1990s, the station opened up a slot in which a different local release was played every day, and it also had a weekly show, "The Psychedelic Boneyard," that featured local music. WPGU's music director at the time boasted that the weekly hour of local music represented significantly more time than any other station in the market devoted to local music, but it should be noted that "The Psychedelic Boneyard" aired at midnight on Wednesday nights—not exactly peak listening time. Moreover, unlike KALX and KUSF, which were willing to air low-budget 45s and even demo tapes, WPGU found it hard to program local music, especially during the day, because:

. . . a lot of the [local releases] that we have are on cassettes, which are not really high quality, and it's hard to be playing a bunch of big name bands, so to speak, major label, and then play something on a cassette which kind of sounds shitty . . . so we try to find the ones on CDs. Well fine, CDs are going to be [on] a bigger label anyway . . .

So during the day we probably lack local music, even though we will definitely support it. If a local band gives a CD out and it fits in with what we're playing, then we'll definitely play it. We played Adam Schmitt [who's on Warner Brothers]. And I know those are kind of the exceptions, because they're on halfway major labels, and they may even do a little something across the nation, which is great.[40]

Ironically, with all its concerns about playing local music, during the time period under study WPGU still set aside more airtime specifically for the purpose of playing local music than did Champaign's community radio station, WEFT. Of course, it is important to recognize that alternative rock and pop are not the only forms of local music, and WEFT's format included a range of non-mainstream musical styles. Many individuals who approached WEFT about doing a show devoted to local music were not interested in alternative rock/pop. As one member of WEFT's programming committee explained, "there [aren't] all that many people . . . involved in the local [alternative music] scene . . . involved in WEFT."[41] However, although there were no WEFT shows devoted explicitly to playing local music, DJs of alternative music shows on the station often mixed local releases with other independent music on their shows, regardless of the quality of the local recordings.[42]

The concept of "locality" in radio, however, is not defined by local music, and even at college radio stations that gave significant airplay to local acts in the 1980s and early 1990s, the extent to which these stations saw their identities as constituted in part by local communities was quite limited. A former college radio music director related this telling anecdote:

> [At] the [1990] New Music Seminar, the panel on college radio was a complete joke. The best thing to come out of it was somebody [who] walked up there and said, "I'm from this little station in Arkansas [and] we need to have more community programming. How do I go about that?" And this is a real issue; every college station has to deal with this issue at some point. And the panel answered back, "This is a music convention. Why are you asking that?" The name of the panel was "College Radio: Let's Talk." College radio is not just music.[43]

The depth of the ambivalence program directors and music directors at student-run college stations felt about local non-music programming was demonstrated by the undesirable time slots, particularly early Sunday morning slots, set aside for these shows.[44]

Even when their music/program directors did not articulate a view of their stations' identities as being constituted in large part by a local community, college radio stations have always been located within a web of local economic practices. In fact, when looking at the economics of alternative music within a locality, it can be difficult to separate out the different institutional entities involved in promoting alternative pop/rock, since their activities have often been intertwined. Many stations, like KALX, sold and continue to sell underwriting, so different Bay Area record stores would sponsor shows put on by KALX. Often the deal was a trade, in which KALX advertised that the show was sponsored by a particular record store, and in exchange KALX received a certain number of free records per week from the store. And these shows were staged in clubs with which KALX also had arrangements.[45] KFJC and KUSF have had similar arrangements with record stores and clubs; in fact, KFJC has often co-sponsored shows with KALX. Many Bay Area performances of well-known alternative touring acts in the early 1990s, however, were sponsored by "Live 105," a commercial alternative radio station. In the space of just one summer week in 1992 in San Francisco, KUSF sponsored a show by Surgery at the Kennel Club; KFJC sponsored shows by KMFDM at Slim's and Alien Sex Fiend at the DNA Lounge; KALX sponsored a show by Course of Empire at the I-Beam, as well as co-sponsoring with KFJC shows by Robert Gordon and Curve. Tickets for these shows were generally available at certain area record stores, primarily Rough Trade, Reckless, and Aquarius, though venues like the Warfield and Slim's (two clubs closely tied to the late Bill Graham's organization) sold tickets through BASS.[46]

Admittedly, most localities cannot support nearly as many live indie music shows as the San Francisco Bay Area. Still, most college radio stations, like most commercial stations, have traditionally had reciprocal arrangements with local businesses. WPGU has worked with Champaign record stores like Record Service. It is notable that WPGU did not have an association with Record Swap, the Champaign retailer that featured independent and import releases. Because it is a commercial station, WPGU's relationships with local retailers often involved advertising deals: for instance, Record Service sponsored "Rockline" on the station. Streetside offered a "CD of the Week" at twenty percent off the regular price that it advertised as featured on WPGU, and in return the store expected sales for the CD would increase since it could be heard on a local radio station. Like most commercial stations, WPGU promoted certain live shows, primarily at Mabel's—a club that booked some alternative acts in addition to more traditional mainstream rock shows— though sometimes at the campus arena. If a band that was being played on the station, such as Alice in Chains, came to the area, WPGU would often sponsor the show and promote it by advertising it on the air, giving away tickets, putting the touring act's record in heavy rotation, and having the act come to the studio and be interviewed on the air. WPGU's promotional activities were not limited to the immediate geographic area: the station also sponsored shows at venues in Chicago and Peoria.[47] College radio stations therefore exist in relation to local businesses and other local radio stations.[48]

The Function of College Radio

Despite their local relationships and identities, college radio stations in part became important to the dominant industry in the past two decades as a valuable source of (primarily male) staff members for national record companies seeking to focus attention on signing alternative artists. College radio historically has not, however, been very useful to commercial radio stations as a training ground for professional broadcasters. According to an entertainment attorney who worked with alternative acts, the most important issue that college radio faced in the 1980s and 1990s did not have to do with the credibility of the music it played or its relationships with local sites; it was "whether college radio serves to prepare people for jobs in the industry, or whether that's a secondary function to actually providing a community access, free-form radio format."[49] In fact, many college stations with mainstream formats cited as a reason for their format choices the inadequacy of stations with non-mainstream playlists for preparing students for professional radio careers.[50] As a former KUSF music director observed:

> [College radio's] really not training people to work in [the broadcast industry], that's for damn sure. It trains people to work at record companies only because it makes them contact people on that schmooze level. It also trains people to work in all kinds of other seedy jobs.[51]

Mainstream, and especially commercial mainstream formats allowed college radio stations to structure themselves in ways much more like professional radio stations than free-form stations. An early 1990s music director at the University of Illinois' commercial, student-run station, WPGU, believed that the format was a great asset to station alumni seeking jobs in radio:

> You've got the door open for you because you work at a real station. If I'm music director at PGU, it's almost the same as [being] music director at any other station of the same size. And that's the great thing, because it's so easy to get a position at the station, and it gives you such an array of choices in the industry, it'll get you in that door.[52]

While this prediction might have been overly optimistic, it underscored the dilemma facing many college radio stations, and more generally, broadcasting programs at colleges and universities in the United States. If college radio stations increasingly came to be seen as places which had as a primary purpose to train future professional broadcasters, then one would have expected more college radio stations to adopt mainstream formats than did.

Still, college radio changed substantially over the course of the 1980s, and the mythic history of college radio cast these changes as detrimental. A number of factors, many of them discussed above, contributed to the institutionalization of alternatively-formatted college radio. *Spin* writer Jim Greer oversimplified the process when he wrote:

> Over time, a massive college radio promotion network was established by major labels eager to cash in on what they rightly saw as a new avenue to record sales. Pressure from the labels, which mostly saw college radio as a convenient tracking device,

or, at best, a farm system for up-and-coming acts, induced many stations to introduce formats dictating which completely manufactured "college rock" bands the station's DJ would be required to force upon unsuspecting listeners.[53]

Greer's tone is indicative of the widely held belief that college radio had gone into decline by the end of the 1980s. His statement contributed to a discourse of college radio that was produced, "through public representations and private memories."[54] Many individuals involved in alternative rock/pop shared similar memories of college radio as an initially free-form medium that became formatted and rigid to better serve the commercial marketplace. In an interview, one indie pop musician invoked the "dominant" memory of what college radio was in the beginning and what it then became:

College radio used to be a really great thing. It filled a big gap, and created something exciting. Now it seems to have gone the other way . . . It's become really homogeneous. There's nothing distinctive. College radio doesn't have that edge, it's not really playing anything that's really alternative anymore. It kind of falls into the same traps [as commercial radio]. College radio, they may play records that are on alternative labels, but there has to be some kind of a "hip-ness" factor for it to get played.[55]

"Knowledge" such as this was the sort that was circulated in private and public contexts, and at least for a particular social group involved in indie music, it became the common sense of the past and present.

The social construction of memory, however, does not merely take place within the inner spaces of and in the conversation among group members; as Paul Connerton states, "Our memories are located within the mental and material spaces of the group":

Groups provide individuals with frameworks within which their memories are localised, and memories are localised by a kind of mapping. We situate what we recollect within the mental spaces provided by the group. But these mental spaces [social theorist Maurice] Halbwachs insisted, always receive support from and refer back to the material spaces that particular groups occupy. (37)

Certainly within discourses of alternative music the college radio station itself has always been a meaningful and contested site. Understandings of the past and present are often tied up with the material space of the radio station, as R.E.M.'s Michael Stipe demonstrated by remembering the early 1980s, a time when "We used to storm the college station here in Athens, and we would play, like the Banana Splits and then a Throbbing Gristle song. . . . [college] radio then was a little bit renegade and kind of wild and fun."[56]

We see again that the social production of popular memory—in this case a memory of college radio in which the 1990s were constituted as a time of decline—always takes place in a situated and contested terrain. While the notion that college radio was at a low point by the early 1990s was widely circulated both publicly and privately, it should in no way be viewed as monolithic. Some pointed to the prominence of formatting and the proliferation of stations playing mainstream music as positive developments that better prepared students for careers in radio. Others would argue that college radio playlists of the early and mid-1980s, which included acts like Billy Idol, U2 and other future major label stars, was less adventurous than popular history would have us believe. Because charts are crucial indicators of success in terms of radio airplay, video airplay and retail sales, it is useful at this point to turn to a discussion of them in order to see how they have influenced the dissemination, and our understanding, of indie music.

Charts

Radio stations, record companies, retail stores, performance venues, and recording artists all value, to varying degrees, the information they obtain from charts in trade papers. And, as *Radio & Records* editor Ken Barnes points out, record companies encourage and value a proliferation of charts; he notes that "[t]he more charts there are, the more chances the label has to create a success story for a record" (41). During the time period under study there were a number of trade papers that included a variety of charts, including *Cash Box*, *Radio & Records*, and *Hits*, but in the world of alternative rock and pop the most important charts were found in *Billboard*, *Rockpool*, and especially *CMJ* and the *Gavin Report*. *CMJ*'s charts were the ones most watched by the industry; its figures were used in programming college radio stations and stocking retail stores.

CMJ debuted in 1979 as the *College Media Journal*, started by Robert Haber, a Long Island resident and former music director at the Brandeis University station, WBRS.[57] In that year CMJ included, among other charts, a New Wave chart and a disco chart. These particular charts were soon phased out, but the format of charts, reviews and columns was established. Initially the magazine's charts were based solely on radio airplay, but in 1981 the magazine added a retail album chart. CMJ in its later form, *CMJ New Music Report*, appeared in 1982, and in the ensuing decade the number of retail and radio reporters passed 700. Institutions included in my study that reported to CMJ were retail outlets Record Service and Record Swap in Champaign-Urbana, Illinois, and Rough Trade and Reckless in San Francisco. Radio reporters included KALX and KUSF in San Francisco. In addition to radio and retail charts (which primarily covered the "alternative" genre, although CMJ has also featured jazz, urban, world, metal, and dance charts), by the early 1990s CMJ featured reviews by editors and editorial staff, and advertisements for current releases. There was no advertising staff at the magazine; instead, editors were responsible for selling advertising space.

CMJ was the foremost trade paper in college radio, the one most read at college stations. Haber acknowledged that because of its prominence, CMJ had a deleterious effect on college radio programming:

> Without a doubt the real negative impact of CMJ is that we've helped to give rise to a college radio version of Top 40—playing different music, of course, but often in just as tight a rotation. You'll still never hear a group like Sonic Youth on a station like Z-100 [a New York CHR with an ultra rigid playlist]; but college radio is often guilty of letting some genres of music fall by the wayside. Blues, for example, is relegated to specialty shows. . . . Though we've had people from ZZ Top to Metallica to Ornette Coleman on our cover, those records have never made our Top 10. There's a lockjaw frame of mind whereby a lot of programmers have just stopped taking chances. I wish they'd read our reviews a lot more than they look at our charts.[58]

Indeed, music critic Robert Christgau saw CMJ as little more than "a programming aid for college radio . . . [w]ith its rah-rah reviews, DIY correspondence, agate playlists, and genrefied charts aimed at genrefied ad bases . . ."[59]

While the CMJ charts were undoubtedly the best known in the college radio industry in the 1980s and into the 1990s, at that time Gavin's college album chart appeared weekly not only in the Gavin Report but in Rolling Stone and on MTV's alternative music show 120 Minutes, so it was the alternative music chart with which the public was probably most familiar. The Gavin Report is a San Francisco–based multi-format trade magazine available, like CMJ, only through subscription. The publication specifically targets radio station program directors instead of the broad-based industry audience that Billboard seeks to reach. Gavin introduced its alternative chart in 1982, which, in the early 1990s, was drawn up from playlists taken from seventy-one reporting college and commercial alternative stations on Monday and Tuesday of each week and those charts took into account only radio play, not record sales. The chart not only appeared in Rolling Stone and on MTV; it was used by MTV to decide what to air on 120 Minutes. In addition to charts, the magazine included reviews and columns, like "Notes from the Underground," and a section devoted to imports and independent label releases.[60] The reviews were written by the editors of each section; i.e. the R&B editor reviewed R&B releases, the alternative editor reviewed alternative releases, and so on. As at most music magazine, the potential existed in this area for conflict of interest, because the record companies whose releases were reviewed were the same ones that advertised in the magazine. Yet the early 1990s alternative music editor at Gavin remarked: "I write up stuff because I like it, or because I know there's an audience for it, and I don't know if that record company is advertising or not."[61]

Gavin may have been a fairly influential publication for alternative music programmers and consumers, but it was no match for industry giant Billboard. Gavin's Alternative chart was somewhat comparable to Billboard's Modern Rock chart, but while *Gavin*'s chart figures were based solely on airplay, since the early 1990s *Billboard*'s singles figures have been based on both radio airplay and retail sales, and its album charts only measure sales.[62] Before the early 1990s, sales numbers for albums were self-reported by retailers and therefore highly suspect. An artist's position on the *Billboard* album chart often had more to do with how much retailers liked that artist than with how many units of the artist's product were actually selling, especially because retailers reported rankings (i.e. which record ranked first in sales, second in sales, etc.) rather than how many copies of each record were sold at a particular outlet. In other words, the best-selling album in the country was not necessarily the number one album in the country according to the *Billboard* chart.[63]

All this allegedly changed when *Billboard* introduced SoundScan technology in 1991. Rather than relying on self-reporting, SoundScan depends on computers at cash registers that scan the UPC bar codes on all recorded music products. SoundScan came with its own set of problems, not the least of which was that major retailers like Tower, Wherehouse, and Strawberries didn't initially report to SoundScan, thus significantly skewing the chart sales figures. Still, the immediate impact of the reporting technology was quite significant for alternative music. Many chart observers predicted that genres whose sales had traditionally been underreported by store managers, such as country, rap, and classical (as well as rock catalogue titles), would chart much higher under the new system, and these predictions proved accurate. What was not predicted, however, was that on the first *Billboard* album chart after the introduction of SoundScan an independent release—N.W.A.'s *Niggz4Life* on the Priority Label—would debut on the chart at Number Two.[64] Less than a year later, former Sub Pop act Nirvana demonstrated the implications of SoundScan figures for the chart success of alternative rock when its major label debut album *Nevermind* reached the top of the album chart. As Nathaniel Wice wrote in *Spin* magazine,

> SoundScan revealed that marginal genres have much stronger sales than previously thought. Nirvana—and N.W.A., Garth Brooks, and Metallica—wouldn't have come close to No. 1 under the old system.[65]

By focusing more attention on types of music that previously did not chart high in *Billboard*, SoundScan made *Billboard*'s charts more relevant to alternative and independent acts. Even so, the majority of bands that received airplay on college radio still did not break through to mainstream success.

Increasingly in the late 1980s and early 1990s, however, there was overlap between the college charts and the mainstream charts, something that was not true in the early- to mid-eighties when few college radio hits made the *Billboard* charts. A former member of a band that frequently appeared near the top of college radio charts noted in 1990:

What's popular on college radio, in the *Rolling Stone [Gavin]* charts, for instance, all those ten items are pretty much always going to be within the *Billboard* Top 100. Five years ago that wasn't true. Five years ago there was little overlap between the *Gavin* and *Billboard* charts. So if those Top Ten *Gavin* items are also in the *Billboard* Top 100, then how different is college music going to be than regular commercial music?[66]

This sort of overlap—a sign in personal narratives of indie music of the genre's decline as it crossed over to the mainstream—could be attributed in large part to the growth of major label alternative music departments in the 1980s and the resulting promotion of alternative acts at the big record companies. Major labels wanted these acts to chart high on the college charts and then cross over to the mainstream charts.

Major labels weren't the only ones interested in chart position: in making decisions a host of other players in the alternative music business looked to charts. Independent labels, which became less and less prominent on the college charts in the 1990s, still found chart numbers quite useful. While a small indie like Parasol, which primarily released singles and pressed only small quantities of any release, generally would not expect to make it onto the *CMJ* or *Gavin* charts, a larger indie like Alias would monitor the chart numbers of its acts. For most indies whose bands made it onto the college or mainstream charts, charting was not an end in itself. A former Rough Trade manager observed that record stores used chart numbers to help determine what records they would stock.[67] An Alias staff member noted in 1990 that having an act on the college charts:

is not per se a goal. It's good to see them on there, because it gives us some indication—however diluted it might be—but it does give us at least an idea [of how much] people are playing [a record] in relation to other records that are out there. It's actually the more records we've had out, the better we do on the charts. And I think a lot has to do with people getting to know the label and getting to know the artists and having the name recognition with Alias.[68]

She found chart information especially useful in promoting records to college radio; charts were a sort of shorthand record labels could use to describe a record's success or potential success to music directors.

Radio, including college radio, uses narrow, "format charts" as aids in programming. Charts like *Gavin's* Alternative chart or *Billboard's* Modern Rock chart show music directors the records that are successful at other similarly-formatted stations and that therefore might be successful at their own stations (see Barnes 41). While the *Gavin* Alternative editor remarked that she hoped that college radio stations were not programming according to what appeared on charts, some music directors found the playlists from reporting stations that were printed in trade papers to be helpful in deciding what artists to add to their playlists. A former college music director explained:

> I used the CMJ chart for regional stuff. If there was some band coming out of New Orleans, I'd look at the college radio station there and see if they're being played a whole lot.[69]

Beyond their impact on what got played on college radio, charts also helped determine whether an indie band got bookings for live performances. At Alias, for instance, there were "more than a few booking agents out there who wouldn't touch the Sneetches because their record did not chart on the CMJ Top 100."[70]

Clearly then the charts that appeared in trade papers had ramifications for recording artists, even though many indie musicians of the 1980s and 1990s denounced the charts and the music that appeared on them, seeing it as less underground or "authentic" than non-chart music. For example, a musician on Parasol commented that he would not like his records to appear on the college charts, because "that would probably mean that my music sucks, or isn't what I'm looking for."[71] But music scene veterans in indie bands generally acknowledged that, good or bad, charts were important gauges of success. Undoubtedly artists derived a certain amount of ego gratification from having records on alternative or mainstream charts. When asked whether it was important to make it onto the college charts, one musician replied:

> I'll be honest—I think it means something. You can say, well, you should really be happy that you made a great record that you're really proud of. And when we first started, when we made our first record, I was totally blown away that we got to work in a real studio. This was like a dream come true. We made the record I always wanted to make, and I was totally pleased, and I didn't care what it did.
>
> And then you start being a band—you start touring, you start thinking "Maybe we can do something with this," and then you see other people get heard or you see other people's records in stores or you see other people make the charts and you think "I know we're better than that," or you think "We're just as good as that." You just start to think "We should be able to do this too."[72]

Artists also realized that chart numbers often determined their futures with labels. Small labels like Parasol generally were not too concerned with whether or how high their acts charted. Furthermore, often high college radio chart numbers did not correlate to high sales. An RCA national promotions representative admitted in the 1980s that "If something does well on the college-radio charts, it's not necessarily going to sell well."[73] Yet at most labels chart numbers could influence how bands were treated. The leader of an indie pop band that was fairly popular on college radio in the 1980s observed in the early 1990s that making it onto the college charts:

> is usually an indicator that your record is going to sell kind of okay—though we've been the exception to that. Usually a Top 5 college radio album will sell 50,000 and above, because the record company tends to get behind it in a way appropriate to that indicator. Enigma didn't really do that for us. I don't think college radio by itself sells too many records. You would think that if record companies saw that you were doing that well they'd say, "Oh, they're doing well—we'll put some dollars into them." And if that happens, you can do better.[74]

A band that charted well and therefore got increased support from its label often would be promoted to Top 40 radio. The former *Gavin* Alternative editor explained that:

> there's a lot of record companies that will just work [a record] to college radio for six weeks [and] see how they get up the charts. If there's enough of a buzz at radio or at retail, they'll work it Top 40. So I think the chart is good for that reason. It helps the artist and it helps Top 40 radio to be a little more willing to take a chance on some [alternative] artists.[75]

While charts were mainly thought of in terms of radio airplay, they also had an impact on what alternative and/or indie videos were played on MTV. A song that makes the Top 5 in the *Gavin* alternative chart was considered for addition to MTV's "Buzz Bin,"[76] which featured an alternative video that was played in heavy rotation for a week, thus receiving the kind of exposure most college radio releases did not normally receive. Video became such an important outlet for indie music in the 1980s and 1990s.

Video

The prevalence of music video in the 1980s had a profound impact on the alternative music marketplace. Without a doubt the primary vehicle for the dissemination of music videos across space and localities in the United States was MTV, though alternative rock and pop videos receive a certain amount of club play. Only with the installation of cable technology in disparate locales across the country and with the fragmentation of the cable audience did an outlet like MTV become possible.[77] The proliferation of cable and satellite technologies made television look more like radio: several stations were competing for fragments of the audience rather than a few stations attracting large general audiences (Frith, *Music* 208). Cable however, with the exception of local access stations and cable-carried broadcast network affiliates, targeted national rather than local audience fragments. MTV, founded by Warner Amex and bought by Viacom in 1986, initially thrived in this environment by targeting "baby boomers" (Lewis 19–20).

In the two decades since it was launched in 1981, however, MTV has re-defined its target audience a number of times. Simon Frith notes that MTV was established as an imitation of Top 40 radio, offering a consistent rotation of product provided by record companies (see Frith, "Video Pop" 95). Indeed, MTV in the 1980s became the closest thing the United States had to a national radio station, as record company executives were quick to point out, and thus it provided them a highly desirable outlet for exposing talent.[78] Evidence showed that MTV did influence audience members to buy records based on viewing video clips on the channel (Lewis 24). It is useful to see videos then not primarily as commodities in and of themselves, but as advertisements for commodities, since the primary benefit accrued by a record company when a video for an act on its roster is aired is publicity for the track. Because the weekly acquisitions meetings at which all clips submitted by record companies were reviewed were open to almost all MTV employees rather than just to a few key decision-makers, record companies claimed that it was difficult to know which employees were actually the ones who make final decisions on the videos that aired. MTV therefore presented itself as somewhat freer from record company influence than, say, college radio, and thus an ideal medium through which to break new talent.[79]

It is important however to remember that a record company, large or small, must believe a new act has a good chance to break before investing money in video production.[80] In his book *Dancing in the Distraction Factory*, Andrew Goodwin outlines what he calls the "Music Video Cycle," in which video production is dependent on sales of company products—including those products promoted through music videos—to media consumers; although ultimately, Goodwin observes, video production costs are largely written off against advertising and promotional budgets (42–43). In any case, video production is intrinsically linked to record promotion and sales, and thus major labels with large budgets are in a better position to produce videos for new artists than indies. Of course, many indies argue that breaking artists to a mass audience through MTV airplay is not one of their top priorities.

Still, the proliferation of indie labels during the 1980s, and the integration of many of these indies into major label corporate structures through distribution deals and label purchases, meant that there were more labels trying to get videos on MTV than there were when the channel first went on the air. By the end of the 1980s, each week MTV was considering between forty and sixty new clips for addition to its rotation, and many of these clips were for alternative rock and pop acts.[81] Tom Freston, Chairman and CEO of MTV Networks, believed that MTV played a crucial role in breaking new acts, many of whom at least started out on independent labels:

... MTV made music more interesting and more relevant to a larger number of people. MTV's been really helpful to a lot of new bands: Jane's Addiction, Black Crowes, R.E.M., to name a few, as well as all the rap artists ... We're perfectly capable of making mistakes from time to time and missing some. But the Black Crowes are a good example: They came in here basically with a good video, they didn't do any kind of incredible promotion with us, and everyone just fell in love with it. We just put it on, and the audience loved it.[82]

Indeed, Freston argued that MTV in the late 1980s and early 1990s was not unlike college radio, stating:

We play a certain amount of mass-appeal hits, but we do have a commitment to the alternative. We may not be as extreme as a college radio station, but I don't think there's a commercial radio station in the U.S. that's as eclectic as MTV, where you can see Public Enemy, Paul Simon, Slaughter, the Cure, Sonic Youth, and Chris Isaak all on one station.[83]

MTV may have played a greater mix of music than most commercially formatted radio stations, but the problem for many alternative acts was not just making it onto MTV, but making onto MTV at a time when most people were awake. In general, alternative rock and pop videos, especially those on independent labels, were ghettoized in MTV's Sunday night alternative music show, *120 Minutes*, which aired between midnight and two in the morning. Having a video on *120 Minutes* certainly did not compromise a band's or label's credibility, the sense that it represented the "authentic voice" of the indie underground. For artists on major labels, however, the fact that most alternative music clips ended up in an undesirable time slot and were often only aired once contributed to the reluctance of many record companies to produce videos for unproven, non-mainstream artists (Negus 97).

For an indie rock or pop band to really benefit from MTV airplay, its video had to air in regular, daytime rotation. Michelle Peacock, vice-president of video promotion and production for Capitol Records, observed that, "You need daytime plays to get attention—at least one good play a day."[84] A few alternative acts achieved success by having videos selected for MTV's "Buzz Bin." "Buzz Clips" in the 1980s and 1990s were typically shown three times a day for about eight weeks; thus, they were shown almost as frequently as MTV's most popular videos in heavy rotation, which aired four times daily. Attention was first focused on the "Buzz Bin"'s ability to sell records when sales for the Red Hot Chili Pepper's album *Blood Sugar Sex Magik* skyrocketed after the video for the single "Give It Away" began airing as a "Buzz Clip." Temple of the Dog, a Seattle "supergroup" made up of members of Pearl Jam and Soundgarden, enjoyed even more marked success when the video for its song "Hunger Strike" was included in the "Buzz Bin." The band's album had been out for fourteen months and had sold only 105,000 copies: after only three weeks in the "Buzz

Bin" the band sold an additional 315,000 units and had the No. 25 album on the *Billboard* Pop Album Chart. The senior vice president of marketing at A&M commented that the record's success was "100 percent attributable to MTV," and an executive at EMI added "We have seen a tremendous correlation between [the "Buzz Bin"] and activity at the cash register."[85]

The vast majority of alternative artists, however, were never included in the "Buzz Bin." In fact, it is notable that the two major "Buzz Bin" success stories were both major label acts. Independent labels on the whole were unable to provide their artists with the large video production budgets necessary to create clips that looked at home amid MTV's slickly produced daytime fare.[86] A typical indie band video experience was related by the leader of a band signed in the 1980s to indie label Enigma:

> We did two nice little videos, I thought . . . Enigma naturally gave the directors nothing to work with—nothing being three or four thousand dollars apiece. Naturally they don't look like hundred-thousand dollar videos, because they're not and there's no way they could. For being such shoestring productions, the directors did an excellent job.[87]

Both videos did air on *120 Minutes*, but never appeared in daytime slots.

Before *120 Minutes* debuted on MTV in 1986, low budget alternative clips by bands like Timbuk 3, the Fleshtones, and Let's Active could be seen on a show called *IRS's The Cutting Edge*. The show first aired in 1983 and was sponsored by I.R.S. records, the independent label to which the Go-Gos, the Alarm, and General Public (and R.E.M., before moving to Warner Brothers), were signed. *The Cutting Edge* was shown on the last Sunday evening of the month and featured a mix of interviews, videos, taped live performances, and on-location segments with host (and Fleshtone) Peter Zaremba. The prominence of I.R.S. recording artists on the show attracted criticism, and the program disappeared a few months after *120 Minutes'* debut.

In the 1990s, *120 Minutes*, and later its half-hour late weeknight counterpart, *Alternative Nation*, became the only MTV slots realistically open to most alternative pop/rock videos. *Alternative Nation* generally programmed according to the *CMJ* and *Gavin* Top Ten College Album charts, which at the time were dominated by major labels, so *120 Minutes* became the place where videos by independent label acts were most likely to appear. But over the years the number of indie acts on the weekly show steadily declined. An October, 1993 edition of *120 Minutes* included seventeen videos. Of those seventeen, only two featured acts that recorded for then-non-major label-affiliated independent labels: Matthew Sweet on Zoo and the band Hazel on Sub Pop. A few videos for acts that recorded for indies that were owned and/or distributed by major labels also appeared, including a video for

Machines of Loving Grace, who were signed to Mammoth (which had become part of the Atlantic Group), as well as three acts on Warner subsidiary Sire/Reprise (Belly, Morrissey, and the Ocean Blue), one on Warner subsidiary Charisma (Curve), and one on Warner subsidiary Virgin (Smashing Pumpkins).

Fully fifteen of the seventeen acts on this typical early 1990s edition of *120 Minutes* were on major labels or major-affiliated labels. Of course, many acts whose videos aired that night and who were on major labels once recorded for indies, including Smashing Pumpkins (on Virgin, but formerly on Caroline), Concrete Blonde (on Capitol, but formerly on I.R.S.), Nirvana (on DGC, but formerly on Sub Pop), and Bad Religion (on Atlantic, but formerly on its own Epitaph label). In contrast, on one typical installment of the program that aired in the fall of 1987, half of the videos—ten out of twenty—were for independent label acts: two for SST bands (Sonic Youth and the Meat Puppets), two for Big Time bands (Huxton Creepers and Love and Rockets), two for Enigma bands (Wire and Game Theory), one each for Relativity (Scruffy the Cat), Rough Trade (Camper Van Beethoven), Homestead (Big Dipper), and Streetwise (New Order).

It is important not to jump to the conclusion, however, that because more bands on independent labels used to appear on *120 Minutes* in its earliest years, the show was more "alternative." Industry trends discussed in the previous chapter, including the acquisition of independents by major labels, major label signings of alternative rock/pop acts like Sonic Youth, and the crossover of some alternative rock acts, like Nirvana, into the mainstream, all helped account for the declining presence of independent labels on the program in the 1990s. Outlets for truly "underground"— and in fact most independent—videos remained limited. Local access cable was one medium through which independent music was disseminated via video. Local alternative video shows, however, generally attract very small audiences in most markets, and therefore have not been seen, at least by the music industry, as crucial sites of new music exposure. As media become still more fragmented and digital technology has become more widely available, the Internet is likely to become the primary source for underground video distribution.

Retail

In looking at the ways in which indie music was disseminated within and across localities in the 1980s and 1990s, there may be no more vital site to examine than the record store. Record stores are not merely retail outlets; they are spaces of social interaction and socialization. Customers often seek advice from, or seek to exchange knowledge with, store employees, and through this process learn not just about various artists, records, and genres, but also about the local music culture.

Record stores are much more amenable environments for discussions of music than live performance venues, especially for those "outside" the local scene who want to discuss music but do not know people in the community who share their interests. In her study of the Liverpool rock scene, Sara Cohen notes that one record store in particular, Probe, became a center for information on and gossip about local music, largely because it (as well as other Liverpool stores), employed musicians and attracted them as customers. As Cohen describes Probe:

> It became a centre for news and gossip on local music. Past employees include two or three well-known rock stars . . . Both shop and office were usually crowded with musicians, some simply passing the time of day. The role played by other record shops besides Probe in the local music scene was not so great although most employed musicians and attracted them as customers, and the managers of one or two also managed bands. (*Rock Culture* 54)

Record stores are therefore not merely sites of commerce; they are social spaces. They are, as Barry Shank observes in his study of popular musical practice in Austin, Texas, daytime centers of music scenes (165). Shank points to Waterloo Records as a center of daytime activity, a place where "Musicians, industry professionals, and fans drop in . . . regularly" (165). The three record stores of the 1980s and 1990s discussed in detail below—Record Swap, Rough Trade, and Record Service—all resembled Waterloo and Probe in their function as daytime centers of scene activity. Because, however, the Champaign-Urbana stores—Record Swap and Record Service—were located in a rather small, Midwestern metropolitan area, unlike Rough Trade in San Francisco (and Waterloo in Austin) they did not generally attract industry professionals and music critics.

At the major Champaign-Urbana independent record stores in the 1980s and early 1990s, including both Record Service locations and Record Swap, the majority of employees were musicians in local bands. In fact, at one point during the early 1990s *all* the regular employees at Record Service's Urbana location were musicians.[88] Rough Trade's employees tended to represent a broader spectrum of participants within the music scene. In all three cases though, the presence of active scene participants meant that these record stores were sites of socialization into the local music scenes. Employees could provide information about local bands and upcoming shows; and other customers were often also scene participants. Some customers spent hours in stores like Record Swap, browsing and talking with scene regulars. Further, because employees chose the music to play on a store's sound system, customers could learn about new bands by spending time in the store. Mall chain stores like Camelot and Musicland do not serve the same function: they are generally located farther away from other sites of scene activity, their employees are often not participants in local music scenes, and the employees also have less input into the artists who are promoted via in-store displays.

Indeed, within any given locality the stores that tend to have the greatest commitment to local alternative rock/pop, and to alternative rock/pop in general, are not the chain stores but are locally owned businesses. These outlets, because they are not parts of national organizations, are primarily defined within a local rather than national context. However, it should be noted that these stores are dependent on one-stops and other regional or national distributors for their products, that most use national charts in deciding what to stock, that many report to national charts like *CMJ*, and that some, like Wax Trax in Chicago and Rough Trade in San Francisco, have enjoyed national and even international reputations.

The Rough Trade store in San Francisco was once associated with an international organization that included a record store in London and record production and distribution companies in the United States and the United Kingdom. According to the early 1990s owner of the Rough Trade store in San Francisco, the store had a national and even international clientele: it had a five thousand name national and international mailing list and received orders from all over the world. There were, at one time, plans for the store to expand into major American and European urban markets.[89] Rough Trade was the exception, however. Most local stores did not particularly see themselves as part of a national or international market. A longtime employee of Record Swap in Champaign, Illinois, commented:

> It seems like Record Swap is something that has changed just periodically as the market has changed. And we really kind of base it on who comes in here and what is going out, not on what other stores are doing. We've been compared to Wax Trax in Chicago for quite awhile, but that was more of a coincidence, [Wax Trax] wasn't something we were modeling [ourselves] after.[90]

In terms of its origins too, the Rough Trade store, which was established in the 1980s as part of a transnational enterprise, was an exception in the world of non-chain record stores. Most had humbler beginnings, like the two Champaign-Urbana stores discussed here, Record Swap and Record Service. Record Swap originated in the 1970s with two brothers who loved music and who initially worked full-time jobs in addition to running the store, which started in Chicago and opened in Champaign in 1979. Record Service began as a student-run cooperative at the University of Illinois in the early 1970s.[91]

Rough Trade also differed from the Champaign stores in terms of the local market it served. While there were several stores in the large San Francisco market that stocked an extensive selection of indie and import alternative rock/pop releases, for much of their existences in Champaign-Urbana, Record Service and Record Swap were the only two stores that serviced the indie/alternative market. Both Record Swap and the main Record Service store were located in "Campustown," a commercial area in the middle of the University of Illinois campus. They were across the street from each other, though Record Service, at ground level and with separate entrance and exit doors, occupied a more prominent space. Record Swap was harder to find; a small sign located at street level pointed customers up a steep staircase, the walls of which were plastered with flyers.

The differences in the physical spaces can be seen as representative of the differences in the sorts of clientele serviced by each store. A manager at Record Service said that Service's campus store sold "a lot of rap, because it's big in the college community, but [the store] caters more to the alternative crowd, the college crowd [and sells] massive quantities of R.E.M. and that kind of stuff"; the Record Swap employee characterized the music sold at her store as "basically alternative."[92] Record Swap in fact specialized in indie and import labels and in buying and selling used records, CDs and tapes. Because Record Swap was essentially a specialty store, it was not really perceived as competing with other stores for customers, as a Record Swap employee explained:

> Because it's a small independent business, we don't deal huge quantities of major labels, but we do try to carry a lot of independents . . . [We carry] things that other stores tend not to carry. We do carry a fair amount of major label stuff, so in that sense any of the stores in this area would compete with us to some extent. [Record Service is a competitor] to some extent. We share clientele . . . We overlap to some extent, but we don't carry identical merchandise.[93]

When a regional chain, Streetside, opened a store across the street from Record Swap in September of 1991, Swap's business was relatively unaffected. The opinion at Record Swap was that Streetside's presence in the market "doesn't seem as though it has impacted us too much, because I think they're pretty much major label, and then we still do a huge amount [of business] in the used market."[94]

Record Service, on the other hand, was affected by competition in the market. Within the Campustown area of Champaign-Urbana in the early 1990s, there were four retail music outlets within a two block area on Green Street: Record Swap, Record Service, Streetside Records, and Discount Den. Because Record Service offered a more mainstream selection of music than Record Swap, and because it also operated a mall store off-campus in Urbana, Record Service was situated rather differently than Record Swap in the local market. The manager of the Lincoln Square Mall store noted that each Record Service location faced a different set of competitors. The mall store was, for instance,

> the only [record] store in Urbana . . . we cater to a lot of the high school and junior high kids. I hear a lot of them talk about Camelot . . . So I would say [our competitors are] maybe Camelot and Musicland at Market Place [Mall], and possibly the campus area.

The campus location was in a different competitive situation:

> Right now Streetside is the main competitor on campus, definitely, since they're two doors down. They came in, and Streetside's emphasis was on having a full line of music—they have a full classical line—they have a lot of space there. A lot of floor space and a lot of inventory.

> Our main edge was price—we undercut their pricing by various amounts on different list prices, and we match or beat their sale price on whatever they advertise—and the fact that they don't carry as much import or independent stuff as we do. They do carry stuff that's popular. They'll have Smashing Pumpkins, but they don't carry as much as we do.

> I think their main vinyl collection is deletion vinyl, like Rose, which we don't mess with, because larger chain stores like Rose can buy larger quantities of cut-out vinyl. Somebody like us, we have to go through a one-stop vinyl cut-out place. So we don't even mess with it anymore, because you could go down to Rose and get great deals on cut-outs, which we have no access to.[95]

The competitive environment faced by Record Service was representative of the situation in which many independent stores found themselves in the early 1990s, a period during which many U.S. stores (especially electronics stores) sold music as a "loss leader," which meant they were willing incur losses in music sales as a way of getting consumers inside the store to purchase more expensive items with higher profit margins (Negus, *Music* 56).

Still, with the exception of Streetside, which moved into the Champaign-Urbana market with the intent of undermining Record Service's customer base, in a small market like Champaign-Urbana each store tried to target a distinct group of consumers. The situation was more complex in the San Francisco area, where several stores competed for the same kind of customer. Amoeba, Aquarius, Leopold's, Rasputin, Reckless, Record Finder, Revolver, Rough Trade, Tower, and Village Music all competed for some segment of the alternative audience. Four of these stores—Amoeba in Berkeley and Aquarius, Reckless and Rough Trade in San Francisco—reported to *CMJ*.

Rough Trade, located on Haight Street, was for a time among the best known San Francisco stores. It was a spacious and prominent store located in one of the main centers of alternative music culture in the San Francisco area. The types of music sold at Rough Trade were indicative of the sorts of music sold at most independent stores in the area. In the early 1990s the Rough Trade store owner noted:

> We mostly sell alternative and independent music. We also carry a lot of imports—we specialize in world music too, international music. We carry all the mainstream stuff too, but we always sell the biggest numbers in alternative music, college music.

The big sellers are bands like R.E.M., the Cure. Also bands like Mudhoney, and some of the other Sub Pop bands—we sell lots and lots of that stuff. Sister Double Happiness, which is a local band. Some of the other commercial alternative music, we sell lots and lots of.[96]

Because of the similarity of its product to that of other stores in the area, Rough Trade struggled to define itself as different from its competitors. Certainly having in-store performances by acts like Tiny Tim helped set the store apart; Rough Trade's owner also believed that employee attitude was important in establishing store identity:

> I think that what sets us apart from everybody else is, I truly believe, that we give the best customer service. We can carry alternative-college music, independent music, without an attitude. So we have a unique staff of people that cater to that. I also believe that although Rough Trade has a reputation of carrying really hardcore and independent and import type music, at the same time we've expanded to include major label alternative product, which has expanded our customer base. We can do both and still be cool.[97]

She claimed that even for those who were not alternative music aficionados, Rough Trade was a comfortable place to shop, because "they can buy Madonna here, they can buy whatever they feel like buying here." Rough Trade also attempted to please the public with in-store performances by local and national acts, which tended not to generate many sales and which were viewed by the owner primarily as a free service the store provided to its customers, largely to generate goodwill.[98]

Although San Francisco was a competitive market for indie music retailers, those competing in the market did not necessarily view the competition as cut-throat. Unlike Champaign, where most of the record stores could be found in a two-block area near campus, stores catering to alternative music audiences in the Bay Area were distributed across a wide geographic area. Reckless, Recycled, and Rough Trade were all located on Haight Street, and therefore were often viewed as competitors. Since Recycled specialized in used product, Reckless and Rough Trade were the stores that directly competed for new music sales in that part of the city. However, while Rough Trade's owner saw Reckless as Rough Trade's most obvious competitor for Haight Street customers, the stores to which Rough Trade was most similar were on the other side of the Bay:

> . . . in what we do, I kind of have a competitive feeling about Leopold's in Berkeley. I used to manage that store, and the woman who runs it now was my product manager . . . they're way far away, but I'll go into [the East Bay alternative weekly paper] and she'll go into [the San Francisco alternative weekly] with advertising and in-stores and that kind of thing. It's a very friendly competition.

> We have kind of a warm working relationship with Amoeba [in Berkeley] too. They do a lot of the same things that we do, but they're so far away it really doesn't directly affect our business. But we look at each other and see what the other's doing.[99]

The reluctance to point to competitors for business and the need to assert that one's record store provided a unique service is quite reminiscent of comments made by individuals at independent record labels. Identity as part of a local independent scene was a process of redefinition that stressed notions of "community" by refusing to acknowledge economic competition while at the same time pointing to the fragmentation, both within and across localities, implicit in claims of "uniqueness."

Independent record stores that specialized in indie rock/pop were by default the outlets for local music, since chain stores usually did not carry product distributed by independent distributors or sold on consignment. Of course, in many localities local musicians signed deals with large indies or major labels and therefore received large-scale distribution. In describing Record Swap's role in disseminating local music, one longtime employee defined as no longer local those acts that had signed with large indies or majors:

> We always distribute local music—we just kind of depend on the band people to bring it in. We mark it up, but not as much as any other item in the store, so it's a small percentage mark-up. We always do it on consignment. Some bands do really well: Lonely Trailer has done pretty decently well, Last Gentleman has done extraordinarily well.

> Didjits really aren't local anymore 'cause they're distributed through Touch and Go. But they do real well. Of course, the Poster Children sell well—but we don't really call them local. After they get signed to a label, then they aren't distributed locally, they just go through the same channels as every other independent thing. But yeah, us and Service are kind of the local market.[100]

A Record Service manager agreed that Service and Swap were the two primarily retail outlets for local music in Champaign-Urbana, but noted that the types of local music that were sold at each store were different, and also that the two Record Service locations differed in the sorts of local music audiences they served:

> Record Service on campus probably doesn't sell more Didjits than Swap does, but they may sell more Difficult Listening. Swap caters to more of the alternative, hardcore crowd . . .

> If there's a local artist that has a tape they have made themselves then [Record Service's ownr] will have them leave it on consignment . . . A college group like Difficult Listening, I know they've sold quite a few of those on campus, but they go to the U of I[llinois], they play parties, they play Mabel's, so their main listening

audience is in the campus community . . . [At the mall store] we may sell more of something like Mistress, which is more of a county metal band—they're not that big in the college area and they play at the Silver Bullet bar and the Alley Cat . . . Last Gentlemen do well in both areas because they have a large crossover audience, they get airplay on WLRW.[101]

Rough Trade, with a larger pool of local talent from which to draw than the Champaign-Urbana stores, aggressively pursued local music and promoted local acts, as its owner explained:

We actually don't have a local music section . . . but we carry hundreds of consignment items for local bands. We merchandize them along with the rest of the product. We go into all the local band issues of BAM and SF Weekly . . . and promote [local] product in those issues.

There're a lot of great bands around town and we like to support them as much as possible. We try to support local bands that may be playing in clubs around town [by] doing in-stores and selling their product before their gig.[102]

In-store appearances were an important as part of the promotional role independent record stores play in college/alternative music scenes. At Rough Trade, it was not unusual to have four different acts, both local and national, making in-store appearances during a single week. While in-stores generally brought crowds of potential customers into the store, often in-store appearances seemed to be more trouble than they were worth. The payoff to the store from these promotions was not always immediate, as Rough Trade's owner explained:

We try not to do in-stores on the weekend because sales tend to drop—you've got the store blocked, and people can't shop. We have a stage we set up, and we have to move the bins out of the way to set the stage up. And they don't tend to generate a whole lot of sales in product. But I think it's one of the best PR things we can do, to offer free things to our customers. I believe in the long run in-stores pay for themselves, but not immediately.[103]

Both Record Swap and Record Service also used in-store appearances as a promotional device, though not nearly as often as a larger, urban store like Rough Trade. Record Swap featured in-store performances by national alternative touring acts like American Music Club, and Record Service hosted record signing events for acts like the dBs.

Promotional activities were an important way in which local independent retail stores were drawn into alternative music's local and national economic networks. As described earlier in the chapter, independent record stores entered into mutually beneficial promotional relationships with local college radio stations through activities like sponsorship of radio programming and offering releases in heavy rotation on local college radio at sale prices. Retail stores also worked with local live venues, selling tickets for local shows. In some cases, venues would even provide displays for local record stores.[104] On the national level, both independent and major labels provided promotional material to retail stores: primarily posters to use in displays, but also other band-related paraphernalia. However, it was up to the discretion of the store owner or manager to decide what promotional material to display. For instance, a Record Service manager created a prominent display for the Sneetches, a fairly obscure band that was among his personal favorites.

Promotional activities that drew customers into record stores became more important than ever in the early 1990s because increasingly, independent stores like Rough Trade and Record Swap faced competition for the local alternative, indie, and import music markets from mail order and the Internet. Mail order and later, Internet, outlets provided individuals who did not live near specialty record stores access to indie and import material; and, as *Spin* writer Johann Kugelberg observed, those who do live near specialty record shops may opt to order records through the mail rather than face "afternoons of fruitless music searches that can seem like archaelogical digs."[105] Many independent labels, like Slumberland and Alias, made their releases available through mail order and the World Wide Web. There were also mail order houses like Ajax in Chicago and Insomnia in Los Angeles that carried releases from a number of indie labels. And finally there were hybrids like Parasol, which offered via mail order a range of indie music on labels like Simple Machines, K, Sunday, Sarah, Summer Shine, and Flying Nun as well as its own indie pop releases.[106] These mail order services posed a direct threat to independent records stores. Not only did they siphon existing buyers from independent stores' customer bases, but, as Mark Fenster explains in his study of the bluegrass music industry, the resulting diminished retail store sales of any given marginal music lessens the incentive for stores to stock the music and for record companies to make that music available in retail outlets. Mail order and the Internet were therefore conceivably damaging to independent labels, because if their releases were not available in even independent record stores, they would have few opportunities to bring in new audience members from the broader record-buying public.[107] As the Internet and mail order grew ever more popular in the 1990s as a way to buy indie pop/rock releases, the tension between alternative music retail and mail order also grew.

Live Performance

Live musical performance is arguably the most immediate means available for disseminating college music, since it locates performer and audience within the same physical space. This physical space is importantly also a social space; one in which, to paraphrase Sara Cohen, participants—audience members and musicians—are united in common activity (1991, 96). Even if they do not explicitly acknowledge it, participants are on some level aware that they share musical knowledge and taste as well as sharing the experience of participating in the live performance. In many cases, as Ruth Finnegan observes of pub rock audiences, generically similar shows at certain venues attract a core of people who, in addition to sharing musical knowledge and tastes, actually know each other (Finnegan 232).

Almost all musicians begin their live careers by playing shows at local venues. The term "venues," however, does not apply merely to bars, nightclubs, auditoriums, and other public spaces; in many communities, a number of bands start their live careers by playing parties. For instance, in Athens, Georgia in the late 1970s, before there was a recognizable Athens "scene," the B-52's debuted at a party, because, in the words of band member Fred Schneider, there was "no place for us to play live except friends' living rooms" (quoted in Fletcher 7). When venues are unwilling to book a particular kind of music, private functions are the alternative. Athens clubs resisted the early B-52's in part because approximately ninety percent of the music in the band's act was prerecorded, a technique that was not widely accepted in live performance at that time (Brown 37).

Even bands able to get bookings at clubs might still play parties. In Champaign in the late 1980s, Hot Glue Gun and Lonely Trailer were among those bands that played parties as well as playing shows at public venues. Still, as most bands develop they seek to move beyond party gigs and get on bills at local clubs. For a club, a popular local band can often make as much money as a national touring act. Therefore, it is generally in the interest of a club to support local music that its management thinks its patrons will like. Most clubs exist off the money made at the bar and a chunk of the door proceeds. However, while money made at the bar is almost always the club's to keep and is used to cover expenses, such as employee wages, the cover charge collected at the door is determined by a number of factors and often split between several parties; a club may end up getting forty percent or less of the door proceeds. Bands generally have contracts that stipulate that they will be paid a certain amount per show, and that is figured into the cover charge. If a band is booked at the club through a promoter, then the promoter will also get proceeds from the door, which tend to inflate the door charge. Sometimes the band itself will be guaranteed a certain percentage of the door. If a band wants to sell its records or promotional t-shirts at a show, the club's management will more often than not require a percentage of the sales be given to the club in exchange for permission to sell merchandise. In the end though, clubs are most dependent on money taken in at the bar. For this reason, they are often hesitant to book bands that bring in large, but non-drinking, crowds.[108] In Champaign, for example, clubs sometimes balked at booking the Last Gentlemen, an extremely popular local band in the 1980s whose fans tended to order more water than beer at the bar.

Clubs have thus traditionally been eager to identify local acts that will bring business both to the door and the bar. The former booking agent at the now-defunct I-Beam club in San Francisco asserted that local bands were the club's "bread and butter . . . because we can't rely on touring bands. There aren't enough of them to go around."[109] Popular local acts often outdraw little-known national touring bands; however, with notable exceptions in all the communities discussed, a heavily promoted national touring act would almost always bring in more revenue than a local band. Because national touring acts are much less available to most clubs than local artists, clubs tend to live tenuous existences. Sara Cohen notes in her case study of the Liverpool rock scene that the vast majority of local acts brought in only a few (about fifteen to twenty) patrons (*Rock Culture* 69), and a similar phenomenon could be observed in alternative music clubs in most United States' college towns in the 1980s and 1990s.

Because of the financial risk involved in booking untested local talent, clubs try to gauge any act's potential profitability. In San Francisco, a city with several venues for live alternative rock/pop, the I-Beam—which, with a capacity of 800 was one of the larger alternative venues—would book a local band if:

> we see the band having a draw, no matter who they are. If they're doing some numbers at the Nightbreak or the Paradise Lounge or the Kennel Club, it can make sense for us to pick them up. But we can't be testing bands here because it's too big of a space to fill. Our role is to get them when they're at the next level after the Nightbreak or the Kennel Club.[110]

When clubs like the I-Beam were consistently able to bring in audiences for local acts, it created a greater demand for live venues. In Athens, Georgia in the early 1980s, for example, there was a proliferation of clubs as local bands, and audiences for these bands, became visible (Fletcher 64).

Not all localities are as supportive of local music as Athens and San Francisco. In Champaign in the early 1990s there were two clubs that booked alternative acts, Mabel's and the Blind Pig, but most local alternative musicians complained that Mabel's, the larger of the two venues and the one that located near campus, was essentially closed to them. The club had begun booking more mainstream local acts—traditional metal bands like Mistress or pop/rock bands widely popular among local college students like Difficult Listening—prompting an indie label owner to state that "Mabel's doesn't book bands like [ours] for various reasons . . . Mabel's doesn't like slam dancing."[111] A local musician added that with the opening in 1990 of the Blind Pig, a smaller club located near downtown Champaign, "it's been both easier and better for bands to find a place to play."[112] Still, local musicians often found their home bases among the hardest live markets to enter.

In a small competitive market like Champaign-Urbana, with only two venues open to alternative rock/pop bands, it was sometimes hard for musicians to get club dates. Some had more success finding opportunities as opening acts for bands in Chicago. Also, in Champaign-Urbana the absence of a noncommercial college station that programmed independent music was perceived as a significant obstacle to developing a following. One musician complained, "It's really hard to get press in this town; it's really hard to get airplay. It's almost not worth it."[113]

Yet even in Champaign local alternative pop/rock bands develop followings by playing at local venues. For those musicians who were able to get shows, playing locally offered an attractive alternative to touring. A musician who played with several Champaign bands and who put out two solo albums on a major label said:

Playing locally was really what kept me going . . . Especially when it got to the point where we weren't able to tour as much or there wasn't enough money to go on tour, and winding up being able to play two or three nights here in Champaign.[114]

Musicians who were ensconced in the local scene often attracted fairly large crowds to their shows simply because they knew so many people. A member of a band composed of several long-time participants in the local alternative scene observed that "if we worked hard enough we could probably get 200 people at our show just by virtue of all the people we know. I think we tend to get so consumed by preparing for the show that we forget to do that a lot."[115] Those who were not yet well-established often had to depend on fortuitous events to get their careers going. For one Champaign-Urbana band, Twiggy, an opening slot for Boston band the Blake Babies at the Blind Pig helped create a live audience for their music, as one band member recounted:

The first time we played we opened for the Blake Babies. We've had really good luck. With the Blake Babies show, everyone knew it was going to sell out, so they'd have to come early to get in. It was really crowded and we only had five songs, two or three of which were covers. It really freaked us out that people were applauding.

Our friends come see us . . . But there's also this group of people who will come and see us who we don't know, we've never seen, we don't know who they are, maybe they don't know who we are. Why would they like us? They don't know us.[116]

But for musicians in any band in the 1980s and 1990s (and of course still today), before they could contemplate booking live dates they had to find a place to practice. In Champaign, which had no indigenous music industry and only a relative handful of bands, finding practice space could be difficult: very few places existed for the primary purpose of allowing musicians to rehearse. The one studio made available for practice cost around eighty dollars a month to rent. So instead, bands tended to practice in people's basements and garages. In fact, musicians often moved into rented houses together in order to have places to practice. A Champaign musician who played in a number of bands recalled the numerous places in which he had practiced:

> Lonely Trailer practices in Tim's basement. He has a house, and we practice in his basement. With B-Lovers and Turning Curious, we used to practice at Faithful Sound. We'd rent that place, and we knew those guys pretty well, so we got it super cheap. And after that place was gone, we practiced in Mark Rubel's loft a couple times, before he got the downstairs. And when he got the downstairs, before it was a studio—when it was just a storage room—we rented that. And then we practiced in the studio while they were building it. Weird Summer practiced there for awhile, and practiced in someone's garage, and in Bob's bedroom.[117]

These sorts of arrangements were fairly typical in college towns, while in a city like San Francisco bands tended exclusively to rent and share practice space separate from their living quarters, since renting a band house was generally not affordable.

Bands that had rehearsed together and were ready to play out in places like San Francisco were generally able to cultivate followings, but it was often hard at first for a band to find its niche in a large market. A member of San Francisco indie band noted that playing locally

> turned us into real survivors. Actually, now it isn't so bad . . . we have a small contingency of fans. San Francisco's a hard place to try to get a big following. The bands that really do well in this city are the ones that fit into a trend. And so people [say], "I heard about this new Cajun polka band". . . and a lot of people go to see it.[118]

This particular band was, at the time, signed to Alias, a label with a strong local reputation, and thus benefited from local promotion done by the record company. Record release parties at local clubs helped bring bands to public attention, as this Alias tour coordinator's account of a Sneetches, X-Tal, and Harm Farm record release party illustrated:

> The I-Beam holds probably close to 800—they crammed over 900 people into that place. It was a free show, but people knew who those bands were, and there was a line out the door to see these bands . . . That was really a big turning point for us, because up until then all our release parties had been opening slots for other bands. So we never really would know how many people were actually there to see our bands.[119]

Because there were a number of small alternative clubs in the San Francisco area— around 1990 these included the DNA Lounge, the Kennel Club, the Paradise Lounge, Nightbreak—it was possible for a band to work its way up to bigger venues, bringing a local following with them as they progressed.

Eventually most bands attempted to build live followings beyond their local bases. Once a band had established a local audience, it often toured regionally to broaden its audience base. If an act had a recording contract with a major label or fairly large indie, then the label would generally set up tours through a promoter in order to push sales of a current release. A Champaign musician signed to Warner Brothers, for example, was sent on regional tours by his record company. The promoter's job, in Keith Negus' words, includes "hiring venues, arranging venues, sorting out public address systems and lighting, employing caterers and security personnel, advertising the show and coordinating the sale of tickets" (*Producing* 130). In some cases, according to Negus, a major label will put new talent on tour with more established acts by paying a promoter and "buying on" to a tour (131).

At the other end of the spectrum, however, were bands with no record deals, many of whom did not employ agents but instead booked their own out-of-town dates, sometimes by sending demo tapes to clubs, but more often by utilizing social and business contacts in other localities.[120] Rather than dealing with large-scale professional promoters such as those described by Negus, little-known bands tended to deal directly with clubs or with small-scale, independent promoters who operate in these localities. Bands played gigs for as little as fifty dollars a show merely to get regional exposure.

Often band members acting as their own agents found that they had trouble getting paid the money they were led to believe by the club owner or promoter that they would be making from a show. Such problems arose because most alternative rock/pop shows were booked by small, independent promoters rather than large promotion companies like Jam and Avalon, and while these promoters were much more familiar with the live independent music scene, they tended to behave less professionally than larger companies. In his *MAXIMUMROCKNROLL* article "The Business of Punk Rock," Ben Weasel listed some of the problems with small-scale promoters:

> Many of them are young and somewhat naive. They're taking on a responsibility that they're not ready for. A lot of times they'll make a guarantee, not pay it and assume the band will have a "punk" attitude about it, not taking into consideration the fact that the band is depending on that money. Often, they view their activities as "underground," and as a result don't advertise, relying on word-of-mouth instead . . . more often than not, nobody shows up and the band walks away with $12.[121]

Because of these sorts of difficulties, a band that wished to continue playing out-of-town dates almost always employed a talent agent to handle bookings and any ensuing problems. A San Francisco entertainment attorney and former talent agent explained why he started a talent agency:

David Stein and I opened a talent agency because everyone was telling us "if you want to help bands, this is the first thing they need." They need someone to represent them, to help them keep working live.[122]

Part of making sure a band kept working live was making sure the club or promoter paid the band its guarantee. Agents had an incentive to pursue this money since they were paid out of the band's live performance income (Brooks 69).

Tours were an important tool by which an act could increase the size of its audience, as this Champaign musician's experiences illustrated:

I think building an audience through touring happens to most bands. If you have 300 people come and see you play, well, maybe not all of them are going to be huge fans of yours, but there's a percentage that will. Playing out of town always gets more people to hear what you're doing and to like what you're doing.

With the Farmboys, we didn't really play out of town that much, but we saw [our audience grow] in the places we'd go play out of town. People would ask us back. With Pop the Balloon we'd start doing mini-tours, like five days in a row or whatever, and that picked up. And then with the Elvis Brothers, that was basically all we did, go play three or four nights a week.[123]

Many bands found that they were actually more popular out of town than they were at home. The Sneetches, for instance, learned through touring that they had a large audience of indie pop fans outside San Francisco. One band member therefore stated that he found playing on the road more enjoyable that playing at home:

Touring has its ups and downs. But when you can go somewhere and it seems like it was worth it to go . . . when there's a packed house with fans you didn't know existed over 3000 miles away, even farther, that definitely helps. That makes up for the local scene.[124]

In general, a band did not tour extensively until it had released a record. Touring served a number of purposes for record companies and artists, not the least of which was enabling acts to offer something more tangible to audiences than a live performance. A Champaign musician with a major label deal explained: "On tour people would come up to me or the road manager or the manager after shows . . . and ask 'Do you guys have a record out?' and the great thing was being able to say 'Yeah, go out and buy it.'"[125] Clearly getting local radio airplay in conjunction with a tour was crucial; artists liked to have their records played on local college, community and/or commercial alternative stations not just when they played in particular towns, but also before they arrived and after they left in order to create audiences for both concerts and recordings. As an *Alternative Press* article pointed out, the alternative bands that were most successful—from R.E.M. to Nirvana to the

Butthole Surfers—were the ones that had established career longevity, popularity, and success through touring, while at the same time receiving significant radio support.[126]

At the level of the record company then, live promotion of product was seen as an effective way to get audiences more interested in acts, of attracting media attention to acts, of gaining at the very least local radio airplay in cities where acts are appearing, and, Keith Negus argues in his book *Producing Pop*, of generating enthusiasm for an act among record company staff members (131). The latter was true primarily of major labels. Though expensive, touring, for acts on independent labels, could be a way to recover the cost of producing an album. For instance, before it signed to Warner Brothers, R.E.M. chose not to take large advances for production from its record company, I.R.S. The advantage was that the band was not indebted to I.R.S.; the disadvantage was that the band could never stay off of the road for too long, since its tours generated the kind of immediate band income that it did not see from record sales (Fletcher 71).

However, some musicians interviewed saw touring as a catch-22: record companies expected tours to build record sales, but tours were only successful if the record the band was supporting was already successful. A longtime Northern California indie pop musician described the dynamic:

> We certainly have the experience where the audience always likes us at shows; everybody has bad nights but usually we get good encores and stuff. But you don't play to 300 people and expect that that's going to turn that city entirely into your city. You have to hit much, much bigger than that. You have to go in with a hit record . . . otherwise, you just get on the road and stay on the road forever. And no show is ever going to turn things around that much . . .
>
> I'd love to think that just touring forever would be the thing that would do it for you. But I've seen too many bands try that and just suddenly be too old to want to do it anymore, with nothing to show for it.[127]

Most touring bands saw very few revenues from their tours, a factor that certainly contributed to cynicism about touring. In setting up a tour, or any live show for that matter, a number of parties that stood to profit were involved, and bands were often at the mercy of people like managers, promoters, record company executives, and venue booking agents.

Managers were generally initially employed by bands as liaisons between artists and record companies by bands actively seeking record company deals. However, managers were also important to touring bands. A good manager handled the business side of a band's career, which included getting bookings. Sometimes the manager began as a friend of the band, as was the case with R.E.M.'s manager, Jefferson Holt, someone who was often cited by indie pop and rock musicians as the model of a perfect manager. Some bands, however, sought professional management. In addition to full-time management/talent agencies, often club owners got involved in band management, and entertainment lawyers also sometimes took on management responsibilities. A San Francisco attorney who had worked with indie bands Camper Van Beethoven, the Sneetches, Soundgarden, Mudhoney, Meat Puppets, and Pylon, not only drafted agreements and helped bands set up partnerships, corporations and publishing companies, but he also worked as a liaison to record labels and to promoters.[128]

In every case, a good manager was someone who allowed a band to develop artistically and kept the band members from getting bogged down in setting up tours or negotiating with record companies. In reflecting on his early band experiences, one Champaign musician emphasized the importance of management:

> We were mismanaged. I think it's really important for bands to have managers . . . it always seems like there's an extra member, a hidden member, that really gets bands out. It's really hard to do everything yourself, unless you're really phenomenal. I think Hüsker Dü did a good job of that. Certainly the Replacements would have been nowhere had they not had a manager who just really forced them to play.[129]

Sara Cohen observes that most of the Liverpool bands she studied correctly assumed that promoters and record companies would be unlikely to deal with bands that lacked managers (*Rock Culture* 60). A manager doesn't just help with a band's business decisions; s/he lends an air of professionalism to the band.

In the 1990s, a well-managed band with an aggressive agent had a chance of landing choice jobs like a spot on the annual Lollapalooza tour, which was staged by the late Bill Graham's company and showcased alternative acts. The tour featured a main stage with headliners like the Red Hot Chili Peppers and a "second" stage for local and lesser-known acts. Unfortunately, dealing with a large promoter did not always serve second stage acts well: many acts complained that they were not paid for their appearances, that there was not food available for them, that they could not sell their merchandise at the concert, and that they were not provided seats at or backstage access to the main show.[130] As tours like Lollapalooza in the 1990s proved to be one of the few profitable ways to present live independent (and major label alternative) music in an economically depressed concert industry, it became more and more difficult for non-major label bands to receive national exposure in live venues.

Clubs like Champaign's Blind Pig and San Francisco's I-Beam were therefore left as the primary venues available to indie pop/rock bands, and the late 1980s and early 1990s were hard for clubs. The I-Beam booking agent of that time contended that packages like Lollapalooza caused significant economic harm to all clubs in all localities, because alternative bands that used to make money for clubs were grouped together in packages and played stadiums and arenas. Since consumers often decided save their money for one big alternative show like Lollapalooza, smaller shows suffer. According to the I-Beam booker in 1991,

> We're just scraping by right now. Business is really bad . . . everything's down at least thirty to fifty percent . . . We're just staying above water. We're hoping we're going to ride through this period. Maybe people don't have as great an interest in live music as they used to.[131]

As the yearly Lollapalooza tour grew bigger in the 1990s, it became a target for critics of the "sellout" of indie music, and important in some narratives of the alternative music's co-optation, and thus, decline.

Such criticisms aside, the overall financial problems in the live music marketplace meant that it was more difficult for clubs in cities like Champaign to attract national touring acts, and in cities like San Francisco with several alternative clubs there was heated competition between venues for desirable acts. The I-Beam may have benefited from being part of a national circuit of similar clubs that included the 9:30 Club in Washington, D.C., the Ritz or Irving Plaza in New York, the Cabaret Metro in Chicago, and the Palace or the Roxy in Los Angeles that promoters chose for many major alternative touring bands. Popular alternative acts that played these clubs would often skip smaller localities, like Champaign, when touring. Furthermore, within a city like San Francisco, smaller venues like the Kennel Club, the DNA, the Paradise Lounge, and Nightbreak in general did not pose much of a threat to most of the larger clubs, like the I-Beam. On the other hand, the I-Beam had trouble with Slim's:

> It's really kind of hard, because all the people who work there are Bill Graham people, so it's almost like a Bill Graham club . . . Slim's definitely is our number one competitor. And the thing is that they were more blues-like, they were never that much trouble for us, but now they've gotten really aggressive and they're paying lots of money.

> Clubs get into a lot of bidding wars around here where the prices skyrocket and the show ends up losing money because the ticket prices have to be so high to accommodate that giant guarantee. That's kind of a common occurrence lately. It's hard to let go though, because there's so little else coming around. You'll end up with a month of local bands.[132]

Despite the competition for shows, the I-Beam booking agent claimed that "all the other booking agents around here are really cool people. We socialize together," and thus pointed to both the overlap between economic and social relationships in music scenes and the potential tensions (e.g. between friendships and business competition) that underlie these relationships.

Sites of indie pop/rock music dissemination occupied disparate physical locations in disparate localities, but popular music practice brought them together in a number of ways. Economic relationships between alternative music institutions within communities—clubs using record stores as ticket outlets, record stores providing product to college radio stations, college radio stations promoting shows at local venues, and so on—made these businesses in many ways inseparable. Because of the nature of their markets, businesses that provided similar products or services often found themselves in complementary as well as competitive relationships. Business relationships also linked institutions across space: indie music created national and transnational economic networks.

It is impossible, however, to separate economics and social interaction. The clubs, radio stations, and record stores were not merely sites of economic practice, they were also sites of audience practice and interaction. Audience members were always implicated in processes of music production, whether they were video viewers or college radio listeners actively engaged in the process of making meaning, CD buyers registering their tastes with SoundScan, or participants united in live musical performances. They were thus also implicated in narratives of indie music's rise and decline, in determining what counted as an authentic expression or practice and what did not. We must examine the social relationships that developed around the institutions and practices of indie music within and across localities; the ways in which, to quote Sara Cohen, people within and across localities used music "to locate themselves in relation to others" ("Localizing" 19).

CHAPTER 5

Locating Subjectivity in Independent Music

The institutions of independent pop/rock music—record stores, clubs, record companies, college radio stations—all helped to locate music scene participants within particular physical spaces, within a structure of social and economic relations, and within received and personal narratives of the local and national histories of indie music. Independent pop/rock music scenes of the 1980s and 1990s were constituted through the practices and relationships that were enacted within social space, including through particular sets of gender relations. They were also defined by the geographical spaces that they occupied. Subjects within independent pop/rock music scenes were complexly positioned on both social and spatial axes. In this chapter I want to take Angela McRobbie's challenge and look at how music scene participants were located on both axes, not "in and through cultural commodities and texts," but "in and through the cultural practices of everyday life" ("Post-Marxism" 730).

Recognizing the centrality of locality in the situated practices of indie pop/rock music is crucial to this study. Indie pop/rock music, more than most forms of pop and rock music in the United States, was identified by locality (Athens, Seattle, Austin, Minneapolis, Champaign, Olympia, etc.), both by participants and by those outside of particular scenes. Therefore, the articulation of alternative music and locality is one that merits examination. However, it is difficult to pin down exactly what is meant by "locality." Does "locality" refer to a tangible, delimited geographical entity or a construct constituted in social relations? Sara Cohen points out the difficulty of settling on one definition or another, observing that locality, "used to refer to a sense of community or affinity that is linked to notions of place and to the social construction of spatial boundaries" ("Ethnography" 129).[1]

These two notions of locality—locality as geographically-defined and locality as socially defined—are inseparable. Localities are constituted both by geographical boundaries and by networks of social relationships. In examining indie music scenes, I think it is important to note that the localities within which music scenes existed were understood and experienced by music scene participants on *both* social and spatial levels. As Jody Berland argues, "social processes can not be understood outside of space" ("Radio Space" 186). Social relationships within indie music scenes, and indie music scenes themselves, were formed and maintained within particular places: within localities and within specific local sites (clubs, record stores, coffee shops, houses).

The focus, however, cannot merely be on any one locality or series of localities. Localities, as both geographic and social sites, do not exist in isolation: they are nodes in social and economic networks and derive meanings from their relationships with and to other localities.[2] Doreen Massey contends that our understanding of what any place (including a place such as "Champaign" as conceptualized as the home of a music scene) means comes only through linking a place to and differentiating that place from places beyond (e.g. by understanding how the Champaign music scene was both like and different from music scenes in Minneapolis, Chicago, Madison, Seattle, and so on). She suggests that we think of places not merely as bounded entities but also as "articulated moments in networks of social relations and understandings" ("Power-Geometry" 66–68). Places like localities are therefore both distinct geographic and social entities and parts of a larger network that is always in flux as relationships between places change.

Sociologist Pierre Bourdieu however ignores the interlocal possibilities presented by phenomena like indie pop/rock music scenes; he writes

> people close to each other in social space tend to be close together—by choice or necessity—in the geographical space; however, people who are very distant from each other in the social space can encounter one another, enter into interaction, at least briefly and intermittently, in physical space. (*In* 127)

While Bourdieu's contention that distances in social space and in geographical space are roughly analogous to one another is undoubtedly true within localities, it fails to take into account the interlocal, geographically distant relationships that form because individuals are located within close proximity of one another in social space and are linked through social relationships. Within the places of indie music scenes it was certainly true that people distant from each other in physical space did, and still do, encounter one another in both social and physical space.

Local scenes are placed in relationship to each other through the circulation of music, knowledge, and style; and they are part of social and economic networks that both structure and are structured by this set of relations. Localities are, as Edward Soja observes, linked to wider and multiple systems of social power (152). Even the most underground levels of independent music production in my case studies were ultimately linked—whether it was because independent labels acted as "farm leagues" for major labels, because some indies signed distribution agreements with or were bought by majors, or because indie marketing strategies (like the seven-inch single) were sometimes adopted by major labels—to the mainstream music industry, and through that industry to global media conglomerates. The geographic and economic margins in this instance did indeed help support the center.[3]

Social Meanings, Practices and Relationships

Two important means by which subjects located themselves within the social space of independent pop/rock music scenes were through genre identification and through personal narrative histories of involvement with the genre. Implicit in these identifications and personal histories was the idea that they constituted a connection with an authentic musical form and set of musical practices, and that these identities were constituted both locally and interlocally.

In identifying with a genre, many interviewees labeled the music with which they were associated as "pop." Responses to the question, "How would you label your music (the music you make/put out on your label/play on your radio show/listen to)?" included "We're mainly doing pop stuff—guitar pop stuff," from the owner of a small record label;[4] "Pop music—of course that's a really generic term," from a musician;[5] "Pop—pop songs," from another musician;[6] and "Beatle-esque pop stuff with nice melodies and clever arrangements," from a record store manager and musician describing the type of music to which he listens.[7]

Not all participants, however, were quite so ready to label their music. Some saw themselves as existing outside the genre niches generally assigned to popular music. One Champaign musician stated of his band's music, "I just say it's acoustic guitar, bass and drums,"[8] while a relatively well-known musician within alternative music's pop subculture did not give a label to his own music and instead explained, "I definitely think of myself as melodically ambitious . . . I'm willing to toss in forty-five chord changes during a song if I think the melody needs that, [and] I also am kind of complex lyrically."[9] There were also those musicians who asserted their music's conformity to certain generic conventions but at the same time argued that their music was different from any existing music. They were willing to give their music the label "pop" but nevertheless contended that their music sounded like no one else's. One musician, complaining about his band's inability to secure a local audience, remarked, "I guess that's one of our problems, there's nobody like us."[10] Another musician stated of his band: "I don't think anyone in town sounds like us . . . I'd say we're pop, but the thing about us, which I think is really neat, is that we don't have a particular sound."[11] Some of those who willingly identified themselves as being associated with "pop" music went to great lengths to clarify what was meant by "pop," as this musician indicated as he tried to define his music:

> I would call it pop music. I would call it wimpy pop music. I would not call it power
> pop. Power pop has now become a term that means a hard guitar band that uses pop

as the format: Nirvana is kind of power pop. Originally power pop was like Badfinger, Big Star—that's power pop. But I refuse to let that label be used for our music . . . I would have to say our music is jangly guitar pop, even though I have a great fear of the R.E.M. comparison.[12]

Identifying one's music so that on the one hand it could be linked to a particular generic tradition but on the other hand it could not be easily categorized or construed as unoriginal was of great importance to musicians in independent pop/rock music scenes.

Because many, though certainly not all, of the music scene participants I interviewed identified the music with which they were associated as "indie pop," I want to explore for a moment the significance of this genre label. Labeling one's own music "pop" was a significant move, one that required a knowledge of how the culture of independent/college/alternative music differentiated between pop and rock. While both indie pop and rock were characterized by simple instrumentation (guitars, bass, drums, and sometimes keyboards) and presentation, indie pop in particular placed high value on melody. When someone chose to define her/his music as "pop," s/he was identifying with one style of indie music—and, implicitly, its practices—*against* other musical styles and their practices, including alternative rock (another genre with which some of my interviewees identified), as well as Top 40 pop, techno, rap, and so on.

Difference is crucial in the formation of subcultural identity, in positioning oneself against dominant cultural forms and practices. Deploying the term "pop" or placing oneself within an "indie pop" tradition that encompasses musicians from Alex Chilton to the Beach Boys' Brian Wilson when describing one's music or tastes was an oppositional move, and, interestingly, one used in many cases to indicate a particularly "authentic" form of expression. The word "pop" evokes something trivial and transitory. Simon Frith ("Rock" 68) argues that "pop isn't a form that progresses," and it was the widespread belief in this truism that makes indie pop powerful. After all, indie pop was *generally* not produced and circulated through the same specific economic and social systems as Top 40 pop music. The relationship between indie pop and mainstream pop music was not truly dichotomous: both genres were marketed as commodities and were therefore implicated in the structures of commercial music production and consumption. However, "indie pop" played with the word "pop." By defining itself as "pop" it placed itself in relation to Top 40 pop music, but it attempted in its conditions of production and consumption, which were idealized as counter to the conditions of chart pop practice (i.e. released on independent labels like Sarah and Slumberland rather than majors, often released in the form of seven-inch vinyl singles rather than on CD, played on college radio rather than CHR, shown on *120 Minutes* rather than during the daytime or on VH-1, etc.), it marked its difference. As indie pop bands like Velocity Girl were signed to major labels in the 1980s and 1990s though, the perceived distance between indie pop and chart pop grew less and less.

Indie pop attempted to construct itself as different from mainstream pop music not merely through romanticized production and consumption, but also through its content. Simon Reynolds argues that indie pop dealt with topics not usually addressed in pop songs—frustration, doubt, ugliness—thus turning pop convention on its head. For Reynolds, the prototypical example of this use of the pop form was the 1980s British band the Smiths, who rewrote youth, according to Reynolds, "in terms of maladjustment, awkwardness, introversion, misery" ("Against" 253–254). Later indie pop acts like Unrest, Heavenly, and Matthew Sweet continued in this vein.

Simon Reynolds locates indie pop's oppositionality in "refusal"; not merely a refusal of rock and chart pop musical conventions and production/distribution practices, but, by embracing the "naivete and purity" of three-to-four minute, verse-chorus melodic pop song, a refusal of mainstream rock and pop's knowingness and musical and lyrical excess ("Against" 39). This sort of "refusal" by indie pop musicians was often conscious. A member of an American indie pop band which was given such labels as "The Association for the nineties," recalled that when the band first started to be played on college radio in the late eighties, "we thought we were being almost rebellious, because it was kind of like playing hard core on an Easy Listening station."[13] Steve Redhead takes the notion of "refusal" a step beyond refusal of generic conventions. For Redhead, the refusal of rock conventions and the embrace of naive song structure by indie pop bands (he cites as examples 1980s British bands Talulah Gosh, The Primitives, and The Darling Buds) was tantamount to a refusal of adulthood and a refusal of citizenship. In a time of diminishing expectations for young people like the 1980s, Redhead argues that "drawing attention to 'innocence' is politically important" (87).

The political importance of indie pop was, however, debatable. Very few interviewees couched their involvement in indie pop in particular or independent music in general in political terms. Yet in describing how they entered into indie pop, interviewees tended to cite common influences, including genres like punk and artists like Alex Chilton, influences that did not fall squarely within the mainstream in popular music histories, and which therefore marked a difference from and even refusal of the musical practices and conventions. At the same time, many common mainstream musical influences were also cited, including the Beatles and the Beach Boys, underscoring a degree of celebration of mainstream practices and conventions within indie pop, albeit practices and conventions that were not representative of the musical mainstream at the time that most of the music scene participants I interviewed began buying records and forming their musical tastes. Listing specific influential musicians and bands, both obscure and well-known, was central in locating oneself within a musical tradition such as indie pop, or, more generally, independent pop/rock music. Some of the explanations of how the older musicians I interviewed entered into indie pop included:

> I remember when I was little I had about seventeen records, and they were all Beatles records. But if it wasn't for punk rock, I probably wouldn't be playing. Until punk rock, it just didn't seem fathomable, you had no idea of what you were supposed to do to have a band.[14]

> I saw the Beatles and I thought, "Boy, this music is really exciting and great, and I'd love to be doing stuff like that" . . . Alex Chilton was sort of the starting point for the cult of eighties American rock that's good. His early seventies band Big Star sold four thousand records or something like that, something really sad, at the time. I think the whole Big Star-inspired subgenre—the dBs and Mitch Easter—spawned a lot of really good stuff, [as did] American new wave: Patti Smith and Television and the Talking Heads.[15]

> The Sex Pistols were important to me because before they happened there was the idea that in order to play music you had to be at a certain level of proficiency before what you were doing was worth anything. Neil Young for his electric guitar playing. The first couple of dBs records for their weirdness, which isn't weird anymore, but it was then [in the late 70s–early 80s]. Television.[16]

Responses from younger musicians included:

> I got my first guitar when I was eleven or twelve. The bands that I liked back then were the Beatles and Queen and the Beach Boys, and then later on Cheap Trick.[17]

> The first band I liked was the Ramones, because after you learn how to play the guitar, you know every Ramones song after two lessons. After them, U2. . . I was young and naive, and I thought they were really sincere. And after that R.E.M. was a big one, and then the Replacements; and then even more so after the Replacements, Hüsker Dü, in terms of originality.[18]

> Musicians who influenced me include Let's Active, specifically Mitch Easter. Alex Chilton and Big Star—all of Big Star. R.E.M.—no one admits that one but I'm too honest—all of the dB's. Then Nikki Sudden, all of the Jacobites. Matthew Sweet, Tommy Keene, for sure. Tommy Keene and [ex-dB] Chris Stamey are my two all-time favorite pop song writers. The Beach Boys; Brian Wilson, rather.[19]

Although many musicians and groups were only named by one interviewee—Nikki Sudden, Neil Young, U2, Queen—much more striking is the number of names that appeared consistently across interviews: the Beatles, the Beach Boys, Alex Chilton, Television, Mitch Easter, the dBs, R.E.M. Also recurrent was punk, either in general or in the form of specific acts like the Sex Pistols, the Ramones, and Patti Smith.

Younger musicians were more likely than their older counterparts to cite as influences acts that gained prominence in the 1980s, like R.E.M. and the Replacements, while 1970s punk acts seem to have made more of an impact on older musicians. Certainly age positioned these musicians somewhat differently in terms of their relationships to independent pop/rock music, but the significant overlap in bands mentioned between age groups indicates that the artists one used to place oneself within this particular musical tradition transcended to some degree age-defined boundaries.

Independent pop/rock music was in part constituted by self-identifications and personal narratives that attempted to position their subjects as part of a tradition of expression that came from the mainstream, but whose situated practices and histories existed outside of the mainstream. A shifting terrain of articulating social and economic practices contributed to the production of identity within alternative music culture. In previous chapters I have discussed the economic practices of independent pop/rock music production and distribution; here I will focus on situated practices. Practices are meaningful within particular historical moments and social and economic contexts, and ultimately in terms of how they contribute to the positioning of subjects within what Bourdieu calls "social space."

The Role of Situated Practice

Within and across local music scenes, practices help define and differentiate groups of participants within social (and often literal) space. In her study of music production and consumption in Milton Keynes, Ruth Finnegan observes that what is understood as music is different to different groups, "each of whom have their own conventions supported by existing practices and ideas about the right way in which music should be realised" (7). Thus, practices are often enacted by groups of participants in order to set themselves apart from participants in other music cultures or subcultures. This process, Paul Willis argues, is governed by a "grounded aesthetic," which is

> the creative element in a process whereby meanings are attributed to symbols and practices and where symbols and practices are selected, reselected, highlighted and recomposed to resonate further appropriated and particularized meanings. (21)

For instance, according to Willis participating in the practices and rituals of spectator sport—identifying with a locality, feeling loyalty to a team, being part of epic rivalries—contributes to a grounded aesthetic of place and belonging, which is founded on an opposition to other places and other ways of belonging.

In looking at the practices that were selected and reselected in a grounded aesthetic of independent pop/rock music and its contexts, it is difficult to separate audience practices from performance practices. Indeed, those practices that attempted to bridge the gap between performer and audience were central in defining independent pop/rock music of the 1980s and 1990s against other kinds of music. An important characteristic of independent pop/rock music performance was the tendency of performers to see stage wear and street clothing as interchangeable. Live performances of independent pop/rock music were marked by a similarity of dress between audience members and performers: indie pop fashion specifically included items like thrift-store clothing, and basic jeans, t-shirts, and sneakers. And often, performers used not-so-symbolic means of lessening the distance between themselves and their audiences. As Sara Cohen (*Rock Culture* 40) observes, the gap between performers and audiences can be narrowed by interpersonal contact that takes place between these two groups at venues before and after shows and between sets. Band members find talking to audience members after the show a useful means of gauging response to the performance, as well as a way to meet people.

Situations like this in which indie musicians sought to interact with audience members were not surprising, because many indie musicians seemed to think of people in the audience as being just like themselves, and indeed, some were. When asked to describe his band's audience, for instance, one musician merely said that audience members were "people who are just into a lot of the same music that we are."[20] Many musicians contended that being in a band, as one put it, "is not a status thing"[21] and that making music—the "true" expression of real people like those in the audience—was what was important. This sort of claim was rather disingenuous, since being a musician did grant one a certain status within independent pop/rock music scenes, and in any event, it was easy to claim that status was unimportant when one not well known within or outside of a particular music scene. However, such claims are integral to a discourse that stressed the similarities, rather than the differences, between performer and audience.[22] The "do-it-yourself" attitude associated with independent music-making in part enabled the discourse and allowed, for instance, a non-musician indie record label owner to comment that "this is an area where . . . somebody who isn't perfect on the guitar or a perfect singer can get into it . . . if I wanted to do it, I probably could pull it off."[23]

The argument that audience members and musicians were somehow interchangeable—that there was *virtually* no difference between them—was also common within this particular construction of independent pop/rock music performers and audiences.[24] In describing the relationship between performer and audience, one musician observed:

> I think all musicians, all really truly good musicians, are big fans; and I think a lot of fans consider themselves musicians. It seems like everyone says, "I'm going to get a band together," "I'm going to take guitar lessons." I'm probably just *slightly* above that because I've actually been on stage a couple hundred times.[25]

The use of "slightly" in this context is significant, because it underscores the *near* interchangeability, rather than the *actual* interchangeability, of performers and audience members. At the root of this near equivalence is practice, as indicated by a record store manager and musician who, upon noting that everyone who works in the store is a musician except for one woman, explained that, "she might as well be. She collects, she likes records, and all that stuff."[26] Participants in alternative music culture often shared practices like collecting that served as markers of knowledge of and interest in the music. Simon Jones notes that the practice of collecting has led young people to embark on their own "archaeologies" of the music in which they are interested, searching out used records and re-releases to trace histories of particular genres (61). Within indie pop culture, for instance, the (re)discovery of the early 1970s band Big Star and the desire to collect records, bootleg recordings, and interviews by a band as a whole and its individual members constituted just this sort of archeology and was a practice by which participants were seen to be united.

Shared social practices—some of which I have already discussed (identifying with a specific musical genre, dressing in a certain way) and some of which I will discuss (participating in particular social networks, frequenting specific spaces)—served to lessen the symbolic space between performer and audience. Furthermore, because audience members at performances were often musicians themselves or friends of the band on-stage, there tended to be a sense of unity between the audience and the performers.[27] A booking agent at an alternative music club explained: "Pretty much all the same people are part of the scene. Behind the scenes, in the audience and on stage, they're all the same group of people."[28] Even if one looked only at audiences in independent pop/rock music performance, there was a certain unity between members based not just in interpersonal relationships but in shared knowledge and practice, as Ruth Finnegan argues of British pub music audiences:

> Pub audiences at musical performances usually contained a core of people who knew each other or at least had the common (and uniting) experience of shared participation in a specific forms of music, aware of the unwritten traditions of that particular pub and usually with the same conventions for listening to musical performance. (232)

All music scenes demand of their participants, both audience members and musicians, a certain level of (sub)cultural competence.

Specifically, shared practices and knowledge in independent pop/rock music culture in the 1980s and 1990s worked to define independent pop/rock music as "authentic" music. The conventions of style that dictated that fans, businesspeople and musicians dress in a similar "ordinary" manner; the musical conventions that eschewed elaborate technology and instrumentation in favor of a guitar-dominated sound; the "do-it-yourself" ethic that told fans that they could easily be in the position of the musicians they admired; and the identification of independent pop/rock music with particular marginal localities (Athens, Minneapolis, Seattle) and small enterprises (micro-indie record labels, non-commercial college and community radio stations, mom and pop record stores) were all part of a discourse and a constellation of practices that constructed independent pop/rock music as somehow more "real" than other kinds of pop and rock music. There was also a sense of shared personal history, of fitting into the narrative of indie music's perceived rise and fall in similar ways.

In *Art into Pop*, Simon Frith and Howard Horne point to "a significant strand of bohemian thought that romanticizes normality" as the motivating force behind the need for authenticity in the face of the artifice of the music industry (21). If the myth of authenticity, as Frith has argued elsewhere ("Towards" 136), is "what guarantees [that] rock performances resist or subvert commercial logic," then this myth was certainly central to independent pop/rock music discourse and practice, which celebrated the ordinariness and accessibility of its stars and placed the music and its culture in opposition to the commercial logic of mainstream music. Yet, as I have demonstrated in earlier chapters, independent pop/rock music during the 1980s and 1990s did not operate in a sphere separate from the commercial music industry. Almost all of the best known college radio acts, including Smashing Pumpkins, Nirvana, the Breeders, and the Lemonheads were on major labels by the 1990s, many of them received airplay on commercial radio, and a large number of bands like Pavement that recorded for independent labels received major label distribution. A system of commercial practice that incorporates marginal musical genres and cultures works to the advantage of consumer culture, which, Mike Featherstone contends

> does not encourage a grey conformism in the choice of goods . . . rather it seeks to educate individuals to read the differences in signs, to decode the minutiae of distinctions in dress, house furnishing, leisure lifestyles and equipment. (Quoted in Tomlinson 21)

So while independent pop/rock music culture's practices and discourse sought to establish an identity for participants and for the music that placed it and them outside the processes of commercial popular music, in fact they were all implicated within the structures of mainstream music, which did not care whether you bought Mariah Carey or Liz Phair, as long as you bought something. And, it might be pointed out, it was the recognition on some level of this economic dynamic at work that made the assertion of independent pop/rock music's difference, its "authenticity," especially vital to participants.

Indeed, part of the irony of the discourse of independent pop/rock music "authenticity" was the degree to which those who contributed to the discourse recognized its contradictions. A member of the band Pavement (which recorded for independent label Matador) pointed out that "The whole commodity side of music is something that people want to know about but don't want to know about . . . Pop music is never gonna be pure, and indie rock has this notion of purity in it."[29] Another indie musician was more explicit in his critique of how the notion of authenticity worked in independent pop/rock music culture:

> Bands and college radio tend to think they're producing music of some sort or another that's better than what's succeeding in the mass commercial market but is less successful because people are essentially manipulated by some structure, some kind of thing in power. You're supposed to in some way feign complete indifference and independence . . . there's a long history of art suffering from pressures from a subculture, just like it suffers from pressure to make money.[30]

Violating certain conventions of independent pop/rock music production and performance could call the "authenticity" of an individual, band, or business entity into question. Generally "selling out" was the charge that was most damaging to authenticity. When a band signed with a major label, when an independent label signed a distribution deal with a major, when a college radio station played a large number of major label releases, or when an artist's song or album became successful on the mainstream charts, the individuals or entities involved always lost credibility in the indie music culture with some members of their original audience(s). Of course some bands, like Nirvana and R.E.M., retained much of their "indie" credibility despite crossing over to the mainstream: this is largely due to the perception that the band remains true to the practices of indie music culture.

Image is also a site at which authenticity is contested. One of the more controversial figures in terms of image in alternative pop/rock music in the 1980s was Michael Stipe of the band R.E.M., because many detractors within independent pop/rock music culture questioned whether the that image Stipe projected—one of, in the words of R.E.M. biographer Tony Fletcher, "a mystical poet"—was an accurate representation of the "real" Michael Stipe. Fletcher explained that according to Stipe's critics, "[Stipe's] persona resembles . . . the cold calculation of a new David Bowie image," and that this assessment was supported by the fact that "Stipe swore the few people who knew of his brief existence in a covers band to secrecy, afraid that such a pastime would detract from his image as an outsider and a musical novice" (87–88). Of course, criticisms such as these ignore the constructedness of *all* images, even the most "authentic" ones, and the debate over the authenticity of Stipe's image demonstrates how an understanding of commercial logic (i.e. the conscious creation of a marketable image) cannot be used to assess the "authenticity" of an artist or other entity. One might question whether Stipe's image as a confused loner was really all that marketable, and one might also wonder whether musicians who appeared to have no explicit public personae, like Kim Deal of the Breeders, were not in fact presenting images of ordinariness that connoted authenticity, as Frith and Horne imply.

Notions about what connotes "authenticity" were constituted within the practices and discourses of independent pop/rock music culture in the 1980s and 1990s and were shared to varying degrees among participants.[31] Within independent pop/rock music practice, social relationships arose that were central to the identification of independent pop/rock music as different from other sorts of music. For many musicians, fans, and businesspeople, friendships were found in the local music scene. One interviewee commented:

> There are a lot of friends of mine who just happen to play instruments and be in bands. The way that I've always seen it is that I got to be friends with these people because of music more than I was friends with these people and then we all reached this point where we started playing music. Everybody that I know, everybody that I'm friends with, is very much involved in music.[32]

For those who had friends who did not share their interest in music, musical taste/interest was still often a criterion in forming friendships, as is indicated by a musician who explained, "I have work friends and music friends. Mostly music friends. And mostly my friends at work are my music-work friends."[33] It is telling here that places (work/local music sites) play a role in friendship formation. And even those who sought friendships outside of the local scene may have found those friendships becoming part of a geographical network of music scene social relations, as this musician described:

> For a while it seemed like the only people I ever hung out with were the people who were in my band and other musicians. It was like, "We're all in this together." Whereas now, I don't know half the bands in town . . . but my friends who aren't part of the music scene tend to get drawn into it, because I don't have much free time, and I don't really go out just to a bar to drink as much anymore. And a lot of my friends will go see a band.[34]

Another musician cited "lack of free time" as the reason that most of his friends were music scene participants of some sort, explaining that "I do a lot of things in music and I hardly have any time to do things not involved with music. And also a lot of people around town are music fans."[35]

Relationships within indie music scenes were not based only on friendships made through involvement in a social network. Many were also business relationships, as is true in many other kinds of work. One participant, a talent buyer for an alternative music club, noted that "It's really hard to separate business and friendship," and she continued:

When you're in this business, the people in the music scene are your friends. All our sound people are musicians, our door people, everybody is a musician. My room-mates are in the music business—one of my roommates works at *Gavin*. Everybody's part of it. There aren't too many people. Everyone kind of sticks together.[36]

An independent record label employee also commented on the difficulty of separating friendships from business:

I live with one of the Sneetches' girlfriends, so I see those guys all the time. I tend to hang out with a lot of musicians, a lot of record people. It gets hard to hang out with people who don't know . . . what you do every day. I think it's a lot more tiring to have to deal with somebody who just has no clue of what I do, who doesn't want to know either.[37]

As is true of other sorts of music scenes, in independent pop/rock music scenes friendships and business relationships were necessarily intertwined in a complex social network, and phrases like "We're all in this together" and "Everyone kind of sticks together" indicated a certain communal feeling exists within scenes.[38] In addition, the sense of interconnectedness among participants within a local independent pop/rock music scene may well have been greater than in other sorts of music scenes, because the high degree of low-budget entrepreneurship (home recording, micro-indie labels, college radio shows, fanzines) within indie scenes created the possibility that each locally situated scene could be a virtually autonomous site of music production, marketing, and circulation.

Locality and Independent Pop/Rock Music Scenes

In the personal histories of indie music scene participants, it was clear that participants were not only positioned (and to a large degree positioned themselves) within a specific constellation of indie music tastes, local histories, and generic histories: they were also located within certain personal relationships and—quite literally located—in certain physical spaces, both of which were of critical importance in the interviewees' narratives. For some, particular physical sites were the central points in stories of how they got involved with independent pop/rock music. A college radio station music director, for instance, placed the station at the center of the narrative of her involvement, noting that, "I was a KALX listener for a couple of years, and I kept saying 'I should go volunteer there,' because at some point I found out anyone could volunteer to work at the station."[39] Similarly, the owner of an independent record store recounted her history as a participant in alternative music culture by listing the particular stores at which she had worked:

I started out as a part-time clerk at a mall record store in suburban Sacramento, and then I just went on from there and was promoted. I actually worked for Wherehouse Entertainment for eight years. I ended up managing Leopold's for a couple years when Wherehouse bought Record Factory. Then I purchased the Rough Trade store out of its bankruptcy.[40]

Specific physical sites also structured the personal narrative of an alternative music club booking agent:

I started when I was eighteen. I got involved in college radio in Chico, then I started putting on independent shows—I started booking shows in halls. I moved to San Francisco and got involved again with college radio at KALX. Then I moved into the I-Beam. I started as a publicist, then within six months I started booking the Biz Club. I went away to Europe for three months. When I came back I did the Kennel Club, and then I went back to the I-Beam.[41]

This last example points not only to the ways in which participants identified themselves with and through specific physical locations and the practices associated with those locations, but it also points, in underscoring the movement from Chico (to Europe) to San Francisco, to the ways in which participants more generally identified themselves with and through particular localities. If we look at the beginning of the personal account of how an editor at an alternative radio trade publication got involved in independent pop/rock music culture, we see that placing one's practices in a specific locality like San Francisco was a powerful way of describing how one entered a particular set of social and economic relations:

I went to high school at Presentation, on Masonic and Turk—it's an all-girl Catholic high school—and when you became a junior you got off-campus lunch. Most of the people went to Haight Street for that. My friends said, "There's USF, there's college guys, they've got a cafeteria—let's go down there." That's basically how my involvement in KUSF started. I remember KUSF put together a Flock of Seagulls show at the Stone, and my friend and I passed out buttons. I just did it because it was fun. I was hanging out with older people and meeting bands.[42]

Not only did this brief narrative invoke multiple physical locations—Presentation High School, Haight Street, the University of San Francisco, the Stone—it included multiple social networks: high school friends, KUSF staff, and band members.

Within all personal narratives, not just personal narratives of involvement in independent pop/rock music scenes, specific places are important. Music scenes, for instance, are largely defined by places within them that are meaningful. What is specifically important in studying independent pop/rock music scenes of the 1980s and 1990s is not *that* places are meaningful—places are prominent and meaningful in all personal histories—it is the particular places (certain clubs, record stores, coffee shops, houses, etc.) that are meaningful. These places were sites of culturally specific practices, and their inclusion in personal narratives positioned narrators within both a specific geographic space and a specific set of social relations. It is therefore not surprising that in discussing their involvement in independent pop/rock music scenes, participants rarely talked about a particular locality's independent pop/rock music scene without mentioning the social relationships in which they were situated within that locality. As in the previous example, narratives often located personal and social events not merely in specific local scenes, but within specific physical spaces within those scenes. A Champaign, Illinois independent record label owner provided a striking example:

> I started working at the Pop Shop in 1982-83, and I hooked up with Steve, who knew everybody else, through that. I grew up here, but before that I really didn't do anything with the music scene. I opened my video and record rental store in '85, and Steve was working for me then. We were doing stuff with the local music scene, just selling cassettes. I hooked up with the Farmboys in the beginning of '85 and was putting out their stuff. I hooked up with them through a friend, because she knew Adam Schmitt. Then [local musicians] Ric and Paul moved into our house.[43]

Not all narratives located relationships within such narrowly-bounded spaces within localities, but in the histories related by almost all interviewees, geography and social relationships clearly intersected, as in this California musician's account:

> A friend of mine and I wanted to form this punk rock band. We couldn't find any musicians in Los Angeles, so we moved up to San Francisco. Of course we found musicians up here, so we had a little punk band. We were called The Wow. And my current band's other guitar player was in a band called If Then, Why. They broke up, we broke up. I started writing songs, and I knew he wasn't playing. I played him some of the songs, and he said, "Okay."[44]

The convergence of social relations and geographical space was also evident in the account given by an Illinois musician, who recalled that his involvement in the Champaign music scene began because, "I was from Decatur, and Nick and Steve and Bernie and I had a band. We used to come to Champaign a lot to see Screams, which was one of our favorite bands. We gradually met people that were in other bands . . . It just kind of snowballed from there."[45]

Moments such as these in narratives, when geographic and social locations were emphasized, tended to be expressed by interviewees as turning points in their relationships to local social and economic structures. They are also often cited as important moments in the upward trajectory of the music scene's history. The following recollection by a Champaign musician underscored the importance of local scene histories in the formation of identity within the relations that constitute a local alternative music scene:

> I played acoustic guitar for a couple years, but I wouldn't have probably thought of playing electric guitar or being in a band if it wasn't for seeing the Vertebrats. I'd never sat in my room before I saw any local bands and say, "I'm going to be a rock star." After about a year of really getting into the local music scene, I just started playing guitar in bands. I think it was just the fact that I started see all these local bands dressing the same way that everybody else did and walking up on stage and playing good music, that was what turned things around for me.[46]

Placing one's participation within this context was a way of asserting the importance of one's position in local music history. For instance, another Champaign musician constructed his involvement in local music as pioneering by articulating his band's relationship in time and space to other bands and local scenes; he claimed "I think we were one of the first completely original local alternative college bands, after the Vertebrats – there was probably no one before them. We were sort of paralleling what the Replacements were doing in Minneapolis without even knowing or hearing of them."[47] By locating his band on a level of importance similar to that of a seminal local band and a nationally prominent band, the musician identified his band as one of local and possibly even national importance, at least within the confines of his narrative.

When contextualizing the production and consumption of independent pop/rock music, localities must be examined, because in the 1980s and early 1990s the production and consumption of alternative music became so closely identified with particular localities. Certain public and private spaces within music scenes provided settings for situated practices such as music performance, music consumption, and social interaction. These subculturally territorialized spaces were the places in which independent pop/rock music (and independent pop/rock music culture) was structured and circulated. Places like record stores, clubs, and bars predictably were sites of alternative music practices; however, within localities *specific* record stores, clubs and bars served as centers of independent pop/rock music subcultural activity within a music scene. Uniform responses were given by most of my interviewees within a locality when they were asked what local establishments they frequented. Among San Franciscans, the list of record stores generally included Rough Trade, Reckless, Aquarius, Revolver, Recycled, Streetlight, and Tower, and the clubs commonly listed were the I-Beam, the DNA Lounge, the Paradise Lounge, Covered Wagon, the Albion, Slim's, and the Kennel Club. Champaign-Urbana, as a much smaller locality than San Francisco, generated a shorter list of establishments: the record stores frequented most by music scene participants were Record Swap or Record Service, though House of the Rising Sound and That's Rentertainment were also named (all four functioned somewhat differently within the market, though all four carried indie rock/pop music in the 1980s and early 1990s and therefore catered to independent pop/rock music scene participants to a much greater degree than large chain stores like Camelot or Musicland.) The venues at which to see bands around 1990 that were mentioned were the Blind Pig and, much less frequently, Mabel's, which was booking fewer "alternative" bands in relation to other sorts of acts.

Intimate knowledge of the public spaces that in part define a local scene is a marker of scene participation, although individual spaces within scenes are meaningful in different ways to different participants. One's familiarity with the nuances of, for instance, live performance venues—the quality of the acoustics, the size of the stage, the geniality of the personnel, the presence or absence of vermin—are part of the store of subcultural knowledge that helps differentiate music scene participants from outsiders. It is important to note, however, that musicians may look at venues primarily in terms of acoustics and management, audience members may look at venues primarily in terms of the ease with which performers can be seen and heard, record labels may look at venues in terms of the number of potential record buyers it can hold, and so on. In other words, what sites of music scene practice mean is largely a function of one's position within the social and economic relations of the scene.

Often there was a general consensus among participants about scene-defining spaces. In Champaign, most agreed that both of the venues that booked alternative bands—Mabel's and the Blind Pig—left something to be desired. Various interviewees described Mabel's as nonsupportive of local, original, and alternative music.[48] On the other hand, complaints about the Blind Pig—a venue that did book local and touring indie pop/rock bands—were common. Overcrowding and ventilation problems were frequently cited. This complaint was typical:

> I've gone to the Blind Pig to see shows, and a lot of the time I just leave, even if it's someone that I want to see. If it's not the smoke, the place is just packed and it's not enjoyable. I'll stay for a couple songs and then just leave.[49]

Clubs, along with independent record stores, are perhaps the most visible sites of interaction within independent pop/rock music scenes. Each provides a different sort of "frame," to use Erving Goffman's term, for social interaction. Goffman's notion of frame is especially useful in looking at how different places within music scenes provide settings for different sorts of social interactions. A frame, according to Goffman, is an identifiable situation that is governed by its own principles of organization; different interactional frames are organized according to different principles (10-11). So, for instance, interactions in clubs operate within a different frame than interactions in record stores. Clubs offer an opportunity for music scene participants and outsiders to gather as an audience to hear live music, and to engage in informal social interaction. Within any locality, there are certain music scene participants that can be counted on to appear at particular shows, and therefore clubs are places at which social relationships within scenes can evolve and be solidified. For those who are not in this network of social relationships (and even for many of those who are) the club framework is a difficult one in which to participate fully. If one knows no one at the show, the frame does not provide that person with anyone with whom to speak: introducing oneself to a stranger in this setting can be quite awkward, and might even be construed as threatening. Because of the noise level in clubs, both when bands are on stage and when recorded music is playing between sets, clubs are difficult environments in which to have conversations and share information.

For someone who was an outsider in an independent pop/rock music scene, an independently owned record store provided a frame more conducive to gaining information about the local scene than a club. The presence of employees behind the cash registers of *all* record stores means that information about recordings or artists is readily available to potential consumers through these employees. The smaller the store, the more accessible the employees are likely to be. Employees at "superstores" like Tower and HMV tend not to be as available to customers for discussions of music as employees at small independent stores. Indie specialty stores provided a framework in which individuals seeking knowledge about independent pop/rock music in general or about the local scene could spend hours looking at records, listening to unfamiliar music on the store's sound system, and talking to employees about music.

In independent stores like Rough Trade and Record Swap that catered specifically to the college/independent/alternative music audience, employees may have been particularly knowledgable about characteristics of the local scene because they participated in it as musicians. This was less true of employees of chain stores in localities that have active music scenes (Camelot in Champaign, for example). It could in fact be said that different types of stores belonged to different types of frames. While it might have been appropriate to ask an employee at Record Swap or Rough Trade whether the new Jesus Lizard record was any good, or what a certain local band, like Champaign's Sidecar Racers or San Francisco's The Grays, sounded like, the same questions in an independent store that catered to a clientele interested in blues music, or in a mall store, probably would not have made sense. This points however to an important observation: indie rock/pop specialty stores were not unlike any other kind of record store. Especially in large localities, there are a number of music scenes (rap, jazz, country, etc.) with independent record stores that fill similar roles as interactional frames. What distinguishes them is both the scenes of which they are part (though there are of course small, independent stores that cater to customers from more than one scene) and the specific musical and social knowledge that is disseminated within the store.[50]

Record stores and clubs were two of the most important sites of social interaction with independent pop/rock music scenes. However, not all sites of independent pop/rock music practice were public places: some were "semi-public" places like college radio stations, independent record label offices, and recording studios. As we have seen, these spaces could be contested sites, places where indie authenticity and commercial pressures, margin and mainstream, came into conflict, even as they were also sites of local practice and had local identities. As social spaces, these places functioned in large part as "workplaces" in which music was produced and circulated and in which interaction took place, but which were not generally available to the public.

Entirely private spaces provided sites for much independent pop/rock music practice as well. Listening to records and the radio, watching videos, talking to others about music, people, and events all could take place in semi-public and private places. Furthermore, within local scenes, some private sites of subcultural practice became publicly known. Houses in which bands and other active music scene members lived often became places to socialize for local insiders. One interviewee recalled that an important way in which he was drawn into the music scene was by living in a house into which three members of various local bands and two record store employees moved.[51] Another interviewee listed the home of a local independent label owner as one of his favorite places to spend time and listen to music.[52] Houses are important practice spaces—all the musicians I interviewed in Champaign-Urbana had rehearsed primarily in houses throughout their careers. And houses could also be performance spaces. In Athens, Georgia, for instance, many of the early important college bands, like the B-52's and R.E.M., performed for the first time in front of audiences at parties. In Champaign, alternative bands like Hot Glue Gun and Lonely Trailer routinely played parties.

In fact, the nature and cost of private and public space within a locality plays an important role in determining whether a local music scene is possible. A musician based in San Francisco explained why it has been difficult for San Francisco to support a music scene, and why towns like Davis, California, in which he formed his first bands while in college, were amenable to the formation of a local scene:

> I think it's really just too expensive in San Francisco for there to be a music scene. It's incredibly expensive to practice. There are clubs everywhere—that's certainly good—but you have to exist and practice too. I had enough trouble with my sort of high-paying computer science job. Lord knows what people who have to subsist off of band money ever do, or people who don't have a college education to justify a fairly high income.

> Davis is a town that doesn't have really high rents, and you can actually rent houses and practice in the houses. There are a couple of little clubs around town—just enough so you can play. A college radio station right in town, so you can walk down with your little band tape and give it to them and get it played on the radio . . .

> Those are the ingredients for a scene. All these little towns like Athens and Austin seem to have these things in common.[53]

The financial possibilities and constraints that existed in localities—especially in terms of the affordability of practice and living space—were central factors in determining whether an active indie pop/rock music scene was possible.

Locating oneself within the physical spaces, social relationships, and history of a local music scene was central in personal narratives of interviewees. Discourse about independent pop/rock music scenes that foregrounds the importance of localities by grouping numerous musicians under descriptions of phenomena like "the Athens scene" or "the Seattle scene" begs the question of the degree to which music produced in localities can be said to express, reflect, and/or reproduce a "local sound." Much indie rock/pop music of the 1980s and 1990s was not recorded on the state-of-the-art equipment available in high-priced recording studios or performed with high-quality sound systems at large venues. Much indie music of the time was recorded on 4-tracks in home recording studios or in relatively inexpensive local commercial recording studios and was performed on locally owned sound systems in clubs. Dependence on locally available and inexpensive sound equipment resulted in the absence of the slick production values that marked much major label music recorded in media capitals like Los Angeles and New York by artists like Madonna and Whitney Houston. Independent music's generally low production values connoted localness, as opposed to urban refinement. Jody Berland makes this point when she argues that Canadian radio stations work to efface markers of "localness" in Canadian recordings by demanding high production values in the Canadian music they program ("Locating" 348). Similarly, American record companies that wanted to "break" alternative artists would generally provide these artists with access to the technical and human resources that make it possible for a record to be produced that would not sound out of place in mainstream AOR, CHR, or "alternative" "Modern Rock" formats.

Although the low production values that characterize much indie/alternative music may be construed as connoting localness, the question of whether any music produced on the media industry's margins reflects the "sound" of a particular locality is open to debate. Some music scene observers maintained that "local sounds" did exist in indie pop/rock. For instance, *Manic Pop Thrill* author Rachel Felder argued:

> A band from North Carolina like Superchunk just sounds right next to local bands like Finger or Polvo; Nirvana makes a good double bill with lesser-known Seattle natives the Melvins and Mudhoney. One region's bands express the feelings, dress, and attitude of that region in a way that another region's bands just can't. (49)

This position has merit. As personal narratives of interviewees indicate, scene participants were for the most part aware of some version of local music history and placed themselves within that tradition, whether it was in Champaign's indie pop scene, San Francisco's punk scene, or Seattle's grunge scene. Bands and audiences were part of social formations in which existing musical practices and traditions impact emerging music. Felder was right to point out that "local bands [are] both influenced by their surroundings and play . . . within them" (14). Locating themselves within a local history of practices helped them define themselves as more authentic, more marginal. As Shane Homan observes in his analysis of music production in Sydney, part of what is important in studying local musical practices is how "mythologies of difference" tied to geographical location have real effects on those who are involved in those musical practices (33).

It would be a leap however to say that because bands influenced and were influenced by the localities with which they were associated that they necessarily embodied a "local sound." Many musicians resented having their music grouped with other music produced in the same locality, contending that their music sounded different. For instance, the tendency to label all alternative Seattle bands "grunge" in the early 1990s came under fire. One Seattle musician complained, "Grunge is sort of a misnomer, because it suggests that all the bands sound alike. I never believed Nirvana sounds like TAD sounds like Mudhoney."[54] And Felder herself had trouble maintaining her position. In the quotation cited above, she stated that Seattle bands like Nirvana expressed the feelings and attitude of their regions; later she changed her mind and argued:

> The real point is that while a band like the Fall reeks of its Manchester home, Nirvana expresses the anger and boredom and depression of living in one of a thousand American towns. And incidentally, to be precise, Nirvana's members are not from Seattle but a smaller town called Aberdeen in Washington [sic].[55] (84)

"Local sound" is an elusive concept because it is a discursive construct. Merely the assertion that a local sound exists leads one to listen for the similarities between bands within a locality: those who seek to find a local sound therefore tend to find it. Sara Cohen contends that "local sounds" are not so much empirical entities as marketing ploys. To quote Cohen, "it also results, perhaps, in the creation and presentation of particular images, sounds, and heritages which marginalize and exclude others" ("Popular" 345). For instance, in Seattle loud "grunge" bands like Nirvana, Pearl Jam, Soundgarden, and Mudhoney came to define the "Seattle sound" in the early 1990s; and perhaps not coincidentally, most of these bands had signed or were in the process of being signed to major labels when discussions of the Seattle music scene became prominent in the mainstream media. Non-grunge Seattle bands like the Posies and Young Fresh Fellows were not generally not taken into consideration in discussions of the "Seattle sound." Likewise, discussion of the Athens music scene in the 1980s and its sound rarely takes into account raucous, non-melodic bands like the Barbeque Killers and the Butthole Surfers. A few groups with similar attitudes and musical styles tend to be seen as defining the "sound" of a locality—R.E.M., the B-52's, and Love Tractor in Athens; the Pixies, Throwing Muses, and Dinosaur, Jr. in Boston; Hüsker Dü, the Replacements, and Soul Asylum in Minneapolis—but a few groups could hardly embody the totality of any locality's "sound."

This is not to deny that there often are similarities between the way bands within any given locality sound. Within music scenes, musicians leave bands and join bands, bands break up and are reformed, and in this process musicians are brought together who have not previously worked together, bringing with them their previous band experiences and musical influences. Over a period of years, as old bands within a scene break up and new bands are formed, the histories of different bands grow evermore entangled. The overlapping paths of musicians in various bands within a local scene undoubtedly results in some similarity in the way these bands sound; however, there are often as many similarities between bands *across* localities as there are among bands *within* localities. Among the bands I listed above, Nirvana may have shared more in common with Soul Asylum in terms of the pop sensibilility of its music than it did with Alice in Chains, and similar arguments could be made about other bands on the list. Indie pop/rock music was not only influenced by intralocal traditions, practices, and social networks: interlocal traditions, practices, and social networks were also integral to the production and circulation of independent pop/rock music, and to the forms of identification through which subjects were located and attempted to locate themselves in the social and physical spaces of alternative music culture.

Interlocal social networks are one of the defining features of local music scenes, and independent pop/rock music scenes in particular.[56] Although most kinds of music scenes are part of interlocal social and economic networks, the low-budget nature of much independent music production (recorded on lo-fi equipment, released on small indie labels) and dissemination (through live performances in clubs, record sales in independent stores and via mail order, airplay on non-commercial radio) made crucial an interlocal social/economic network that was able to aid in the circulation of a band's music to receptive audiences. Two former San Francisco bandmates described how highly valuable these networks could be to a band without major label tour support:

Musician #1: When we started touring, there was a social network that had been set up by R.E.M.'s people when they started touring in 1982 or 1983 that adopted us. And they helped us out so much—we stayed at people's houses. They just passed us along from place to place. That was immensely helpful. They showed us around towns we were unfamiliar with, stuff like that. And by the time we were making enough money to stay in hotels or drive vans around, they would come with us for several shows. It's like an underground community.

Musician #2: The social network is still very important. It provided me with "ins" in the industry, it provided me with places to stay, it provided me with friends. It's a great thing.[57]

The members of many bands relied on interlocal social networks when they toured. And, as a Champaign musician explained, it was sometimes through touring that scene participants became aware of how they were linked to people in other localities:

People come to me asking about certain people in certain towns. Tonight I'm going to go see Die Kreuzen, who we always used to stay with every time we played Milwaukee. If they were in town, they expected to stay with us. We're part of a group where you see someone every six months or every three months, and it's just understood that if they need a place to stay they can stay with someone else in this group. There are lots of people you come in contact with who are in this same boat.[58]

Interlocal neworks such as these, because they brought institutions and people in disparate local scenes together in broader systems of cultural production and dissemination, underscored the degree to which economic structures of indie music articulated with social practices. A *Gavin Report* editor gave another example of the overlap between interlocal economic and social relationships within independent pop/rock music:

You're out there, you're in the music business, you're meeting people from clubs, you're meeting bands, you're meeting managers, you're meeting people at the record stores – people you see at the same shows over and over again, eventually you just start to know them. And eventually, this network forms. It's sort of scary how if you just keep talking with somebody, you know the same people.[59]

A staffer at California-based independent label Alias emphasized how business dealings worked specifically to form interlocal networks:

It's really funny, but with as much local stuff as we do, we end up having to communicate with a lot of people in different parts of the country to get stuff done. I can probably name somebody in every state, in every major city, who either has to do with an indie label, a record company, publishing, or sales.[60]

Interlocal social relationships could be cultivated for business purposes. A San Francisco booking agent used her friendships with people in Los Angeles' alternative music scene to attract Southern California acts to the club at which she worked:

I have a lot of friends in LA, and I've always made a point to be part of that scene and have some kind of visibility there. I don't think other booking agents have made that step. I always make it a point to bands' press people, and that's probably why we get inundated with all kinds of bands calling us from all over the place. A lot from LA.

When I was in law school, it was weird, I met these people at a party at USC law school, and they said, "We've heard of you—you're the one who quit booking live to go to law school." A lot of people knew who I was, which was really kind of weird.[61]

One might argue that these sorts of economic and social networks occur in all businesses and therefore were not specific to independent pop/rock music scenes. However, direct personal connections between people in different localities were particularly characteristic of independent pop/rock music. Independent pop/rock music's grassroots institutions, including micro-indie labels, fanzines, and mail order businesses, were often operated by a very small number of people, and their survival depended on the contacts made within this social/economic network. While independent pop/rock music was too closely tied to the musical mainstream to constitute a true "underground," the systems of independent production and distribution that existed in all independent pop/rock music scenes operated on such a narrow economic margin that participating institutions within a scene and beyond it had a vested interest in supporting like institutions. Cooperation, even among supposed competitors, helped to ensure the continued existence of a network of more or less underground institutions that struggled to maintain an independent existence in the shadow of the mainstream music industry.

For this reason it is not surprising that, as discussed earlier, unlike most businesspeople, individuals involved in independent pop/rock music's institutions of production and dissemination were often loath to describe themselves as competing with others in the same business. Rather than focusing on difference, they pointed to the ways in which they were connected through shared knowledge, interests, and institutions to those one might suppose were their competitors. The owner of a small Champaign-based indie pop label described how he was linked to founders of indie pop labels in other localities, rather than how he was different or separate from them:

The people we deal with who sell our records are the same people that Albert sells his to and that Maz sells his to and that Clint sells his to. We all know each other because we all sell the same stuff and we all deal with the same people. Everybody knows everybody in this little clique. They're all over the country. And we know people in England that do the same stuff, and we know people in Australia that do the same stuff.

If I were to go to San Francisco, I've got a bunch of people I could call that would say, "Oh, you're Geoff from Parasol." And I would know who they are and what kind of music they listen to . . . But you have to find the right people. We could go anywhere and find somebody who knew who we were, but we couldn't just randomly pick people.[62]

He argued that specific networks were often rather small; he said, "Once you go outside your genre of music, it falls apart. If Sub Pop knew who we were, it would be by some weird, freak thing."

These observations demonstrate the importance of thinking of independent pop/rock music's social and economic structures as *overlapping* networks in which genre, geography, position in the independent or alternative music industry, and other factors located subjects within one or more social networks. The circulation of information through these networks enabled a sharing of subcultural knowledge that supported Will Straw's assessment (378) that "points of musical reference are likely to remain stable from one community to another"; the influence in the 1980s of Alex Chilton's early seventies band Big Star on musicians in locations ranging from North Carolina to Illinois to California and even to Scotland bears witness to this. A Champaign indie pop musician felt that he was part of an musical subculture, because, as he put it, "the guys in Velvet Crush, Alan Clapp in California, and I all know these labels that are really small . . . and these great pop songs."[63] Shared musical knowledge, especially within subgenres, was important in the formation and maintenance of interlocal social networks.

Will Straw argues that interlocality makes alternative music scenes somewhat paradoxical; they are part of a "musical cosmopolitanism" that allows the localism that marks their characteristic "small-scale infrastructures of production and dissemination" to be "reproduced, in relatively uniform ways, on a continental and international level" (378). Localism is itself therefore already interlocal. Indeed, locality and interlocality are inseparable: both coexisted within independent pop/rock music scenes in the 1980s and 1990s. Yet I would argue that within these interlocal networks factors like genre, geography, and subject position within webs of social and economic relations are constantly being re-articulated to one another, and therefore indie music scenes were never stable, and they always varied in character from one locality to another.

The specificity of each locality cannot be overlooked. Straw fails to take interlocal differences into account and makes something of an overstatement when he contends that bands find it possible to successfully "circulate from one local scene to another" (378). Variations between localities due to scene histories and current influences—the sorts of "local circumstances" to which Straw refers—mean that the reception of any band or type of music will vary from one local scene to another. Some local scenes are more receptive to indie pop, others to alternative rock, others to hardcore—traditions within local scenes are clearly important in determining how certain types of music are received. In addition, Straw's statement that "the relationship of different local or regional scenes to each other is no longer one in which specific communities emerge to create a forward movement to which others are drawn" is also problematic. The visibility of the Seattle alternative rock scene in the early to mid-1990s and the way that "grunge rock" was identified as the "Seattle sound" contradicts Straw's argument. Specific communities or regions *were* seen as spearheading alternative music movements. In the eighties there was the "jangly," melodic rock of bands from North Carolina and Georgia like R.E.M., Let's Active and the Connells; the psychedelic pop of California bands like the Three O'Clock, Jellyfish, and Dream Syndicate; the hardcore indie rock of Minneapolis bands like Hüsker Dü, Soul Asylum, and the Replacements; and so on.

Ultimately, locality and interlocality were inseparable notions in independent pop/rock music. Local scenes were distinctive because of their differences from other local scenes, yet they were also always linked to other local scenes through the circulation of music, knowledge, and style. These economic and social networks connected even the most economically marginal institutions of independent pop/rock music production and dissemination with the dominant music industry and all of its ancillary structures. Independent pop/rock music scenes were thus sites of interaction that were linked to wider and multiple systems of social power.[64]

Gender in Indie Pop/Rock Music Formations

Indie pop/rock music was also linked to wider systems of social power through its gendered practices. Because of its attempts to remain outside the machinations of the mainstream music industry, it appeared to present opportunities for women and girls not usually available in the field of popular music. Narrative histories of the rise of indie music often note its relative lack of patriarchal power relations and openness to women at all levels. Women's experiences in the culture and economic structures of alternative music, however, often contradicted the common wisdom and suggested that the gendered power relations of mainstream music production and consumption were to a large degree reproduced in indie music culture in the 1980s and 1990s. Within the realm of practice, gender differences that contradicted the notion that a unitary identity could exist among participants in indie pop/rock music scenes were quite evident, and thus were a particular locus of tension and struggle in systems of independent music production, dissemination, and consumption.

The narrative histories of indie music scenes that argue that indie music offered women and girls a space outside the mainstream music industry and rock/pop music culture reflect the experiences of many scene participants. In many ways indie music offered a *relatively* uncolonized space in which girls and women were accepted in non-traditional roles: as musicians, as record label owners and employees, as college radio disc jockeys, as entrepreneurs, as music journalists. Still, since the economic and social structures of indie music did not operate wholly independently of the mainstream music industry, many of the industry's patriarchal structures and practices were reproduced in the relations that governed indie pop/rock's production, distribution, and consumption. The received history of indie pop/rock culture as an egalitarian space was not borne by out by many women's experiences. Indie music, like mainstream rock and pop, remained a primarily male domain.

Personal histories of situated practices are central in understanding the many ways in which women and girls engage with popular music, including indie music. In Britain in the 1970s, and in response to the largely music-oriented and almost wholly male working-class subcultures constructed by cultural studies scholars, Angela McRobbie and Jenny Garber posited female subcultures in which activities centered not around the male-defined domain of "the street" but the female-defined domain of "the bedroom." McRobbie and Garber argued that the bedroom is as important a space as the street; it is the space in which teeny bopper culture is accommodated and in which pop records provide the background music for teenage rituals, as well as for domestic tasks like babysitting and housework ("Girls and Subcultures"). The "bedroom culture" intervention was important, because it not only pointed out that girls and women engage with popular music differently than their male counterparts, but also because it pointed out that girls and women *do* engage with popular music.

This certainly should not be seen as the only way in which girls and women are involved in pop and rock music though. Subjects' lived experiences are crucial to any study that attempts to draw conclusions about cultural contexts and meanings. Stories of these experiences need to be collected because they, in the words of the Personal Narratives Group, "illuminate the significance of the intersection of individual life and historical moment, [and] address the importance of frameworks of meaning through which women orient themselves in the world" (23). In the specific case of pop and rock music, in order to understand both the similarities and the differences between subjects' gendered understandings of rock and pop music culture, we must examine how the practices and relations of this culture are lived by its participants. For instance, as Sue Steward and Sheryl Garratt discovered when they examined female experiences of pop music culture, unlike adolescent boys, who *tend* to talk about the instruments, equipment and equipment used in pop and rock, teenage girls *tend* to talk more about lyrics, about whether a song is danceable, and about the stars themselves. These practices make it more difficult for aspiring female musicians to assimilate into the broader rock culture, because they haven't talked about the music technically and structurally while growing up (110–112). Similarly, Mavis Bayton's study of female rock and pop musicians reveals that unlike male musicians, few women learn to play songs by ear because they lack confidence in their ability to work the songs out, a result of the tendency of adolescent girls not to be part of music-making peer groups. The incentive to learn songs in this way comes only from being in a band. And only when they can identify themselves as musicians do these women feel they can legitimately talk to musicians at shows without being seen as groupies (243 & 254).

In looking specifically at women's experiences within the major record companies, it is not surprising to discover that women in all areas of the mainstream industry complain that they are ghettoized in particular departments, like Publicity. In *Producing Pop*, Keith Negus writes:

> Women I spoke to in both the United States and Britain frequently spoke of the way in which higher management and key decision-making jobs were dominated by an "old boys network" or "boys club"—a milieu in which women were not welcome. (126–127)

It might be reasonable to assume that because independent labels of the 1980s and 1990s, in theory at least, operated outside the mainstream of the music industry, their anti-mainstream philosophy encompassed a rejection of the well-documented sexist practices of the dominant systems of music production and circulation. The DIY ethic embraced by the independent scene, and the notion that indie music was marginal and an outlet for true expression by real people, would indicate that participation was wide open to anyone who wanted to give it a try. Male personal histories of indie music bore this out. A male indie musician and record store manager observed there was something inherent in indie scenes that made them less sexist: "I think there's less gender conflict in alternative music, for some reason. It's just more of a unity."[65] A male former buyer for Rough Trade's distribution arm agreed, saying, "I don't think there's any sexism within the independent music sector . . . a lot of it's just drive," and explained,

> Here's the way I see it. When I started at Rough Trade, everyone [got] paid five bucks an hour. It's not a glamorous thing. People are there because they're really into it and they want to do it. So there's no way to discriminate. If someone really wants to do it, is excited about it, they'll get that job.[66]

Women who worked at independent labels, however, often disagreed with this assessment. A Rhino Records employee did not see much difference between the gender politics of major labels and indies, complaining that

> With record companies, it's all a boys' club. Women in this business are allowed to do one thing; they're allowed to be publicists. The publicity department [at Rhino] is almost ninety percent women. [A&R] is the last place where you'd find women;

and added sarcastically,

> What do women know about music? Give me a break.[67]

Another woman, who left Bomp! records because of the discrimination she faced there and began the Frontier label in 1982, agreed:

> ... people say to me, "I can't think of any women A&R people, I can't think of any women head-of-promo. I'm sure a large part of that is out-and-out sexism. But it might be that women . . . would probably rather do what we do—the isolationist thing—and not have to dirty themselves up with what you've got to do to be. . . . really, really successful in this business.[68]

But the fact is that even women who had little trouble attaining fairly high positions in the independent music business eventually ran into problems that they believed were the result of gender bias. San Francisco–based indie Alias grew quite a bit during the early 1980s and eventually had both male and female employees, but for several months in the early 1990s the label's staff was entirely female. The then-director of college radio promotion and tour coordinator at Alias admitted that this created a rather sheltered environment, but observed that the all-female staff still encountered problems in a male dominated field, most notably in dealing with some male bands:

> A few months ago, we finally had to put our foot down with a band and say, "This song doesn't sound good, and we don't want to put it out. Either you re-mix it or we're not putting it on the record." . . . We really did have to come down and just say, "This was mixed horribly. How many vocal takes did you do?" "Well, one." And they were kind of like, "Tell us exactly what you want."

> Well, of course, technically none of us is qualified to go, "There's too much low end," and they just used that as such a big point against us. . . . It was all of a sudden, "You're not qualified to tell us [what's wrong]." [And we said], "Just because we don't know the technical terms doesn't mean we don't have valid points about not releasing this song."

> We all talked about it here at length and decided there are times that we're going to have to stand firm, and *all* of us are going to have to get behind that person. We were just saying, if there was one guy who was working here who would run into the studio and say, "Hey guys, that part doesn't sound that good," they'd probably reconsider it immediately. [69]

This anecdote points to unequal power relations in independent music production and demonstrates that independent labels were not necessarily a utopia in the 1980s and 1990s for women interested in working at record companies. Indies, however, as places that especially attracted younger men and women to label jobs, might have been one of the first sites at which the traditional structures of gender relations were undermined. Singer Diamanda Galas, who recorded on Mute, claimed, "A lot of the younger guys are more radical thinkers in general. They're not just these music industry idiots—you know, your typical breeder type that gets into the music business to score with women or something."[70] Yet clearly independent labels had much work to do in this area.

Still, within the sphere of music retail, women's personal histories indicated that they ran into fewer problems of discrimination and blatant sexism at independently owned stores than they did at chain stores. For example, a female indie record store owner who formerly worked in the Wherehouse organization, remarked that "when you get into the real large retail companies, women face a lot of limitations. I've just fortunately never experienced them myself." Yet she also noted, without a trace of irony, that "as long as I've gone above and beyond whatever's been expected of me, I've really had few stumbling blocks in my way." Whatever the gender-related problems she encountered in the Wherehouse chain, or avoided by outperforming her male counterparts, she thought it was important to use her position as a business owner to support other female business people: "I, whenever I can, like to utilize other women's services. Our attorney is a woman."[71]

Women also made inroads into the male-dominated music industry as booking agents at clubs that showcased independent music. San Francisco in the late 1980s and early 1990s provided a particularly striking example, because most of the booking agents at San Francisco's alternative clubs at that time were women. Yet despite the prevalence of women, problems still existed. Female booking agents claimed that they were paid less and taken less seriously than their male counterparts and that they were kept out of the male network of promoters, managers, agents and club owners. Sometimes this exclusion affected the kinds of shows that were booked. In San Francisco in the late 1980s, when a group of women who worked in the local indie music scene staged a series of benefits called "Voices for Choice," they ran into resistance. One of the organizers thought that the feminist nature of the benefits made some male scene members leery of participating. She recalled that "There were a lot of people that weren't allowed to participate. Their club owners wouldn't let them because they thought it was too controversial."[72] In many ways, then, while alternative club owners, promoters and agents might have liked to have positioned themselves outside the musical mainstream, their practices often reinscribed the system they disavowed.

Similar problems existed for women who worked at college radio stations, although college radio was certainly a site from which music by female *rock* musicians was disseminated to a much greater degree than mainstream commercial radio stations in the 1980s and 1990s. Female pop music artists were mainstays of commercial radio, but few female rock singers, and even fewer female rock musicians, were played on commercial radio. Those who did receive airplay, like Bonnie Raitt and Heart, tended to play music that fit rather easily in traditional, commercially successful rock genres (i.e. Raitt's blues-rock, Heart's power ballads). Female-

dominated bands like L7, Scrawl, and PJ Harvey, whose music did not follow established rock conventions, became college radio stars even as they were ignored by
commercial radio.

Indeed, college radio stations, as they were popularly constructed in indie music's
received narrative history—student-run stations that served reasonably large campus communities and whose playlists tended to emphasize indie or alternative rock
and pop—were hospitable places for female staffers (more so than for minorities),[73]
but inequities between males and females still existed. Because of the perceived lack
of professionalism at many college stations and the free-form formats professed by
many music directors, it would seem that college radio stations might have been
more likely to allow access to groups traditionally marginalized by the radio industry, like women. And to a degree, this was true. While at college stations there
tended to be, as one former college DJ put it, "a plurality of males over females,"[74]
many women did become program directors and music directors as well as on-air
personalities. KALX's female music director noted that many of KALX's managers
were women, but, in her words, "I'm not sure I could say on air it's fifty-fifty."[75] The
plurality of males over females, which in general was disproportionate compared to
the percentages of males and females in campus populations, certainly bears more
investigation. Why were women less likely to become active in college radio? Was
it because they were socialized to feel uncomfortable using technology, or perhaps
because their experiences of music were often different from men's and less compat-
ible with involvement in college radio, or because of any number of other possible
reasons? Whatever the answers, several people I interviewed involved with college
radio held a fairly optimistic view of gender relations in college radio. When specifically asked about how women fared in college radio environments, interviewees
(especially men) commonly responded with remarks like "College radio is pretty
fair to everybody," and "Everybody's much more willing to treat each other just like
regular people."[76]

Despite these comments, problems of unequal power relations between men and
women were present in college radio, largely because of the numerous ways in
which college radio in the 1980s and 1990s was tied to the broader music industry.
Although some women moved from college radio to positions in the music industry,
this was not necessarily proof of abundant opportunities open to women via college
radio. According to a male former KUSF music director, "The industry bigwigs
aren't saying, 'Oh gee, college radio seems to be doing a lot of good stuff with
women these days. Let's hire a few.' That doesn't happen."[77] And a male KFJC program director cynically added:

> The professional level of the music business is a pretty nicely sexist little place . . . it
> gives women professional experience before they go become secretaries at A&M. It
> is available to women as much as it is also fully available to people who lisp, and

people who can't read, and people who don't know how to follow punctuation. College radio is pretty much open to all these people.[78]

While college radio may have given women reasonably open access to the airwaves, they often found their post-college radio industry prospects less promising than those of their male counterparts.

The women I talked to who were involved in college radio agreed that the power many of them exercised at their stations was not indicative of the state of affairs in the music industry as a whole. Ultimately, in both the mainstream industry and the structures of college music, the white male hegemony prevailed, as one woman who was a music director at a Bay Area college station stated:

> The record industry and I think for the most part the college radio scene are pretty much run by white people and largely male-dominated. I think it's pretty much men calling the shots. There are women [in college radio], and there's definitely more of a space for women, people of color, gay people, that are marginalized elsewhere . . . but it's not Mecca. I think the standards are still set by society's norms—we all come from that anyway, even if we are on the edge, or indie, or whatever.[79]

As she implied, the interrelationship between the marginal practices and institutions of college music, the mainstream music industry, and society in general meant that indie music in the 1980s and 1990s could never be outside the dominant ideology of music production and dissemination. The gendered experiences of practices and institutions within indie music formations demonstrated the degree to which college music's social and economic structures, despite their professed "independence" from the mainstream, reproduced patriarchal relations and to a degree circumscribed the possibilities of women and girls within them.

Subjects within indie music scenes were multiply positioned by their generic identifications, by their senses of local identity, by overlapping social and economic relationships, by their understanding of the narrative history of indie music, by a constellation of situated practices, and by gender identity. Such multiple positioning within social and economic networks, locality and interlocality, and personal and popular memory underscores the need for conjunctural analysis of formations like indie pop/rock music scenes. Indie music production, dissemination, and social relations were sites of continual negotiation, and rearticulation. The complexity of this case study points to the need to rethink some of the ways in which cultural formations have traditionally been analyzed.

CHAPTER 6

Theorizing Independent Music Formations

The existence of the indie pop/rock formations described in the previous chapters indicates a broader need in popular music studies, and media studies as a whole, to address the complicated nature of the web of personal, social, historical, geographical, cultural, and economic relations and identifications involved in the processes of production and consumption. This study has tried to look in detail at several of these elements in an attempt to address a tradition of audience analyses that failed to examine institutional and ideological apparatuses, and industry analyses that posited simplistic models of participants in production and consumption. It is also posed as an alternative to the textual analysis approach to the study of popular texts: not that such interpretations are not valuable, but the personal narratives of those involved in the networks that create, disseminate and engage with these texts are also valuable. Pierre Bourdieu's notions of "habitus" and "fields of practice" are particularly useful in looking at independent music scenes as social, cultural, economic, and local phenomena. As this study has demonstrated, indie music formations were characterized by deeply intertwined local and interlocal social and economic networks that make a complex understanding of these relations, and of the personal narratives of the participants and the broader historical narratives associated with indie music, of primary interest.

Scene vs. Community vs. Art World

The terminology used to describe social and cultural formations plays a key role in determining the objects of interest examined by the researcher. For this reason I chose the term "scene" because "scenes," as I have discussed them, encompass both the geographical sites of localized musical practice and the social and economic networks that exist within these contexts. Instead of the concepts of "community" and "world," Will Straw proposes that "scene" be used to describe the interrelationship of musical practices within a geographical space. Straw describes a musical scene as that cultural space in which a range of musical practices coexist, interacting with each other within a variety of processes of differentiation, and according to widely varying trajectories of change and cross-fertilization. (373)

I believe that "musical practices" should not refer narrowly to the particular activities of musical composition, performance, and appreciation, but also must include the range of economic and social practices through which music is created and circulated within and across localities.

"Scene" is preferable to two other terms often used to describe similar formations: "community" and "world." "Community" is inappropriate: although communal feelings and shared musical practices exist within music scenes, they do not necessarily constitute a community. Will Straw objects to the use of the word "community" because it

presumes a population group whose composition is relatively stable—according to a wide range of sociological variables—and whose involvement in music takes the form of an ongoing exploration of one or more musical idioms said to be rooted in a geographically specific historical heritage. (373)

Straw's interpretation of music "community" seems to coincide with the way that "community" has been traditionally conceptualized within social science: as an observable "social fact" that can be measured through an examination of constituent parts (A. Cohen 71). Even if Straw does not mean to indicate that this is how he sees "community," the definition he puts forth alludes to the baggage that the word "community" carries with it. Sociologists in the early twentieth-century—including Chicago School sociologists like Robert Park and Louis Wirth, and German sociologist Ferdinand Tonnies—tended to contrast the small, stable, integrated "community" (Gemeinschaft) with the large, impersonal, alienating city (Tonnies' "association" or Gesellschaft) (Giddens 95-100). The residual connotation of stability and integration which remains from this sociological tradition makes "community" an unsatisfactory word to apply to indie music formations, which tend to be fragmented along lines of genre, age, gender and so on,[1] and in which individual participation is often transient.

One might accept that the connotations of stability, integration, and—to go back to Straw's definition—geographical delimitation, are no longer strongly associated with "community": indeed, while geographical constraints may have traditionally been characteristic of "communities," the word "community" is now often used to describe groups whose members are located at disparate physical sites, and there is a growing body of research on "virtual communities" formed by computer networks. Yet one might also question whether tangible communities of any sort actually exist. Anthony Cohen argues that communities cannot be understood as observable social facts, as givens that can be fully comprehended and explained through the examination of constituent parts. He contends:

Community exists in the minds of its members, and should not be confused with geographic or sociographic assertions of "fact." By extension, the distinctiveness of communities and, thus, the reality of their boundaries, similarly lies in the mind, in the meanings which people attach to them, not in their structural forms . . . the reality of community is expressed and embellished symbolically. (98)

In doing my research, I did not specifically ask interviewees whether they thought they were part of an indie music "community" and if so, what constituted that community and what specifically was meaningful within this community. I agree with Sara Cohen's argument that communities are constructed symbolically amongst their members, and thus I do not believe "community" is an appropriate label of the subject of my research.

An alternative to "community" used in some research is the term "world." In her study of music making in Milton Keynes, Ruth Finnegan calls local networks of music-makers and audiences "musical worlds." Finnegan borrows the term from sociologist Howard Becker, who uses the more general term "art world" to describe the people and practices associated with any artistic production. Art worlds

consist of all the people whose activities are necessary to the production of the characteristic works which that world, and perhaps others as well, define as art. Members of art worlds coordinate the activities by which work is produced by referring to a body of conventional understandings embodied in common practice and in frequently used artifacts. (Becker 34)

Finnegan uses the idea of a "world" to apply both to those worlds constituted in people's interactions within a local context and to those largely symbolic worlds that link individuals across local boundaries by means of shared knowledge, taste, and belief (188), although apparently not through direct or indirect social and/or economic relations. The concept of a "musical world" thus becomes rather slippery, and the word "world," with its all-encompassing connotations, is not well-suited to describing the relationships between people and practices located in different geographic areas, since presumably people in different localities could at once belong to the same musical world and to different musical worlds. The term "scene," as Straw discusses it, grounded in the idea of shared sets practices and shared cultural spaces, was thus the term of preference in this analysis.

Popular Music Studies

Historically, much scholarly work on popular music consumption is constituted by readings of musical texts. Musicologists, for instance, examine the musical structures of pop and rock songs. According to Susan McClary and Robert Walser, "The chords, melodic contours, and metric structures must be grasped analytically or else one has no way of addressing how in material terms the music manages to 'kick butt'" (290). Conversely, analysts rooted in literary theory produce readings of popular music texts and phenomena, as in this example by Simon Reynolds:

> But the whole discourse of noise [music]-as-threat is bankrupt, positively inimical to the remnants of power that still cling to noise. Forget subversion. The point is self-subversion, overthrowing the power structure in your own head. The enemy is the mind's tendency to systematize, sew up experience, place a distance between itself and immediacy. The American bands understand this, instinctively. (*Blissed* 59)

Both musicological and literary forms of interpretation place the writer in a privileged position in which s/he presumes to possess the tools to uncover what the music really means. Pierre Bourdieu argues that semiotic approaches such as these are inherently flawed because

> The semiologist, who claims to reveal the structure of a literary or artistic work through so-called strictly internal analysis, exposes him or herself to a theoretical error by disregarding the social conditions underlying the production of the work and those determining its functioning. (*Field* 140)

Semiotic and institutional analyses are by themselves inadequate for understanding cultural production in general and indie pop/rock music scenes in particular. In the case of indie scenes examined here, not only were these formations important sites of musical production and innovation, they were implicated in complex social and economic networks, and they were sites of often inseparably circular practices of production and consumption. Because these networks were composed of fans, musicians, college and community radio disc jockeys, record label staffers, record store employees, and so on, theories which rest on assumptions of the separate roles of consumers and producers are inadequate to explain the complicated processes that took place both within and across indie music scenes. Only a very few studies have attempted to explain and contextualize such local popular music practices, and many studies have tended not to investigate interlocal practices that are equally meaningful.[2] What studies by scholars such as Ruth Finnegan, Sara Cohen, and Barry Shank recognize is that music in local (or any) settings cannot be understood as merely "meaning" in its lyrics; meanings are inextricably linked to the music's contexts and social uses.

This book has not presented the formations that it describes as subcultures, in the sense of the research on subcultures that came out of the Centre for Contemporary Cultural Studies in the 1970s. Socioeconomic class was not at the center of my analysis. Within indie pop/rock music scenes, social spaces are often inseparable from the spaces of economic production and consumption, and the social roles of participants cannot be understood outside of their economic roles. While subcultural theory is based in a set of assumptions about the relationship between a particular economic system—capitalism—and a particular social structure, the microeconomics of subcultural youth formations are rarely (if ever) explored.

Nor in this book was participation in indie music's social, cultural, and economic practices seen necessarily as a way as to resist dominant power. Those who make such arguments about audiences' various forms of engagement with popular culture tend to use the term "resistance" somewhat loosely, implying but not demonstrating a conscious politics of resistance on the part of the marginalized pop culture consumers under study.

Ultimately, popular culture consumption is never independent of capitalist power. Even fan reappropriations of pop culture artifacts serve capitalist logic by distributing capitalist products to wider audiences. It is important to keep in mind that under capitalism, consumption is to some degree structured. Within popular music, genres, conventions, economic practices, and other institutionalized norms work to maintain the ideological dominance of the leisure apparatus that is already in place. When looking at the economic, historical, social and cultural dimensions of indie music formations, one must remember that tactics that appear resistant can in fact illustrate the degree to which capitalism constrains music scene participants and alternative music fans in general. Frith notes, for instance, that it is "because they lack power that the young account for their lives in terms of play, focus their politics on leisure" (*Sound Effects*, 201). The hegemonic forces that seek to contain revolution in the political arena at the same time package it for leisurely consumption: in the late 1980s and even still today, sometimes in the form of the "resistant" music of indie or alternative rock. Moreover, without dominant, mainstream musics against which to react, independent music cannot be independent. Its existence depends upon dominant music structures and practices against which to define itself. Indie music has therefore been continually engaged in an economic and ideological struggle in which its "outsider" status is re-examined, re-defined, and re-articulated to sets of musical practices. The webs of economic and social relationships that in part structured intra- and inter-local indie music scenes and the practices that held together these networks of often contradictory relationships were thus of central interest in my study.

Fields of Practice

Because of the complex relationships involved, a study of indie music scenes can certainly benefit from Bourdieu's emphasis at all levels of analysis on both social and institutional factors. In order to understand any form of musical (or indeed, cultural) product, it is inadequate to examine texts in isolation from the extra-textual social and historical conditions of their production (Garnham and Williams 215; *Field* 11 & 19).

At all sites of cultural practice, including sites of indie pop/rock music practices, social and economic practices of consumption and production are virtually inseparable. Social interactions take place at places of economic production; economic relationships often also serve as meaningful social relationships. Indie pop/rock music scenes cannot be understood independent of their social or economic practices, and Pierre Bourdieu's work on "fields" and the practices of cultural production and consumption is particularly useful in understanding this. According to Bourdieu, any social formation is made up of several "fields" of practice—including the economic field, the political field, the educational field, and the cultural field (where the practices of indie music scenes would largely be found)—which are hierarchically organized. These fields provide the contexts, the sets of objective social relations, in which agents act. As Randal Johnson explains of fields:

> Each field is relatively autonomous but structurally homologous with the others. Its structure, at any given moment, is determined by the relations between the positions agents occupy in the field. A field is a dynamic concept in that a change in agents' positions necessarily entails a change in the field's structure. (6)

A field therefore enjoys a degree of autonomy from other fields; at the same time, all fields in a social formation must be understood in relation to a set of social conditions that are best explained by Bourdieu's notion of the "habitus." According to Bourdieu, a habitus is a system of:

> durable, transposable dispositions, structured structures predisposed to function as structuring structures, that is, as principles which generate and organize practices and representations that can be objectively adapted to their outcomes with presupposing a conscious aiming at ends or an express mastery of the operations necessary in order to attain them. Objectively "regulated" and "regular" without being in any way the product of obedience to rules, they can be collectively orchestrated without being the product of the organizing action of a conductor. (*Outline* 72)

As Nicholas Garnham and Raymond Williams describe it, "The habitus is not just a random series of dispositions but operates according to a relatively coherent logic, what Bourdieu calls the logic of practice. . . . [it] is a unified phenomenon. It produces an ethos that relates all the practices produced by a habitus to a unifying set of principles" (213). A habitus can, in Johnson's words, "generate practices in multiple and diverse fields of activity . . . [and these practices] inevitably incorporate the objective conditions of their inculcation" (5). Thus, while fields, such as the cultural and the economic, may be relatively autonomous (e.g. the process of popular music composition is relatively autonomous from the process of major label mass marketing), they are linked by sets of practices, or logics of practice, incorporated into a habitus and enacted across fields.

We can usefully speak in this instance, as Bourdieu does, of specific class habitus. The idea of class habitus, however, is not sufficient to explain production, consumption, and social practice in indie music scenes: generation, gender, and ethnicity also help shape indie music contexts. But Bourdieu's work is relevant to the study of indie music formations because he is not particularly interested in merely cataloging patterns of cultural consumption according to class habitus, although this is one aspect of his research. Rather, he is interested in a broader understanding of how a range of cultural practices is linked to a range of habitus (Garnham and Williams 214).

Fields and habitus intersect at a number of sites and in a number of practices. For Bourdieu, most actions "are the product of an encounter between a habitus and a field; that is, between two more-or-less completely adjusted histories" (*Field* 91). When the habitus and the field are largely, to use Bourdieu's term, "in agreement," the individual agent implicated in both need not resort to rational calculation in order to choose an action. The unconscious dispositions of the habitus provide satisfactory guidance. Bourdieu uses the example of the relationship between writers and the publishing industry to illustrate the interaction between habitus and field. In Bourdieu's example, in order to select the publishers to whom to send their manuscripts, authors envision specific publishers as occupying specific positions within the space of the publishing industry. Authors therefore target certain publishers with their manuscripts, based on their perceptions of their own writings and on their images of the publishers. At publishing houses the manuscripts are, as Bourdieu explains,

> coloured from the outset by a series of determinations (e.g. "interesting but not very commercial," or "not very commercial, but interesting") stemming from the relationship between the author's position in the field of production (unknown author, consecrated author, house author, etc.) and the publisher's position within the system of production and circulation ("commercial" publisher, consecrated or avant-garde). . . Because subjective intentions and unconscious dispositions contribute to the efficacy of the objective structures to which they are adjusted, their interlacing tends to guide agents to their "natural niche" in the structure of the field. (*Field* 134)

The dispositions of the habitus of the author therefore lead him/her to a publishing house which is the product of a similar habitus and which should be most amenable to publishing his/her work.

The interrelationship between habitus and field in musical production works much like the publishing example described by Bourdieu. Musicians perceive certain record labels as being positioned within the domain of music production in a way that would tend to mark those labels as favorably or unfavorably disposed toward the music of particular artists. For instance, a little-known Midwestern artist who composes and plays melodic, guitar-oriented "indie pop" music might see Parasol in Champaign, Illinois as the ideal label for his/her music. Parasol, as a small independent label that largely specializes in melodic pop, would be more inclined to put out a record by an unknown artist working in this genre than a major label like Sony. Within the sub-field of indie pop music production, as in all fields of cultural production, perceptions of the positions of various agents by various other agents— and the positions themselves—are products of essentially unconscious dispositions and adjustments that tend to steer agents toward their "natural niches" within a specific field.

When thinking of indie pop/rock music as part of the field of cultural production, it is especially useful to consider Bourdieu's notion of the "field of restricted production." This field is a subdivision of the field of cultural production (Bourdieu places it in opposition to the "field of large-scale production"), and one form of field into which habituses are incorporated. Although when Bourdieu writes of the field of restricted production he is referring to the production of what is commonly considered "high art," in fact, the concept of "production for producers" or, slightly more broadly, production not intended for a large-scale market (Johnson 7), is applicable to many areas of cultural production, including indie music. Bourdieu sees the field of restricted cultural production as characterized by an

> almost perfect circularity and reversibility of the relations of cultural production and consumption resulting from the objectively closed nature of the field of restricted production enable the development of symbolic production to take on the form of an almost reflexive history. (*Field* 118)

This inseparability of production and consumption posited by Bourdieu exists in indie music scenes, where it can be virtually impossible to distinguish cultural producers from consumers, since many scene participants simultaneously occupy both positions in social space.

The field of restricted production is also characterized by the following set of values described by Randal Johnson: "Economic profit is normally disavowed (at least by the artists themselves), and the hierarchy of authority is based on different forms of symbolic profit, e.g. a profit of disinterestedness, or the profit one has on seeing oneself (or being seen) as one who is not searching for profit" (15). Indeed, individuals involved in the production of college music, including musicians, record label owners and employees, and college radio staff, tended to espouse this same lack of interest in profit and popularity. Individuals involved in the underground of small "micro-indie" labels certainly saw themselves as part of a field of restricted cultural production. They catered to very small audiences of highly knowledgeable consumers, many of whom were themselves producers of sorts (e.g. musicians, fanzine editors, small label and record storeowners, college radio staffers).

The celebration of non-commerciality within indie music points to a weakness in Bourdieu's conceptualization of the terrain of cultural production. The subfields of large-scale production and restricted production defined by Bourdieu are presented as distinct; however, as the case of indie pop/rock music production demonstrates, such distinctions are not always easy to make. Within the broad domain of alternative music production over the past two decades, one finds both commercially successful major label acts that began on independent labels and whose work reaches a mass audience, and little-known, non-commercially successful, independent label acts whose work is known to a small number of individuals. Between these two extremes were artists who were neither widely known nor terribly obscure, and who did not operate solely within one or the other sub-field of cultural production described by Bourdieu. Certain forms of music and practice (for example, vinyl pop singles on "micro-indie" labels which only sold a few hundred copies) were better able than others to maintain a distance from large-scale cultural production.

Independent pop and rock music production (and, I would argue, almost any field of cultural production in a capitalist society), even at its most underground levels, has never been fully autonomous from the economic field. In every field, argues Bourdieu, there is a relative mix of economic capital and specific forms of cultural knowledge, competences and/or dispositions—"cultural capital"[3]—that positions individual agents hierarchically in social space (see *In* 128). Bourdieu therefore does not grant the economic field determinative power over other fields. At the same time, he argues that economic and institutional structures are highly influential within cultural production. As Johnson explains of Bourdieu's theory,

> Literature, art and their respective producers do not exist independently of a complex institutional framework which authorizes, enables, empowers and legitimizes them. This framework must be incorporated into any analysis that pretends a thorough understanding of cultural goods and practices. (10)

Although the reference is not specifically to economic institutions, such structures are clearly part of the framework of cultural production with which Bourdieu is concerned. Indeed, Bourdieu must take economic relations into account, because his method is intended to explain structures and processes of cultural production on three levels of social reality at which economic institutions of cultural production and dissemination are salient: (1) the position of the particular artistic field within the dominant relations of power in society, which he calls the field of power; (2) the positions and characteristics of the agents within the structure of the specific artistic field; and (3) the cultural producers' habituses (*Field* 14).

Moreover, Bourdieu contends that within any social/historical context one cannot simply attempt to study the broad social groups that in part constitute it, but one must also examine the social relationships that help position individual agents in social space ("Social Space" 723). According to Bourdieu, "To speak of a social space means that one cannot group just anyone with anyone while ignoring the fundamental differences, particularly economic and cultural ones" (726). Bourdieu also allows that differences between individuals and groups besides economic and cultural differences can be important. He argues that "The social world may be described and constructed in different ways in accordance with different principles of vision and division, and that we are socialized to recognize the relationships between particular practices and particular positions in social space" (*In* 132). Understanding any local music scene requires a study of both positions in social space and social practices. Ruth Finnegan points to the centrality of social relationships in music scenes when she writes:

> The pathways of musical practice involve people in a series of cumulatively overlapping social relationships. These in turn relate them both to each other and, through the series of personal networks, institutional links, and social order of space and time necessarily implicated in each of these pathways, to other elements in social life. This extends not just within a single town but also much more broadly to national institutions and the many country-wide musical worlds and their pathways. (329)

Finnegan's description of the ways in which subjects are implicated, through social relationships and practices within localities, in interconnected regional and national (and, I would argue, international) social and institutional networks is quite applicable to the study of indie pop/rock music.

In addition to social relationships, any number of practices by music scene participants in the localities I examined—what sorts of music they bought and where they bought it, with whom they socialized, whether and where they attended live performances, whether they were in bands and what sorts of music their bands played, whether they worked at record stores or college radio stations, what sort of clothes they wore, and so on—positioned them relatively as participants or non-participants in a music scene, and also helped position them within the social space of the scene. Bourdieu's work emphasizes the central role played by specific practices within a cultural field in which individuals inside (and sometimes outside) the field make distinctions about the legitimacy of any individual agent's participation.

In recent years "practice" has become a more prominent concept in critical analyses of social and cultural structures and processes. Angela McRobbie has argued for the need to study "identities in practice" and to integrate such study into broader analyses of social formations (730). Within popular music studies, a fair amount of research has focused on social and cultural practice with notable contributions by

Mavis Bayton, who examines the practices through which women become, and come to identify themselves as, musicians; Ruth Finnegan, who looks at the practice of music-making across a wide variety of musical genres in Milton Keynes; and Sara Cohen, who focuses on two bands in her study of the situated practices of rock culture in Liverpool. The latter two works are of particular note, because they not only foreground the study of practice, they also foreground issues of space in general and locality in particular. For Finnegan and Cohen, the study of musical practices is the study of located (and local) practices.

Indeed, one weakness in Bourdieu's work is his failure to adequately acknowledge the interrelationship between geographic space and social practices and processes. Although Bourdieu makes occasional reference to the relationship of social space to geographical space, he does not fully explore the intersection of these two vectors. The importance of physical space to the practices and social relationships of indie pop/rock music scenes cannot be overemphasized. As much as music scenes are social spaces delineated by social practices, they are also local spaces, so questions of the role played by locality must be addressed in any study of indie music formations. Geographer Doreen Massey notes that how we think of spaces and places is integral to how we experience and conceptualize the world ("Politics" 143). Positioning in social space cannot be viewed outside of physical or geographical space, since, just as space is socially constructed, so, in Massey's words, is "the social is spatially constructed" (146). Specifically, Massey contends:

> . . . we need to conceptualize space as constructed out of interrelations, as the simultaneous coexistence of social interrelations and interactions at all spatial scales, from the most local level to the most global . . . [conversely], all social phenomena/activities/relations have a spatial form and a relative spatial location . . . The spatial spread of social relations can be intimately local or expansively global, or anything in between . . . there is no getting away from the fact that the social is inexorably also spatial. (155)

In looking at the local, regional, national, and international social and economic networks that constituted indie music formations, I have argued that the relationships and practices of indie music scenes both created and were created by constructs of locality and interlocality.

It is not enough, however, to locate indie pop/rock music scenes within spaces and places; they must also be understood within historical moments, and specifically within the social, cultural, economic, political, and spatial relations that constitute the present conjuncture.[4] Conjunctures are fluid. Pierre Bourdieu, for instance, is careful to historically locate many of his examples of cultural production, but his discussion of historical contexts tends to privilege the reproduction of social and economic structures rather than historical change. Garnham and Williams argue that the process of reproduction encompasses not only "replication," which they rightly indicate is the sense in which Bourdieu thinks of reproduction, but also "reformation," which "points us towards the spaces that are opened up in conjunctural situations in which the dominant class is objectively weakened . . ." and which allows for shifts in the social structure and the alignment of entities in social space to take place (222–223). Therefore, while it is crucial to take into account the specificities of cultural, social, and economic practices when studying indie music scenes, it is also crucial that these practices be understood within the context of a highly specific set of conjunctural relations.

In the 1980s and early-1990s, the socioeconomic and cultural context in the United States was characterized by a recognition of the limits of economic opportunity for members of all races and social classes.[5] Christine Griffin cites the Center on Budget and Policy Priorities when she states that

> The USA entered the 1980s with many of its citizens experiencing a worse standard of living than thirty years previously. Severe cuts in social and welfare programmes and in public housing projects, and rising poverty levels, produced a situation in which young people, and especially working-class young people and young people of colour, were suffering more than at any time since the Second World War. (33)

Although such social and economic shifts were primarily felt by the working and lower classes, their impacts were felt throughout the social structure, including by the largely white, largely middle-class participants in local indie music scenes. Angela McRobbie argued that British youth, including middle-class youth, in the 1980s and early 1990s had been impacted by "Deindustrialization, class realignment, the changing place of women, and the consolidation of black people at the bottom end of the labour hierarchy" ("Shut Up," 412). Certainly the general conditions of deindustrialization and of social and class realignment to which McRobbie points in Great Britain were also present in the United States. However, as Griffin argues, features that distinguish the two societies mean that conditions in the United States and Britain cannot be conflated. She writes:

> The rise of the New Right is common to 1980s Britain and the USA, but the pattern of youth unemployment, the diversity of the two labour markets, variations between British and US economic and political systems, welfare provision and educational institutions all contribute to the many differences between Thatcher's Britain and Reagan's USA. Forms of opposition, negotiation, and survival have also varied on both sides of the Atlantic. (199)

An example of how young people in the two countries react differently to a similar set of conditions within similar, but not identical, conjunctures is presented in McRobbie's analysis of British rave culture. In both the U.S. and Great Britain, young people face certain dangers ("drugs, cigarettes, alcohol, unprotected sex, sexual violence and rape, ecological disaster") and demands (to be responsible in their sexual behavior, to be good citizens and act on issues of social and political issues of relevance to them, to earn a living wage, to marry, and to raise a functional family) (422). McRobbie explains that many British youths have dealt with these pressures by escaping into the style (aerobics gear combined with props of childhood, like pacifiers), drugs (Ecstasy), and music (acid house and techno dance musics) of rave culture, which never gained widespread popularity in the United States but which creates a social, cultural, and physical space of avoidance and abandonment.

Although "rave" culture did not become as widely adopted by youth in the U.S. as it was by those in Britain, a dynamic similar to that of rave resonated through youth culture/subcultures in United States in the 1990s. Indie music formations in the United States, like the British youth (specifically rave) subcultures described by McRobbie, exhibited economic, social, and cultural tendencies to both operate outside the mainstream (as in rave culture) and to be part of it (as in the desire to make skills of subcultural production marketable). On one hand, indie music culture in the 1980s and early 1990s posited its institutions, generic conventions, and, to a lesser degree, style as somehow "authentic," and, if not oppositional, then at least alternative to mainstream popular music culture; but on the other hand, participants in indie music culture were aware of the numerous ways in which indie pop/rock music was implicated in hegemonic economic and cultural structures. The tension between these two recognitions was manifested in the everyday situated practices of participants in local music scenes of San Francisco, California, and Champaign-Urbana, Illinois interviewed for this study, and was played out, on economic, cultural, social, and spatial fronts.

While this book has striven to be empirical in its method, whenever one attempts to construct an ethnographic and/or historical account of a social phenomenon, one engages in a highly interpretive activity. For instance, this book began with a history of indie music derived from interview data and archival records. However, we must keep in mind that while the project of uncovering the "true" history of indie music is tempting, it is impossible. Traditionally, ethnographic and historical narratives have been presented as accounts of what "really" happens or has happened. In discussing ethnographic writing practices, Mary Louise Pratt underscores a central problem in ethnographic and historical discourse:

> . . . one still hears expressed as an ideal for ethnography a neutral, tropeless discourse that would render other realities "exactly as they are," not filtered through our own values and interpretive schema. (27)

Of course Pratt's point is that such a discourse is impossible. Precisely because all data gathered in social scientific endeavors like history and ethnography are filtered through our own values and interpretive schema, events can never be depicted exactly as they occur or occurred.

One way in which we can see individual interpretive schema at work among participants in indie music scenes is by noting that events in individuals' lives take on great significance in retrospect when tied to events that brought indie music to the attention of mainstream institutions and audiences. For instance, one person whom I interviewed pointed out that the independent music scene in Athens, Georgia began to achieve national recognition at the same time he began working at an independent record store. Another interviewee emphasized that she worked at the University of San Francisco's college radio station, KUSF, at a time when several people who achieved prominent positions in various arms of the alternative music industry emerged from the station.

Observations like these point to the necessity of collecting and reporting life stories in accounts of musical forms and their cultures, and in accounts of engagement with all cultural forms in order to effectively illustrate the roles played by economic, social, cultural and spatial practices. Indie music scenes, and the identifications of their participants, are constituted by disparate elements that can only be understood by looking at webs of relations, and at popular narratives and personal histories. The themes that have recurred throughout this analysis are most certainly recurrent themes found in other social and cultural formations, and are worthy of further complex investigation.

Notes

Chapter 2: Telling the Story of Independent Music

1. *Spin College Music Report* April 1991: 3.
2. Personal interview, 16 July 1991.
3. Personal interview, 19 December 1991.
4. Personal interview, 30 December 1991.
5. Personal interview, 16 July 1991.
6. *Spin College Music Report* April 1991: 3.
7. As David Hesmondhalgh notes in the case of the U.K., "'Indie,' the term increasingly used in the British music press from the mid-1980s onwards, started to become a genre—a sound and a look—as much as an economic category" (270).
8. Barry Simons, personal interview, 2 August 1990.
9. Susie Racho, personal interview, 1 August 1990.
10. Jonathan Segal, personal interview, 31 July 1990.
11. Linda Ryan, personal interview, 2 August 1990.
12. Felder claimed that each alternative music sub-genre had a distinct look. She asserted, "Just as male and female miasma fans dress the same, in loose t-shirts and jeans . . . fans of American guitar bands have a specific look. De rigueur fashions for grunge fans include Doctor Marten boots . . . and over a t-shirt . . . a lumberjack shirt . . ." (88). Though there may be tendencies among fans of certain genres to dress in certain ways, the uniforms described by Felder were in no way "de rigueur"; there were many grunge fans who did not own Doc Martens or flannel shirts, and many "miasma fans" who wore things other than loose t-shirts and jeans.
13. Mike Levy, personal interview, 15 July 1991.
14. 1992, p. 3.
15. *NBC Nightly News* 9 June 1994.
16. Gail Countryman, personal interview, 16 July 1991.
17. Scott Miller, personal interview, 2 August 1990.
18. Geoff Merritt, personal interview, 19 December 1991.
19. Adam Schmitt, telephone interview, 17 June 1992.
20. Geoff Merritt, personal interview, 19 December 1991.
21. The Popular Memory Group observes that popular memory works most powerfully when it unites people in beliefs about social improvement or decline (248). A narrative of indie music such as this which situates the genre's aesthetic peak in the mid-eighties and

its decline in the late eighties and early nineties mirrors the way in which popular memory as articulated by the mass media—perhaps most explicitly in Donald L. Bartlett and James B. Steele of the *Philadelphia Inquirer's* series of articles and subsequent book *America: What Went Wrong?*—constructs that period of time in the United States in economic terms. Notions of rise and decline play an important role in popular memory.

22. Bill Barol, et al., "Rock Around the U.S.A," *Newsweek* 16 June 1986: 70–71.

23. Jonathan Segal, personal interview, 31 July 1990.

24. Anita Rivas, personal interview, 16 July 1991.

25. Scott Miller, personal interview, 2 August 1990.

26. Victor Kummenacher, personal interview, 31 July 1990.

27. Geoff Merritt, personal interview, 19 December 1991.

28. Mike Levy, personal interview, 15 July 1991.

29. Barry Simons, personal interview, 2 August 1990.

30. *Spin College Music Report,* April 1991: 20.

31. Gail Countrymen, personal interview, 16 July 1991.

32. Susie Racho, personal interview, 1 August 1990.

33. Linda Ryan, personal interview, 2 August 1990.

34. Craig Marks, et al., "A to Z of Alternative Music," *Spin* February 1993: 40.

35. Andy Schwartz, "6IX 4OR 82: R.E.M.," *New York Rocker* January 1982, 49.

36. Barol et al. 70.

37. Both of the well-known Minneapolis indie acts that signed early to major labels—Hüsker Dü and the Replacements—disbanded. Soul Asylum, a Minneapolis band which put out its debut album in 1984 on the independent Twin/Tone label, achieved chart success with a *Billboard* Top Ten single in 1993, seven years after the band was featured in the *Newsweek* article.

38. Jeff Evans, personal interview, 19 December 1991.

39. Victor Kummenacher, personal interview, 31 July 1990.

40. Interviewed in *MAXIMUMROCKNROLL* July 1992: 76.

41. Ted Friedman, "Graduates of College Rock," *Spin College Music Report* April 1992: 16.

42. Various excerpts from Samual Nathan Schiffman, "Nirvanification," *MAXIMUMROCK-NROLL* July 1992: 101–102.

43. Marks 46,

44. "Rockbeat: Lollapalosers," *Village Voice* 18 August 1992: 78.

45. The attraction of alternative music for advertisers is described in Stuart Elliott, "Alternative Music is Piquing Interest as a Marketing Tool," *New York Times* 21 August 1992: n.p.

46. "College Music Round-Up," *Spin Guide to College Music* April 1992: 4.

47. David Fricke, "R.E.M.'s Southern-Fried Art," *Rolling Stone* 7 November 1985: 50, and Tony Fletcher, *Remarks: The Story of R.E.M.* (New York: Bantam Books, 1990) 46.

48. Quoted in Jeff Tamarkin, "Bobby Haber: Ten Years After," in CMJ: The First Decade, 1979–1989 (Albertson, NY: College Media Inc., 1989) 182.

49. Robert Christgau, "The Time of Their Lives," *Village Voice* 26 March 1991: 67.

50. See "Michael Stipe: The Rolling Stone Interview," *Rolling Stone* 5 March 1992: 49, and Fletcher 57.

51. Quoted in "Michael Stipe" 49.

52. Quoted in Fricke 50.

53. Mark Glaser in "Staff Infections: CMJ's Favorite Records, 1979–1989," in *CMJ: The First Decade* 70.

54. *Billboard* 13 July 1985: 46.

55. "The Best . . . And the Rest," in *CMJ: The First Decade* 162.

56. "Going for Baroque," *Spin*, March 1991: 28.
57. For many R.E.M. fans, though, the band became less "authentic" when lead singer Michael Stipe actually began enunciating lyrics clearly, around the time of *Life's Rich Pageant*. Lyrics that were impossible to understand acted as a sign of the band's "authenticity" for many fans. For many songs on the R.E.M.'s early albums Stipe did not write full sets of lyrics, and so many of the syllables he sang were not words at all. This certainly marked R.E.M.'s early material as oppositional to mainstream pop; it also led many critics to dub *Murmur*, R.E.M.'s first full-length album, *Mumble*.

Chapter 3: Producing Independent Music

1. Tommy Mottola, "The 90s: Fasten Your Seatbelts," *Billboard* 30 June 1990: W-12.
2. Hale Milgrim, "The Promise of the '90s," *Billboard* 30 June 1991: W-10.
3. Al Teller, "Developing the Talent to Stay on Top," *Billboard* 30 June 1990: W-28.
4. Ed Rosenblatt, "Spanning the Full Spectrum of Music," *Billboard* 30 June 1990: W-23.
5. The increasingly important role played by licensing in popular music is extensively discussed by Fenster. Also see Bob Buziak, President of RCA Records, "Creativity and Consolidation in the '90s," *Billboard* 30 June 1990: W-34.
6. Rosenblatt W-23.
7. Ahmet Ertegun, CEO, and Doug Morris, President, Atlantic Records, "The Challenge of the '90s," *Billboard* 30 June 1990: W-29.
8. Ertegun and Morris W-9.
9. Geoff Merritt, personal interview, 19 December 1991.
10. David Fricke, "The Underground Empire." *Rolling Stone* 18 December, 1986/1 January 1987: 121.
11. Quoted in Daniel Fidler, "Dischord," *Spin* February 1991: 74.
12. Quoted in Ben Weasel, "The Business of Punk Rock," *MAXIMUMROCKNROLL* January 1992: 2 (of article). *MRR* catered to the American punk/hardcore audience (the genre that spawned Nirvana and encompassed bands like Helmet, Jesus Lizard, and Fugazi), and its content tended to exhibit a more overt concern about issues of "authenticity" than indie pop/rock magazines like *The Bob* (which tended to feature more melodic, less noise-oriented act like R.E.M., Teenage Fanclub, and Beat Happening.)
13. Weasal 2.
14. Quoted in Grant Alden, "Grunge Makes Good," *Spin* September 1992: 52.
15. Michael Roux quoted in Bill Whitmer, "Trials, Triumphs on Local Band Scene," *Daily Illini*, Finals Edition, December 1989: 41.
16. Boston band Dumptruck, for instance, found itself being sued by its label, Big Time, when it attempted to sign with Polydor. However, soon after it filed the lawsuit, Big Time's poor management practices landed the label in bankruptcy. Later, Nine Inch Nails (Trent Reznor) and the Connells, two of the most profitable acts on indie label TVT, made it widely known that they were unhappy with their TVT deals and wanted to leave the label. Members of the Connells claimed that the only way they could get out of their TVT contract was to break up the band (Doug Macmillan and Mike Connell, personal interview, 21 November 1992.) Trent Reznor reportedly "sold his soul" to TVT when he signed with the label (Neil Strauss, "You Looking at Me?" *Village Voice* 27 October 1992: 92).
17. Mike Levy quoted in Robb Moore, "Sneetch Attack," *The Bob* Summer 1990: 5.
18. Dave Auchenbach of Small Factory quoted in Evelyn McDonnell, "NMS After Dark," *Village Voice* 30 July 1991: 75.

19. Samual Nathan Schiffman, "Nirvanafication," *MAXIMUMROCKNROLL* July 1992: 99.

20. Weasel 1 (of article).

21. "Rockbeat: The Final Chapter." *Village Voice* 4 June 1991: 57.

22. Jason Cohen, "The Indie Shuffle," *Option* March/April 1990: 13.

23. Weasel 7 (of article).

24. Geoff Merritt, owner/founder, Parasol Records, personal interview, 19 December 1991.

25. Uli Elser, personal interview, 1 August 1990.

26. Jim Greer, "New Music Preview," *Spin* January 1992: 30. See also Jason Cohen, "Eyeballing the Indie Action," *Option* January/February 1993: 19.

27. Schiffman 101.

28. Susie Racho, personal interview, 1 August 1990.

29. Jonathan Segal, personal interview, 31 July 1990.

30. Matt Allison, quoted in P. Gregory Springer, "Back to the Garage," *Champaign-Urbana News-Gazette Weekend* 17 February 1989: 9.

31. Anne Heller, "Superchunk," *New Route* December 1991: 20.

32. Schiffman 101.

33. Schiffman 102.

34. Fidler 74.

35. As Fenster explains: "Larger stores and chains are supplied directly through the branch distribution system, while smaller store purchase merchandise for slightly higher prices from independent distributors" (102). Because the distribution arms of major labels own and run the branch distribution system, the music that is readily available in the stores in which most records buyers purchase music is music that comes through the major label pipeline. The degree to which major labels control distribution makes clear why distribution agreements are desirable for many independent labels. Fenster notes that in 1988 the major distributors handled over 83% of the music industry's total output, and about 10% of this was independent label product (102). Independent labels that operate through independent distributors, therefore, tend to be shut out of most retail stores. In the smaller stores, many of which cater to specific listening audiences, major label-produced and/or distributed records are often more expensive than in chain stores.

36. RCA Records President Bob Buziak, W-34.

37. Quoted in Cohen, "Indie Shuffle" 14.

38. Quoted in Cohen, "Indie Shuffle" 14.

39. Quoted in Cohen, "Indie Shuffle" 14.

40. Information from Robert Christgau, "Rockbeat: Ice-T Blinks," *Village Voice* 11 August 1992: 88; Cohen, "Indie Shuffle," 13; Cohen, "Eyeballing" 19; and Fenster 94.

41. Quoted in Robinson et al. 42.

42. Simon Frith explains this cyclical pattern in "Video Pop: Picking Up the Pieces." Most music industry observers agree that the industry has for the past several years been in a period of consolidation as the major companies buy out the larger independent labels. Some note that the late 1980s-early 1990s greatly resembled the 1930s and 1940s, a time when the music industry was dominated by three major labels: RCA Victor, Columbia, and Decca.

43. Cohen, "Indie Shuffle" 18.

44. See Fenster 94, and "CMJ Radio Top 150," *CMJ New Music Report* 15 November 1993: 20.

45. Nirvana, for instance, established a large underground following in the late 1980s on the basis of its live performances, singles, and Sub Pop album *Bleach*, well before its major label debut and mainstream breakthrough album *Nevermind* (1991) was released.

46. Fricke 121.
47. Uli Elser, personal interview, 1 August 1990.
48. Paul Kiely, personal interview, 2 August 1990.
49. "Reality Used to be a Friend of Ours," *Voice Pazz and Jop* 3 March 1992: 18–19.
50. Mike Levy, personal interview, 15 July 1991.
51. Alden 55.
52. Robert Hilburn, "Record-Company Execs Still Eager to Gamble Millions on Superstars," *Louisville Courier-Journal* 24 January 1992: E10.
53. Quoted in Cohen, "Indie Shuffle" 16.
54. "Reality" 18.
55. Nathaniel Wice, "How Nirvana Made It," *Spin* April 1992: 58.
56. Wice 58.
57. Wice 58.
58. Jim Greer, "Major League," *Spin* September 1992: 78+.
59. Michael Kaplan, "Getting a Good Rep," *Rolling Stone* 26 March, 1987: 115–116.
60. Mottola W-12.
61. Quoted in Fricke 122.
62. Jonathan Segal, personal interview, 31 July 1990.
63. Scott Miller, personal interview, 2 August 1990.
64. Jason Cohen, ". . . And In With The New," *Spin* January 1993: 37.
65. Cohen, "Eyeballing" 19.
66. Cohen, "Eyeballing" 19.
67. Quoted in Cohen, "Eyeballing" 19–20.
68. Cohen, "Eyeballing" 20.
69. "Rockbeat: The Final Chapter" 57.
70. Jason Cohen, "The Rough Trade Fiasco," *Option* September/October 1991: 15.
71. Uli Elser, personal interview, 1 August 1990.
72. Elser, personal interview, 1 August 1990.
73. Perhaps the best-known "country" artist on Rough Trade was Lucinda Williams, who left Rough Trade and, after receiving much interest from major labels, signed with Chameleon (distributed by Elektra, which is owned by Warner Brothers.) Although songs written by Williams were made popular by mainstream country artists like Mary Chapin Carpenter and Patty Loveless, Williams herself is not widely popular with country music audiences. Her early appeal was primarily to fans of indie music.
74. Uli Elser, personal interview, 1 August 1990.
75. Uli Elser, personal interview, 1 August 1990.
76. Uli Elser, personal interview, 1 August 1990.
77. Stated by Elser in personal interview, 1 August 1990.
78. Uli Elser, personal interview, 1 August 1990.
79. Gail Countryman, personal interview, 16 July 1991.
80. Cohen, "Rough Trade" 18–19.
81. Simon Frith, "Britbeat: Duff Trade," *Village Voice* 4 June, 1991: 61.
82. Cohen, "Rough Trade" 18.
83. Jonathan Segal, personal interview, 31 July 1990.
84. Victor Krummenacher, personal interview, 31 July 1990.
85. Susie Racho, Alias Records, personal interview, 1 August 1990.
86. Racho, personal interview, 1 August 1990.
87. Mike Levy, quoted in Moore 5.

88. Racho, 1 August 1990.

89. Racho, 1 August 1990.

90. Racho, 1 August 1990.

91. Racho, 1 August 1990.

92. Racho, 1 August 1990.

93. Racho, 1 August 1990.

94. Racho, 1 August, 1990. Ironically, shortly after I conducted this interview Alias signed (at least) two more San Francisco bands, even though the label closed its San Francisco office in 1992.

95. David Snyder, "A Single Thought," *The Bob* Summer 1990: 22.

96. Gail O'Hara, "Jangly, Fuzzy, Cute, and Twee" *Spin*, October 1992: 116.

97. A few of the "poppier" local musicians, like Ric Menck and Paul Chastain (currently of the Providence, Rhode Island-based band Velvet Crush) and Matt Allison, put out singles on Iowa City's Bus Stop label. For a short while after that Bus Stop founder Brian Kirk moved to Champaign but then returned to Iowa City.

98. Quoted in Springer 8.

99. Springer 8.

100. Some information taken from Ben Fenske and Amy Flammang, "Poster Children . . . On Second Thought," *Sound Seen* Fall 1990: 11.

101. Geoff Merritt, Parasol Records, personal interview, 19 December 1991.

102. Merritt's recorded music (albums and CDs) rental business, part of his That's Rentertainment video rental store, allowed members to rent music overnight for a nominal fee. Complaints from a local record store owner led to the closing of That's Rentertainment's music rental business in July, 1987.

103. Personal interview, 19 December 1991.

104. O'Hara 116.

105. McDonnell 75.

106. Geoff Merritt, personal interview, 19 December 1991.

107. Geoff Merritt, personal interview, 19 December 1991.

108. Johan Kugelberg, "Mail Supremacy," *Spin* April 1993: 34.

109. Personal interview, 19 December 1991.

110. Geoff Merritt, personal interview, 19 December 1991.

111. Geoff Merritt, personal interview, 19 December 1991.

112. Geoff Merritt, personal interview, 19 December 1991.

113. Fidler 74.

114. Victor Krummenacher, Camper Van Beethover, personal interview, 31 July 1990.

115. Scott Miller, personal interview, 2 August 1990.

116. Mike Levy, personal interview, 15 July 1991.

117. Information gathered from Anthony DeCurtis, "R.E.M.'s Brave New World," *Rolling Stone* 20 April 1989: 48–54+; and Tony Fletcher, *Remarks: The Story of R.E.M.* (New York: Bantam Books, 1990) 105-106.

118. Adam Schmitt, telephone interview, 17 June 1992.

119. Schmitt, telephone interview, 17 June 1992.

120. Quoted in Gina Harp, "My Bloody Valentine," *Puncture* May 1992: 21. For similar views from Seattle bands, see Alden 55-56.

121. Jonathan Segal, Camper Van Beethoven, personal interview, 31 July 1990.

122. Fletcher 39.

123. Greer, "New Music" 30.

124. A description of Adam Schmitt's situation in Erika Rosenberg, "Future So Bright," *Daily Illini Diversions* 21–27 June 1991: 3.

125. Adam Schmitt, telephone interview, 17 June 1992.

126. Victor Krummenacher, personal interview, 31 July 1990.

127. Eric Gladstone, "Bonfire of the Inanities," *Alternative Press* January/February 1992: 10.

128. Zoo was an independent when Sweet signed, but became part of BMG.

129. Phil Strang of Record Service, quoted in Springer 9.

130. Patrick Hawley, personal interview, 19 December 1991.

Chapter 4: Disseminating Independent Music

1. Herbert H. Howard and Michael S. Kievman, *Radio and TV Programming* (Columbus: Grid Publishing, 1983) 30–32, 268–69.

2. Anthony DeCurtis, "Tastemakers," *Rolling Stone* 25 September 1986: 84.

3. Scott Miller, Game Theory and the Loud Family, personal interview, 2 August 1990.

4. Irene Nexica, music director, KALX (University of California at Berkeley), personal interview, 23 June 1992.

5. Mike Levy, The Sneetches, personal interview, 15 July 1991.

6. Paul Kiely, former music director, KFJC (Foothill College), personal interview, 2 August 1990.

7. Kiely, personal interview, 2 August 1990.

8. KFJC and KALX, early alternatively-formatted college radio stations, were profiled in Lynn Hirshberg's "Radio Goes Back To School," *Boulevards* April 1980: 29–31.

9. Quoted in Richard T. White, "Who (or What) is College Radio Listening To These Days?" *Alternative Press* January/February 1992: 12–13.

10. Ted Friedman and Raymond Rogers, "Schmoozin' On Up," *Spin College Music Report* April 1990: 18.

11. Quoted in Karen Schoemer, "College Radio Crosses Over," *Rolling Stone*, 4 October 1990: 140.

12. Jonathan Segal, Camper Van Beethoven, personal interview, 31 July 1990.

13. A 1983 *Rolling Stone* article by Steve Pond entitled "College Radio's Brave New Wave" described KUSF as "one of the most influential and least-formatted college stations in the country" (29 September, 1983: 86).

14. Anita Rivas, booking agent, I-Beam, personal interview, 16 July 1991.

15. Irene Nexica, personal interview, 23 June 1992.

16. Mike Levy, personal interview, 15 July 1991.

17. Quoted in DeCurtis 83.

18. DeCurtis 83.

19. Friedman and Rogers 17.

20. Laura Schmidt, "Can College DJs Bite the Hand that Feeds Them?" *U: The National College Paper* March, 1992: 19.

21. Although promoters did, and still do, also use concert tickets, threats to cut service from the record company, and other inducements to encourage airplay.

22. Quoted in Friedman and Rogers 17.

23. Sean Ross, "When College Outlets Play the Hits," *Billboard* 4 November 1989: 13.

24. Some of this information is from Ross 13.

25. Ross 13.

26. Ross 14.

27. "Sturgis," personal interview, 16 June 1992.

28. Personal interview, 16 June 1992.
29. Sturgis, music director, WPGU, personal interview, 16 June 1992.
30. Adam Schmitt, personal interview, 17 June 1992.
31. Mark Fenster, WEFT program committee, personal interview, 8 March 1992.
32. Adam Schmitt, telephone interview, 17 June 1992.
33. Susie Racho, personal interview, 1 August 1990.
34. Paul Kiely, personal interview, 2 August 1990.
35. Clearly community radio stations like WEFT in Champaign-Urbana, which are specifically programmed to provide material not available on any other radio stations within a market, did not see themselves in competition with other stations for audiences.
36. Irene Nexica, personal interview, 23 June 1992.
37. Ted Taylor, personal interview, 2 August 1990.
38. Irene Nexica, personal interview, 23 June 1992.
39. Ted Taylor, former KUSF music director, personal interview, 2 August 1990.
40. Sturgis, personal interview, 16 June 1992
41. Mark Fenster, personal interview, 8 March 1992.
42. Mark Fenster, personal interview, 8 March 1992.
43. Susie Racho, personal interview, 1 August 1990.
44. An example of this was given by Paul Kiely, former music director at KFJC, who said of his tenure, "[Because KFJC was] not . . . run by a university in any way, shape or form, public affairs was tailed to the absolute minimum that was required by the FCC. I buried it."
45. Irene Nexica, personal interview, 23 June 1992.
46. As listed in *SF Weekly*, 3 June 1992, and *The Bay Guardian*, 3 June 1992. Live 105 also put on several shows during early June, including Skankin' Pickle and Yothu Yindi at Slim's and The Soup Dragons at the Warfield.
47. Sturgis, personal interview, 16 June 1992.
48. As well as, at least implicitly, other local and national media with which they compete for their share of the radio audience: television, computer services, magazines, newspapers, etc.
49. Barry Simons, personal interview, 2 August 1990
50. In the Ross article, the program director of a college radio station that programmed adult contemporary music observed that at most college stations students were not being properly trained; they were allowed to do whatever they wanted on the air. And the general manager of a Top Forty-formatted station argued that "the consistent air product . . . allows other departments—sales, promotions, etc.—to have a tool with which [to] learn their crafts also" (13).
51. Ted Taylor, personal interview, 2 August 1990.
52. Sturgis, personal interview, 16 June 1992.
53. Jim Greer, "Present Tense," *Spin* November 1992: 126.
54. In the words of the Popular Memory Group, Johnson et al. 207.
55. Mike Levy, from personal interview, 15 July 1991, and also as quoted in Robb Moore, "Sneetch Attack," *The Bob* Summer 1990: 5.
56. Quoted in Greer 126.
57. All historical information on CMJ is from *CMJ: The First Decade, 1979–1989.* (Albertson, NY: College Media, Inc. 1989).
58. Quoted in "Bobby Haber: Ten Years After," *CMJ: The First Decade* 181.
59. Robert Christgau, "'The Smart People',' *Village Voice* 19 November 1991: 92
60. All background information on the *Gavin Report* is from a personal interview with Linda Ryan, Alternative Music Editor at the *Gavin Report*, 2 August 1990.

61. Linda Ryan, personal interview, 2 August 1990.
62. Until 1991, the singles chart combined sales and airplay, but was split into two separate charts—one for sales and one for airplay—when SoundScan was introduced (see "Rockbeat: Lost in the Supermarket," *Village Voice* 19 April 1991: 78).
63. "Rockbeat: Lost in the Supermarket" 78.
64. "Rockbeat: Priority Adventures," *Village Voice* 18 June 1991: 73.
65. Nathaniel Wice, "How Nirvana Made It." *Spin* April 1992: 58.
66. Jonathan Segal, Camper Van Beethoven, personal interview, 31 July 1990.
67. Uli Elser, personal interview, 1 August 1990.
68. Susie Racho, personal interview, 1 August 1990.
69. Ted Taylor, former music director, KUSF, personal interview, 2 August 1990.
70. Susie Racho, personal interview, 1 August 1990.
71. Patrick Hawley, personal interview, 19 December 1991.
72. Mike Levy, The Sneetches, personal interview, 15 July 1991.
73. Quoted in Schoemer 137.
74. Scott Miller, Game Theory and The Loud Family, personal interview, 2 August 1990.
75. Linda Ryan, personal interview, 2 August 1990.
76. Linda Ryan, personal interview, 2 August 1990.
77. And, in the 1980s, cable shows like the USA network's *Night Flight* often featured alternative acts like Cabaret Voltaire and Kate Bush. TBS also occasionally included alternative clips in its weekend late-night video show *Night Tracks*. Local access cable created the possibility of low-budget local music video programs, and some local broadcast stations also produced their own music video shows. Beyond television outlets, unsuccessful attempts were made in the early 1980s to place video jukeboxes in bars and clubs. Far more successful has been the retail sale of video clip compilations and videotaped concerts by alternative acts like the Cure and R.E.M.
78. For example, Gil Friesen, president of A&M Records, said that "more important than the video [itself]. . . . is that MTV is the one national radio station that exists in America." Quoted by Steve Pond in "Gil Friesen," *Rolling Stone* 17–31 December 1987: 104.
79. Fred Goodman, "Who Do You Blow?" *Village Voice* 6 August 1991: 41.
80. See, for instance, Keith Negus' *Producing Pop*, in which Negus quotes David Steele, a marketing manager at Virgin, who says "In a lot of cases we are waiting until we are virtually sure that a track's going to happen before we go ahead with a video" (97).
81. Goodman 41.
82. Quoted in Lisa Robinson, "Mr. MTV," *Spin* January 1992: 54, 83–4.
83. Quoted in Robinson 55.
84. Quoted in Goodman 41.
85. All "Buzz Bin" information from "Buzzing the Masses," *Louisville Courier-Journal, Scene* 22 August 1992: 11.
86. The exception was rap videos, which too were often made by independent labels with small budgets. These videos on the whole were also relegated to blocks of rap programming, which sometimes appeared in the morning.
87. Scott Miller, personal interview, 2 August 1990.
88. Jeff Evans, Record Service manager, personal interview, 19 December 1991.
89. Gail Countryman, personal interview, 16 July 1991. (The expansion never happened, and the Rough Trade store in San Francisco closed in the late 1990s.)
90. Brenda Nielsen, Record Swap, personal interview, 30 December 1991.

91. Brenda Nielsen, personal interview, 30 December 1991; and Jeff Evans, manager, Record Service, 19 December 1991.

92. Brenda Nielsen, personal interview, 30 December 1991; and Jeff Evans, manager, Record Service, 19 December 1991.

93. Brenda Nielsen, personal interview, 30 December 1991.

94. Brenda Nielsen, personal interview, 30 December 1991.

95. Jeff Evans, personal interview, 19 December 1991.

96. Gail Countryman, personal interview, 16 July 1991.

97. Gail Countryman, personal interview, 16 July 1991.

98. Gail Countryman, personal interview, 16 July 1991.

99. Gail Countryman, personal interview, 16 July 1991.

100. Brenda Nielsen, personal interview, 30 December 1991.

101. Jeff Evans, personal interview, 19 December 1991.

102. Gail Countryman, personal interview, 16 July 1991.

103. Gail Countryman, personal interview, 16 July 1991.

104. Anita Rivas, personal interview, 16 July 1991.

105. Johann Kugelberg, "Mail Supremacy," *Spin* April 1993: 34.

106. Kugelberg 34; and Geoff Merritt, Parasol founder, personal interview, 19 December 1991.

107. See Mark Fenster, "The Articulation of Difference and Identity in Alternative Popular Music Practice," dissertation, University of Illinois, 1992.

108. Or fans who, as a group, often tried to smuggle in cheap liquor from elsewhere. See Ben Weasel, "The Business of Punk Rock," *MAXIMUMROCKNROLL* January, 1992: 3 (of article); and Roman Kozak, *This Ain't No Disco: The Story of CGBG* (New York: Faber and Faber, 1988) 118.

109. Anita Rivas, personal interview, 16 July 1991.

110. Anita Rivas, personal interview, 16 July 1991.

111. Geoff Merritt, personal interview, 19 December 1991.

112. Adam Schmitt, telephone interview, 17 June 1992.

113. Don Gerard, personal interview, 19 December 1991.

114. Adam Schmitt, personal interview, 17 June 1992.

115. Don Gerard, personal interview, 19 December 1991.

116. Patrick Hawley, personal interview, 19 December 1991.

117. Nick Rudd, personal interview, 30 December 1991.

118. Mike Levy, personal interview, 15 July 1991.

119. Susie Racho, personal interview, 1 August 1990.

120. Sara Cohen (*Rock Culture* 67) describes a similar process in Liverpool.

121. Weasel 3 (of article)

122. Barry Simons, personal interview, 2 August 1990.

123. Adam Schmitt, telephone interview, 17 June 1992.

124. Mike Levy, personal interview, 15 July 1991.

125. Adam Schmitt, telephone interview, 17 June 1992.

126. White 14.

127. Scott Miller, personal interview, 2 August 1990.

128. Barry Simon, personal interview, 2 August 1990.

129. Don Gerard, personal interview, 19 December 1991.

130. Evelyn McDonnell, "Rockbeat: Lollapalosers," *Village Voice* 18 August, 1992: 78.

131. Anita Rivas, personal interview, 16 July 1991.

132. Anita Rivas, personal interview, 16 July 1991.

Chapter 5: Locating Subjectivity in Independent Music

1. Sara Cohen ("Localizing" 7) discovered in her Liverpool research that residents, while all part of the same locality, had different experiences of that locality and often different definitions of what constitutes that locality, and might use the term "Liverpool" to describe only one element of the city's population. An elderly Jewish man, for example, used the terms "Liverpool" and "this town" even when referring only to the city's Jewish community.

2. As Mike Featherstone points out, "The drawing of a boundary around a particular space is a relational act which depends upon the figuration of significant other localities within which one seeks to situate it" (1993, 176).

3. The relationship of government to local music production is also an important area of study. However, because I am focusing on local music scenes in the United States rather than Great Britain, I am not examining the activities of local governments in promoting local music, a practice that seems to be much more salient in Britain than it is in the U.S. Researchers at the Institute of Popular Music at the University of Liverpool have examined local Liverpool policies toward popular music, and John Street has detailed how the Norwich city government helped to finance and oversee the management of a performance venue. Street notes that Norwich government authorities, like the Greater London Council before it, wanted to promote locally a "pluralistic musical culture," in order to "combat the damaging economic and cultural consequences of transnationalization," and therefore to encourage a sense of a local musical identity in response to the globalization of almost all popular music forms (see Street).

4. Geoff Merritt, Parasol Records, personal interview, 19 December 1991.

5. Mike Levy, The Sneetches, personal interview, 15 July 1991.

6. Adam Schmitt, personal interview, 17 June 1992.

7. Jeff Evans, personal interview, 19 December 1991.

8. Don Gerard, personal interview, 19 December 1991.

9. Scott Miller, The Loud Family, personal interview, 2 August 1990.

10. Don Gerard, personal interview, 19 December 1991.

11. Patrick Hawley, personal interview, 19 December 1991.

12. Patrick Hawley, personal interview, 19 December 1991.

13. Personal interview, 15 July 1991.

14. Mike Levy, personal interview, 15 July 1991.

15. Scott Miller, personal interview, 2 August 1990.

16. Nick Rudd, personal interview, 30 December 1991.

17. Adam Schmitt, personal interview, 17 June 1992.

18. Don Gerard, personal interview, 19 December 1991.

19. Patrick Hawley, personal interview, 19 December 1991.

20. Mike Levy, personal interview, 15 July 1991.

21. Adam Schmitt, personal interview, 17 June 1992.

22. Sara Cohen finds a similar discourse at work in the Liverpool independent music scene. She quotes a member of the band Half Man, Half Biscuit as saying that, "With our band there's no difference between being on stage and being in the living room" (*Rock Culture* 82).

23. Geoff Merritt, personal interview, 19 December 1991.

24. This characteristic is not exclusive to indie pop/rock. Simon Frith ("The Magic" 159) noted the same characteristic of folk music culture.

25. Don Gerard, personal interview, 19 December 1991.

26. Jeff Evans, personal interview, 19 December 1991.

27. Cohen makes a similar point in *Rock Culture in Liverpool.*

28. Anita Rivas, personal interview, 16 July 1991.

29. Quoted in Jim Greer, "Big Slack Attack," *Spin,* April 1994: 100.

30. Personal interview, 2 August 1990.

31. In this context, I use the word "participants" to refer not only to those who are publicly engaged in the creation, commerce, and circulation of independent pop/rock music, but also to those who are involved in the private consumption of independent pop/rock music.

32. Adam Schmitt, personal interview, 17 June 1992.

33. Scott Miller, personal interview, 2 August 1990.

34. Don Gerard, personal interview, 19 December 1991.

35. Patrick Hawley, personal interview, 19 December 1991.

36. Anita Rivas, personal interview, 16 July 1991.

37. Susie Racho, personal interview, 1 August 1990.

38. Frith, in "'The Magic That Will Set You Free,'" discusses the myth of rock community and notes that this myth is not one of how a community makes music, but rather it is about certain kinds of communal experience. In looking at the particular social and economic networks that are the focus of my study however, I am looking at a level someone between the general level of mass consumption and the very particular level of music production. Certainly the sort of myth of community Frith describes exists in independent pop/rock music scenes.

39. Irene Nexica, personal interview, 23 June 1992.

40. Gail Countryman, personal interview, 16 July 1991.

41. Anita Rivas, personal interview, 16 July 1991.

42. Linda Ryan, personal interview, 2 August 1990.

43. Geoff Merritt, Parasol Records, personal interview, 19 December 1991.

44. Mike Levy, the Sneetches, personal interview, 15 July 1991.

45. Jeff Evans, personal interview, 19 December 1991.

46. Adam Schmitt, personal interview, 17 June 1992.

47. Don Gerard, personal interview, 19 December 1991.

48. Of the Mabel's staff, one musician said, "I don't care for the people there," while another said he didn't enjoying going there because "then you have to put up with all the assholes who work there."

49. Nick Rudd, personal interview, 30 December 1991.

50. Although I have focused on places primarily characterized by the performance or dissemination of music, music scene participants did not like to be defined only by their involvement with music and often cited non-music-related places as significant in their lives. For example, when asked what local establishments they frequented, some scene participants named places that weren't generally listed by other interviewees. A Champaign musician indicated his multiple positioning as music scene participant and college student by noting that he also likes to spend time at a local coffee house, of which he says, "Sometimes I take homework or a book, but of course I just go there to talk to my friends." A San Francisco interviewee, after naming the DNA Lounge and the I-Beam as hang-outs, underscored the diversity of his taste by adding, "and Kimball's East—I go to see jazz. There are actually some good jazz clubs in the East Bay." Another San Franciscan connoted his "literariness" by saying, after mentioning that he frequents the I-Beam, Kennel Club, and Albion, "My favorite bar to hang out at is Vesuvio's in North Beach. It's where all the Beat poets used to hang out in the late fifties and early sixties. It's right next to City Lights

bookstore." And a third San Francisco scene participant foregrounded beer connoisseurship as a key part of his identity when he stated:

> When I go out, it's generally either to Donnington Park, which is a tiny place that serves only English beer and has darts; or the Tornado, which is the only beer and wine bar that serves a million types of beer; or where I work, which is a pub also. Eighteen draft beers.

He not only asserted his difference from others in the local scene by patronizing places that are off-the-beaten-music-scene-path, he also does so by eschewing some places closely identified with the local scene. Of the Albion, he says:

> The Albion is kind of important, even though it's a really despicable place, because "hip" music people, music scene people, go there. It has a little back room; I performed in the back room. In this idiot article in *BAM* they called it "the new Folk City." It's run by people that are in this band X-Tal. The bar is a real underground music scene hip cat place. It's usually crowded, which I don't like at all, and it takes awhile to get the beer.

These interviewees all indicated a desire not to be solely identified with a music scene and the spaces it has territorialized, but to be multiply identified with a variety of public places.

51. Geoff Merritt, personal interview, 19 December 1991.
52. Patrick Hawley, personal interview.
53. Scott Miller, personal interview.
54. Daniel House, Skin Yard, quoted in Grant Alden, "Grunge Makes Good," *Spin* September 1992: 55.
55. In fact, two of the three members of Nirvana's final lineup—Kurt Cobain and Krist Novoselic—grew up in Aberdeen. The third member, Dave Grohl, was from Virginia. At other points in the book, Felder contradicts her own argument that bands from a particular geographical area express that area's feelings, dress and attitude. For instance, she makes the transition from discussing Boston-based bands to talking about Belleville, Illinois' Uncle Tupelo by saying, "Uncle Tupelo may not be from the Boston area, but its sound evokes a similar sense of Americana" (73).
56. A key problem with both of the seminal works on local music scenes—Ruth Finnegan's *The Hidden Musicians* and Sara Cohen's *Rock Culture in Liverpool*—is that they focus on local practice without much consideration of the relationship of local practice to practices in other localities. Finnegan, however, acknowledges and to some degree describes this process, and Cohen, in her more recent work, has begun to address the issue of interlocality. For a more developed critique of Finnegan and Cohen, see Kruse, "*Rock Culture,*" and "Subcultural Identity."
57. Jonathan Segal and Victor Kummenacher, personal interview, 31 July 1990.
58. Don Gerard, personal interview, 19 December 1991.
59. Personal interview, 1 August 1990. In a similar vein, Gail Countryman, owner of the Rough Trade record store in San Francisco jokes, "On many occasions over the years I have said there are only fifty people in the world, and they all work in this industry" (Personal interview, 16 July 1991).
60. Personal interview, 1 August 1990.
61. Personal interview, 16 July 1991.
62. Geoff Merritt, personal interview, 19 December 1991.
63. Patrick Hawley, personal interview, 19 December 1991.

64. This is a paraphrase of what Edward Soja argues about the nature of localities in general (152).
65. Personal interview, 19 December 1991.
66. Uli Elser, Buyer, Rough Trade, personal interview, 1 August, 1990.
67. Caroline Lambeck, personal interview, 31 July 1991.
68. Lisa Fancher, quoted in Seana Baruth, "Behind the Rock Scene: Women Wedge In," *The Guardian* 13 May 1992: 6.
69. Susie Racho, personal interview, 1 August 1990.
70. Quoted in Baruth 6.
71. Gail Countryman, personal interview, 16 July 1991.
72. Anita Rivas, personal interview, 16 July 1991.
73. As constituted in popular discourse, college radio was traditionally perceived as a "white" medium. This construction of college radio is quite dangerous, because it ignored the significant number of stations broadcasting from historically African-American schools. For the most part, however, college radio stations at racially mixed schools, in the words of Anthony DeCurtis, "have reflected the white, essentially middle-class tastes of the media kids behind the mikes" ("Tastemakers, *Rolling Stone* 25 September 1986: 84). While stations may have attempted to serve minority audiences and to put non-white DJs on the air, these attempts were often little more than tokenism, with scant recognition of the differences that existed within and across ethnic groups. Take, for instance, this remark by WPGU's music director:

    > . . . we support an increase in minorities too, because we have very few minorities that work at the station. We have one show that is directed toward the minorities in a way . . . it's like urban rap and dance. So in a way it's kind of geared toward the black community. (Personal interview, 16 June 1992)

    To think that there was a single "black community" within the student body that could be addressed by one radio show was naive and ignored the variety of ethnic groups (Latino, Chinese, Vietnamese, Hispanic, Indian, Arab, etc.) which comprised the minority population present on most large, historically-white, college campuses in the 1980s and 1990s.

    It should be noted, however, that through the 1980s college radio as a whole became more aware of its problems with race, and many stations sought to address the absence of artists of color on their playlists. In fact, college radio stations were recognized for supporting rap music before commercial radio, including urban commercial stations, made a commitment to the genre. College radio remained one of the few places where controversial hardcore rap can be heard.
74. Mark Fenster, WEFT programming committee, personal interview, 8 March 1992.
75. Personal interview, 23 June 1992.
76. These particular comments are from interviews with Paul Kiely, former KFJC program director, and Boris Butkov, former DJ and producer at KUSF, 2 August 1992.
77. Personal interview, 2 August 1990.
78. Personal interview, 2 August 1990.
79. Irene Nexica, personal interview, 23 June 1992.

Chapter 6: Theorizing Independent Music Formations

1. Certainly within any indie music scene there was no single unifying community. If anything, in the words of Colin MacCabe, "we are all members of numerous collectivities, numerous communities, which often hold contradictory beliefs" (quoted in Redhead 14).

2. The most prominent work in this area has been done by Ruth Finnegan (1989), Sara Cohen (1991) and Barry Shank (1994).

3. This summation of the term "cultural capital" is taken from Randal Johnson's introduction to *The Field of Cultural Production* (7).

4. Geographer Edward Soja extends the notion of conjuncture to include a spatial component.

5. Gender, as argued in Chapter 5, does not fit quite so easily here, since there has been an uninterrupted increase during the past decades and to the present in the number of occupational fields in which women are represented and in the earnings of women: even though these figures remain disproportionately lower for women than men.

References

Azerrad, Michael. *Our Band Could Be Your Life: Scenes from the American Indie Underground 1981–1991*. Boston: Little, Brown and Company, 2001.

Barlett, Donald L., and James B. Steele. *America: What Went Wrong?* Kansas City: Andrews and McMeel, 1992.

Barnes, Ken. "Top 40 Radio: A Fragment of the Imagination." *Facing the Music*. Ed. Simon Frith. New York: Pantheon, 1988.

Bayton, Mavis. "How Women Become Musicians." *On Record: Rock, Pop, and the Written Word*. Ed. Simon Frith and Andrew Goodwin. New York: Pantheon, 1990. 238–257.

Becker, Howard. *Art Worlds*. Berkeley: University of California, 1982.

Berland, Jody. "Locating Listening: Technological Space, Popular Music, Canadian Mediations." *Cultural Studies* 2.3 (1988): 343–358.

———. "Radio Space and Industrial Time: The Case of Music Formats." Ed. Tony Bennett, et al. *Rock and Popular Music: Politics, Policies and Institutions*. London: Routledge, 1993.

Bourdieu, Pierre. *The Field of Cultural Production*. Ed. Randal Johnson. New York: Columbia University Press, 1993.

———. *In Other Words: Essays Towards a Reflexive Sociology*. Trans. Matthew Adamson. Stanford, CA: Stanford University Press, 1990.

———. *Outline of a Theory of Practice*. Trans. Richard Nice. Cambridge: Cambridge University Press, 1977.

———. "The Social Space and the Genesis of Groups." *Theory and Society* 14 (1985): 723–744.

Brooks, Clive. *How to Form a Successful Band*. London: Virgin Books, 1989.

Brown, Rodger Lyle. *Party Out of Bounds: The B-52's, R.E.M., and the Kids Who Rocked Athens, Georgia*. New York: Plume, 1991.

Cohen, Anthony. *The Symbolic Construction of Community*. London: Routledge, 1985.

Cohen, Sara. "Ethnography and Popular Music Studies." *Popular Music* 12,2 (1993): 123–138.

———. "Localizing Sound." Keynote Address. International Association for the Study of Popular Music International Conference. Stockton, CA, 17 July 1993.

———. "Popular Music and Urban Regeneration: The Music Industries of Merseyside." *Cultural Studies* 5.3 (1991): 332–346.

——. *Rock Culture in Liverpool: Popular Music in the Making.* Oxford: Oxford University Press, 1991.

Connerton, Paul. *How Societies Remember.* Cambridge: Cambridge University Press, 1989.

Dannen, Frederic. *Hit Men.* New York: Vintage Books, 1991.

Decker, Scott. "Memory Serves: Our Back Pages 1979-1989." *CMJ: The First Decade, 1979-1989.* Albertson, NY: College Media Inc., 1989. 6-64.

Felder, Rachel. *Manic Pop Thrill.* Hopewell, NJ: Ecco Press, 1993.

Fenster, Mark. "The (Ab)uses of Popular Music History." *ONETWOTHREEFOUR* (Winter 1990): 7-22.

——. "The Articulation of Difference and Identity in Alternative Popular Music Practice." Dissertation. University of Illinois, 1992.

Finnegan, Ruth. *The Hidden Musicians: Music-Making in an English Town.* Cambridge: Cambridge University Press, 1989.

Fletcher, Tony. *Remarks: The Story of R.E.M.* New York: Bantam Books, 1990.

Fornatale, Peter, and Joshua E. Mills. *Radio in the Television Age.* Woodstock, NY: The Overlook Press, 1990.

Frith, Simon. "'The Magic That Can Set You Free': The Ideology of Folk and the Myth of the Rock Community." *Popular Music* 1 (1981): 159-168.

——. "Music for Pleasure." *Screen Education* 34 (1980): 51-61.

——. *Sound Effects: Youth, Leisure, and the Politics of Rock 'n' Roll.* New York: Pantheon, 1981.

——. "Rock and the Politics of Memory." *The Sixties Without Apology.* Ed. Sohnya Sayres et al. Minneapolis: The University of Minneapolis Press, 1984. 59-69.

——. "Towards an Aesthetic of Popular Music." *Music and Society: The Politics of Composition, Performance and Reception.* Ed. Richard Leppert and Susan McClary. Cambridge: Cambridge University Press, 1987. 133-150.

——. "Video Pop: Picking Up the Pieces." *Facing the Music.* Ed. Simon Frith. New York: Pantheon, 1988. 88-130.

Frith, Simon, and Howard Horne. *Art Into Pop.* London: Methuen, 1987.

Garnham, Nicholas, and Raymond Williams. "Pierre Bourdieu and the Sociology of Culture: An Introduction." *Media, Culture and Society* 2 (1980): 209-23.

Giddens, Anthony. *Sociology: A Brief but Critical Introduction.* 2nd Ed. San Diego: Harcourt Brace Jovanovich, 1987.

Goffman, Erving. *Frame Analysis: An Essay on the Organization of Experience.* Cambridge: Harvard University Press, 1974.

Goodwin, Andrew. *Dancing in the Distraction Factory: Music Television and Popular Culture.* Minneapolis: University of Minnesota Press, 1992.

Griffin, Christine. *Representations of Youth.* Cambridge: Polity Press, 1993.

Hesmondhalgh, David. "Post-Punk's Attempt to Democratise the Music Industry: The Success and Failure of Rough Trade." *Popular Music* 16.3 (1998): 255-274.

Homan, Shane. "Losing the Local: Sydney and the Oz Rock Tradition." *Popular Music* 19.1 (2000): 31-49.

Jensen, Joli. *The Nashville Sound: Authenticity, Commercialization, and Country Music.* Nashville: Country Music Foundation Press, 1998.

Johnson, Randal. "Editor's Introduction: Pierre Bourdieu on Art, Literature and Culture."

The Field of Cultural Production. By Pierre Bourdieu. Ed. Randal Johnson. New York: Columbia University Press, 1993. 1–25.

Jones, Simon. "Music and Symbolic Creativity." *Common Culture.* Ed. Paul Willis. Boulder: Westview Press, 1990. 59–83.

Kruse, Holly. "*Rock Culture in Liverpool,* by Sara Cohen." *Tracking: Popular Music Studies* 4.1 (1992): 28–30.

———. "Subcultural Identity in Alternative Music Culture." *Popular Music* 12.1 (1993): 33–41.

Laing, Dave. *One Chord Wonders: Power and Meaning in Punk Rock.* Milton Keynes: Open University Press, 1985.

Lewis, Lisa A. *Gender Politics and MTV: Voicing the Difference.* Philadephia: Temple University Press, 1990.

McChesney, Robert W. *Rich Media, Poor Democracy.* New York: The New Press, 2000.

McRobbie, Angela. "Post-Marxism and Cultural Studies: A Post-script." *Cultural Studies.* Ed. Lawrence Grossberg, Cary Nelson, and Paula Treichler. New York: Routledge, 1992. 719–730.

———. "Shut Up and Dance: Youth Culture and Changing Modes of Femininity." *Cultural Studies* 7.3 (1993): 406–426.

McRobbie, Angela, and Jenny Garber. "Girls and Subcultures." *Resistance Through Rituals.* Ed. Stuart Hall and Tony Jefferson. London: Hutchinson, 1976. 208–222.

Massey, Doreen. "Politics and Space/Time." *Place and the Politics of Identity.* Ed. Michael Keith and Steve Pile. London: Routledge, 1993. 141–161.

———. "Power-Geometry and a Progressive Sense of Place." *Mapping the Futures: Local Cultures, Global Change.* Ed. Jon Bird, Barry Curtis, Tim Putnam, George Robertson, and Lisa Tickner. London: Routledge, 1993. 59–69.

Miege, Bernard. *The Capitalization of Cultural Production.* New York: International General, 1989.

Negus, Keith. *Music Genres and Corporate Cultures.* London: Routledge, 1999.

———. *Producing Pop: Culture and Conflict in the Popular Music Industry.* London: Edward Arnold, 1992.

Perry, Steve. "Ain't No Mountain High Enough: The Politics of Crossover." *Facing the Music.* Ed. Simon Frith. New York: Pantheon, 1988. 51–87.

Personal Narratives Group. *Interpreting Women's Lives: Feminist Theory and Personal Narratives.* Bloomington: Indiana University Press, 1989.

Popular Memory Group. "Popular Memory: Theory, Politics, Method." *Making Histories.* Ed. Richard Johnson, Gregor McLennan, Bill Schwarz, and David Sutton. Minneapolis: University of Minnesota Press, 1982. 205–252.

Pratt, Mary Louise. "Fieldwork in Common Places." *Writing Culture.* Ed. James Clifford and George Marcus. Berkeley: University of California Press, 1986. 27–50.

Redhead, Steve. *The End-of-the-Century Party: Youth and Pop Towards 2000.* Manchester: Manchester University Press, 1990.

Reynolds, Simon. "Against Health and Efficiency: Independent Music in the 1980s." *Zoot Suits and Second-Hand Dresses: An Anthology of Music and Fashion.* Ed. Angela McRobbie. Boston: Unwin Hyman, 1989. 245–255.

———. *Blissed Out: The Raptures of Rock.* London: Serpent's Tail, 1990.

Robinson, Deanna Campbell, et al. *Music at the Margins: Popular Music and Global Diversity*. Newbury Park, CA: Sage, 1991.

Shank, Barry. *Dissonant Identities: The Rock 'n' Roll Scene in Austin, Texas*. Hanover: Wesleyan University Press, 1994.

Smith, Anthony. *Age of the Behemoths*. New York: Priority Press, 1991.

Soja, Edward. *Postmodern Geographies: The Reassertion of Space in Critical Social Theory*. London: Verso, 1989.

Steward, Sue, and Sheryl Garratt. *Signed, Sealed, and Delivered: True Life Stories of Women in Pop*. Boston: South End Press, 1984.

Straw, Will. "Systems of Articulation, Logics of Change: Communities and Scenes in Popular Music. *Cultural Studies* 5.3 (1991): 368–388.

Tomlinson, Alan. "Consumer Culture and the Aura of the Commodity." In Alan Tomlinson (ed.), *Consumption, Identity, and Style: Marketing, Meanings, and the Packaging of Pleasure*. London: Routledge, 1990. 1–40.

Tunstall, Jeremy, and Michael Palmer. *Media Moguls*. London and New York: Routledge, 1992.

Willis, Paul. "Symbolic Creativity" and "Common Culture." *Common Culture*. Ed. Paul Willis. Boulder: Westview Press, 1990. 1–29 and 128–152.

Name Index

Index

M U S I C
[M E A N I N G S]

GENERAL EDITORS: STEVE JONES, JOLI JENSEN, & WILL STRAW

Popular music plays a prominent role in the cultural transformations that are constantly reshaping our world. More and more, music is at the center of contemporary debates about globalization, electronic commerce, space and locality, style and identity, subculture and community, and other key issues within cultural and media studies.

Music[Meanings] offers book-length studies examining the impact of popular music on individuals, cultures and societies. The series addresses popular music as a form of communication and culture from an interdisciplinary perspective, and targets readers from across the humanities and social sciences.

For additional information about this series or for the submission of manuscripts, please contact:

Acquisitions Department
Peter Lang Publishing
275 Seventh Avenue, 28th Floor
New York, NY 10001

To order other books in this series, please contact our Customer Service Department:

(800) 770-LANG (within the U.S.)
(212) 647-7706 (outside the U.S.)
(212) 647-7707 FAX

or browse online by series:

WWW.PETERLANGUSA.COM